HE WHO IS

HE WHO IS

A STUDY IN TRADITIONAL THEISM

By

E. L. MASCALL, D.D.

Professor of Historical Theology
in the University of London;
Emeritus Student of Christ Church, Oxford;
Priest of the Oratory of the Good Shepherd

*Les purs philosophes disent sans cesse : recommençons ; le
philosophe chrétien peut seul dire : continuons*
A. D. SERTILLANGES

Ita ergo philosophandum est in fide
JOHN OF ST. THOMAS

ARCHON BOOKS
1970

To
MY MOTHER
Mulier timens Dominum ipsa laudabitur

SBN: 208 00901 9
Library of Congress Catalog Card Number: 76-95026
Printed in the United States of America

CONTENTS

INTRODUCTORY ESSAY

IT is gratifying to an author to know that one of his books is still in demand more than twenty years after its first appearance, but, if its subject is in any degree alive and developing, he can hardly fail to reflect how different it would have been if he had written it at the later date. In default of a complete rewriting of the book from start to finish, I think the most useful task that I can perform in the present Essay will be to give some indication of the more important material dealing with its subject which has appeared since the first publication of the book in 1943 and of its sequel, *Existence and Analogy*, in 1949.

It was no part of my purpose in either of these books to provide an answer, except by implication, to the violent onslaught on the very possibility of natural theology (or indeed of theology of any kind) which, in a variety of metamorphoses, has occupied much of the effort of English-speaking philosophers since the publication of A. J. Ayer's *Language, Truth and Logic* in 1936. My own contribution to that debate is embodied in a small work entitled *Words and Images* which was published in 1957, while some reflections on its more recent phases will be found in the first chapter of my *Secularisation of Christianity* (1965). R. W. Hepburn's *Christianity and Paradox* (1958) is an out-and-out major offensive, impressive for its seriousness and sincerity; T. R. Miles's *Religion and the Scientific Outlook* (1959) is slightly less out-and-out. R. B. Braithwaite's celebrated Eddington Memorial Lecture of 1955, *An Empiricist's View of the Nature of Religious Belief*, attempted to reinterpret Christian theism in strictly empiricist[1] and moral terms; in this sense, he stands out as a forerunner of such recent writers as Schubert M. Ogden (*Christ Without Myth*, 1961), Paul van Buren (*The Secular Meaning of the Gospel*, 1963) and, perhaps in some aspects, J. A. T. Robinson (*Honest to God*, 1963), though all of these writers are concerned much more with reinterpreting theism in secular terms than in constructing arguments for its truth. The ultimate ancestor of the movement would in fact seem to be Ludwig Feuerbach, whose *Essence of Christianity*

---

[1] Traditional cosmological theism is, of course, "empirical" in the sense that it takes as its starting-point the world of our sense-experience, but not, like the positions mentioned above, in holding the objects of our senses to be the only or the ultimate realities.

appeared as long ago as 1841. The whole technique of reduc-
tionism, with its programme of retaining the traditional language
of Christian theism while replacing its transcendent reference by
a purely finite and empirical one, has been drastically criticized
by Hugo A. Meynell in his short and incisive work *Sense, Nonsense
and Christianity* (1964). On some of the recent experiments in
this technique I have written at length in *The Secularisation of
Christianity* and I shall say nothing more about them here. Other
marches and counter-marches in the field of basic theology are
manifested in such volumes as *New Essays in Philosophical Theology*
(1955), edited by A. G. N. Flew and A. MacIntyre, the symposium
Metaphysical Beliefs (1957), by S. Toulmin, R. W. Hepburn and
A. MacIntyre, and P. Munz's *Problems of Religious Knowledge*
(1959). Two important collections which are traditional in their
conclusions if not always in their methods are *Faith and Logic*
(1957), edited by B. G. Mitchell, and *Prospect for Metaphysics*
(1961), edited by I. T. Ramsey; I. M. Crombie's essay in the
former and H. D. Lewis's in the latter are specially worthy of
notice. I. M. Ramsey's somewhat individual approach is expounded in his lecture *Miracles* (1957) and his books *Religious Language*
(1957) and *Christian Discourse* (1965); and if I am doubtful whether
a really satisfactory defence of traditional Christian theism can be
constructed on his lines, this is not because I have any doubts
that traditional Christian theism is what he is defending. The late
M. B. Foster's suggestive but cautious *Mystery and Philosophy*
(1957) should not be forgotten.

It was one of the main purposes of the present work and its
sequel to argue that the real function of the famous Five Ways of
St. Thomas Aquinas was not to provide five independent arguments for the existence of God from finite beings, but to manifest
by five different expositions the character of finite beings as
radically dependent on a transcendent, self-existent infinite
Being; the Five Ways are, I maintained, unified on the finite
and not on the infinite level. This does in fact give my approach
a good deal in common with that of such writers as A. M. Farrer,
Mark Pontifex and Illtyd Trethowan,[1] who, while having less
respect than I have for St. Thomas's Five Ways, see the basis
of an argument for theism as consisting in an intuition or "contuition" of God and finite being together in what Farrer calls

[1] M. Pontifex, *The Existence of God* (1947); M. Pontifex and I. Trethowan, *The Meaning of Existence* (1953).

the "cosmological relation". I have discussed Farrer's great work
Finite and Infinite (1943) at some length in *Existence and Analogy*.

As very close indeed to my own position, I would single out
G. F. Wood's unjustly neglected book *Theological Explanation*
(1950) and the earlier chapters of H. D. Lewis's *Our Experience
of God* (1959). Had space permitted, I should have liked to include
a full discussion of Bernard Lonergan's brilliant but heartlessly
monumental work *Insight* (1957), which places the notion of
contuition on the broadcast basis and applies it to every conceivable
branch of human thought; I can only refer the reader to my review
of it in *Theology* of February 1958 and to the issue of *Continuum*
of Autumn 1964, which is wholly devoted to Lonergan's life and
work. I should also draw attention to the sympathetic and search-
ing criticisms of my own arguments by Trethowan in his *Essay in
Christian Philosophy* (1954); I believe that our positions are in
fact closer to each other than they then appeared to be. The
outlook of Miss D. M. Emmet's *Nature of Philosophical Thinking*
(1945), which I also discussed in *Existence and Analogy*, is in some
respects similar to Ramsey's; her own reflections on my position
were given in a review-article in *Theology* of December 1949.

The assault on natural theology from the biblical revela-
tionists has continued, but it has become extremely complicated
and confused. Such typical figures as Karl Barth and Gustaf
Aulén continue to insist that the First Cause of the philosophers
has simply nothing in common with the God of Christian Faith—
an assertion practically identical with that made by W. R.
Matthews, a theologian of a very different type[1]—and, though
Rudolf Bultmann could rightly claim to be a biblical theologian
of a kind, they seem to be equally convinced that the God of
Christian Faith has little in common with the God of Bultmann.
This, however, is hardly the place in which to initiate a discussion
of the issues raised by the introduction into the theological realm
of the existentialist philosophy of Heidegger and his school.
(Here it may be well to emphasize that the "existentialism" of
St. Thomas[2] has little in common with the "existentialism" of the
Heideggerians.) Bultmann has been the object of passionate attack
and defence, but little of either has come from the angle of natural
theology or of rational philosophy; one of the few such critiques—
and it is a very powerful one indeed—is provided by H. P.

[1] *God in Christian Thought and Experience*, p. 104, cit. in the present work, p. 105 *infra*.
[2] Cf. *Existence and Analogy*, ch. iii.

Owen's *Revelation and Existence* (1959). The Bultmannite "reduc-
tionism", with its various aspects—existentialist, mythological,
psychological and the rest—has been brilliantly dissected in the
first part of Walter Künneth's *Theology of the Resurrection* (1951).
To turn to Barth, a remarkably penetrating discussion of his
rejection of natural theology has quite recently been given by
Hugo Meynell in his small book *Grace versus Nature*; while
generously describing Barth as the greatest living theologian, he
argues that, while Barth has shown one type of natural theology—
that which sets itself up as the arbiter of what is and is not
"revelation"—to be incompatible with revelation as that is
traditionally understood, he has not shown that human reason
as such is utterly incompetent in matters of faith. Whether the
other giant of modern Protestant thought, Paul Tillich, is to be
described as a supporter of natural theology is difficult to determine; most of those who reject natural theology would describe
him as one, while many of those who defend natural theology
would deny him the title. After the ultra-Kierkegaardian polemics
of Kenneth Hamilton (*The System and the Gospel*, 1963) and the
more moderate assessments of J. Heywood Thomas (*Paul Tillich:
An Appraisal*, 1963) and A. J. McKelway (*The Systematic Theology
of Paul Tillich*, 1964), it is still too early to pass a final judgment
on his achievement, but it seems safe to say that his position can
hardly be described as that of traditional theism. Miss Dorothy
Emmet has made a valiant attempt to clear up some of the ob-
scurities in an article entitled "The Ground of Being" in the
Journal of Theological Studies of October 1964. I refer later on in
this Essay to the comments of B. Mondin on certain elements
in the teaching of both Barth and Tillich.

I urged in my book *Words and Images* (1957) that a satisfactory
doctrine of theistic discourse would have to take into account
the epistemological function of images as well as of concepts.[1] A. M.
Farrer had already anticipated me in his Bampton Lectures
The Glass of Vision (1948), and in that and other books he has given
some very striking and sometimes controversial applications of
this principle. It has also received attention in such books as
F. W. Dillistone's *Christianity and Symbolism* (1955), Gilbert Cope's
Symbolism in the Bible and the Church (1959) and A. C. Bridge's
provocative and evocative *Images of God* (1960). Some of my
own reflections on these various trends may be found in a mono-

[1] Op. cit., pp. 109 ff.

graph entitled *Theology and Images* (1963); I think that, while there has been a great deal of valuable and fascinating writing about the concrete use of images, both material and mental, in Christian history (and here I would mention as worthy of special commendation Gervase Mathew's most illuminating work *Byzantine Aesthetics* (1963)), the theoretical problem of the epistemological function of the image, especially its function in Christian theology, needs far more attention than anyone has yet given it; such attention might, I suggest, forge a much needed link between systematic and biblical theology.

An outstanding event in the Thomist realm has been the appear-ance of the first volumes of the new Dominican edition of the *Summa Theologiae* (this form of the title seems now to be accepted as more authentic than *Summa Theologica*). The scale is extremely lavish and, without the Supplement, the three Parts will run to sixty volumes; in each there is printed the Latin text with English translation (usually free and sometimes even colloquial) *en face*. There are ample Introductions, Notes, Appendices and Glossaries; the different volumes have been assigned to a variety of scholars, not all of them Dominicans. Questions ii to xi of the *Pars Prima* were assigned to Fr. Timothy McDermott, but additional appendices were contributed by Fr. Thomas Gilby. While lucid and helpful, his comments are rightly devoted to balanced expositions rather than to brilliant idiosyncratic suggestions. With regard to the disputed reading in the Third Way (cf. p. 46 *infra*), the text omits the word *semper*, while giving it as a variant reading in the footnote, and the translation makes sense with the robust rendering "Now everything cannot be like this." In the Fifth Way, *Aliqua quae cognitione carent, scilicet corpora naturalia* is oddly taken in the translation as referring to *all*, and not merely *some* bodies obeying natural laws. I may perhaps be allowed to refer to my review of this volume in *Blackfriars* of September 1964 for further comments.

A great part of the present work and of its sequel is devoted to the study of the arguments for God's existence put forward by St. Anselm and St. Thomas Aquinas; these I have taken as typical of the essentialist and the existential[1] approach respectively. I have since made a more detailed consideration of the question and have taken into account Karl Barth's interpretation of Anselm, which seems to me to be quite perverse, and Edward Sillem's

[1] Not "existentialist", in the Heideggerian sense!

interpretation of St. Thomas, which seems to me to be quite brilliant.[1] My conclusions are embodied in an article entitled "Faith and Reason: Anselm and Aquinas", which was published in the *Journal of Theological Studies* of April 1963. This is now included as an Appendix to the present book.

The basic problem with which I was concerned is one which has puzzled all students of St. Anselm and St. Thomas, namely that each of them embeds what professes to be a purely rational proof of the existence of God in the early part of a writing—the *Proslogion* and the *Summa Theologiae* respectively—which quite clearly assumes from the start that God exists and is what the Christian revelation assumes him to be. My answer is that each of them begins with a definition of God which comes to him from the Christian revelation—the *Quo majus nihil . . .* and the *Qui est* or *ipsum esse* respectively—but that the definition is of such a character that the existence of the being to whom it corresponds would seem to be capable of a purely rational proof; the definition comes from revelation, the argument does not. The two definitions are very different, and even more different are the two metaphysical contexts in which they are placed. One is that of Being identified with essence, the other that of Being identified with *esse* or existence. Where they are both profoundly Christian is in identifying God with Being. From the Thomist's point of view St. Anselm's argument was a brilliant and praiseworthy, but unsuccessful, first attempt at a task which St. Thomas discovered how to perform successfully. But both the *Doctor Magnificus* and the *Doctor Angelicus*—were, as I see it, concerned with the same Christian work, *fides quaerens intellectum, philosophari in fide*. I would add that I am glad to find that, if my impression is correct, the view which I have formed of St. Anselm's intention is supported by the very learned introductory essay and commentary which Dr. M. J. Charlesworth has provided in his recent edition of the *Proslogion* and the allied documents.[2]

Two of the basic doctrines underlying the theme of the present book are those of existence and analogy, and it was because it became clear to me that, while I had made extensive use of them, I had given them little explicit consideration that I devoted the sequel *Existence and Analogy* to a detailed discussion of them. For

[1] K. Barth, *Fides quaerens intellectum* (1958, E.T. 1960); E. Sillem, *Ways of Thinking about God* (1961).
[2] *St. Anselm's* Proslogion (1965).

the principle of the primacy of existence over essence and for the view that, while essence is grasped in a concept, existence (*esse*) is affirmed in a judgment, I was heavily indebted to M. Étienne Gilson. The relation between these two constituents of being has been treated by him, both historically and philosophically, in his book *L'Être et l'Essence* (1948), which came into my hands only after I had written *Existence and Analogy;* I was happy to find that it confirmed the general outlook which I had come to hold. A somewhat modified and rearranged English version of his book was published in 1949 under the title *Being and Some Philosophers;* in the second edition (1952) he replied, as I think successfully, under the heading *Sapientis enim est non curare de nominibus* (itself a tag from St. Thomas), to accusations made by Fr. L. M. Régis and Fr. J. Isaac, that he had, substantially and not merely verbally, departed from the position of Aquinas himself. In the foreword to *The Christian Philosophy of St. Thomas Aquinas* (1957; the English translation of the fifth edition of *Le Thomisme*, 1944) he adds his own voice to the chorus of protest against Cajetan being taken as the authentic interpreter of the Angelic Doctor and asserts that Bañes, in spite of an unfortunate lapse concerning accidents having an *esse* of their own, is by far the "most Thomistic of all the Thomists whom it is [his] privilege to know" and eminently so concerning "the notion of the act of being (*esse*) which is the very core of the Thomistic interpretation of reality." "It is," he says, "a sad commentary on the present situation of Thomistic studies that the text of Bañes is almost impossible to find, while another commentary, as misleading as it is painstaking, is still considered the quasi-official interpretation of the doctrine developed by Thomas Aquinas in his *Summa Theologiae*." Characteristically he adds: "This surprising fact perhaps only confirms the time-honoured truth that God does not intend to save man through metaphysics. Still, if we must metaphysicise, it is important that we should do so in the proper way."

On the place of analogy in natural theology I have seen no reason to modify substantially the position which I expounded in chapter v of *Existence and Analogy*. I am, however, glad to draw attention to some of the more important contributions to the study of both analogy itself and St. Thomas's understanding of it which have appeared in the intervening period. For an admirable exposition which, while taking full account of variant interpretations, is basically faithful to what might be described as the "classical" view (namely, that propounded by Cajetan in the early sixteenth century) it would be difficult to improve on James F. Anderson's *Bond of Being* (1949). However, from a number of quarters the validity of Cajetan's view has been radically called in question. Hampus Lyttkens, in his masterly work *The Analogy between God and the World* (1952), traced the history of the concept of analogy from Plato and Aristotle through Albertus Magnus to Thomas Aquinas, and then from St. Thomas's successors to the present day. He did not hesitate to accuse the Angelic Doctor of inconsistencies and changes of opinion. Rejecting the common division of St. Thomas's use of analogy under the two headings of (1) analogy of proportion or attribution and (2) analogy of proportionality, he added two further headings of (3) analogy designating an image from its prototype and (4) analogy designating a cause from its effect. He saw this last type of analogy as primary and, contrary to the grand Thomist tradition, he asserted that the theistic use of analogy of proportionality can be made coherent only by an appeal to the casual analogy and also that analogy of proportionality does not hold a central place in St. Thomas's thought. He ascribed to St. Thomas the view, which I have also urged, that, while the use of analogy is involved in the discussion of the nature of God, it is not directly implicated in the arguments for God's existence. I would however suggest that Lyttkens's discussion suffers in places from being conducted too exclusively in logical, rather than in metaphysical terms. Thus, having made the classical distinction between *res significata* and *modus significandi*, he tends to take analogical predication as simply a combination of equivocal predication as regards the *res* with univocal prediction as regards the *modus*. This interpretation of analogy as a logical conjunction of univocity and equivocity, which is also found in I. M. Bochenski, is a typical example of the effect of a logical interpretation of what is essentially a metaphysical problem.

George P. Klubertanz, who praises Lyttkens's pioneering work, has himself undertaken, in his book *St. Thomas Aquinas on Analogy* (1960), a re-investigation, based on a close analysis of all St. Thomas's mentions of analogy. He accepts Lyttkens's fundamental criticisms of the traditional interpretations (that is, in the main, those of Cajetan, Sylvester of Ferrara and Suarez). While discussing, in great detail and with insight, he holds that St. Thomas had no general theory of analogy, though his use of it was remarkably harmonious and consistent. Ralph McInerny, in *The Logic of Analogy* (1961), also repudiates the Cajetanian formulation, which, he says, results from taking Greek usage as regulative. For him, the doctrine of analogy in St. Thomas is purely logical and in no way metaphysical, though he stresses that this does not imply that the things which are named analogically are logical entities. "It is," he says, "*things* as known which are named and sometimes named analogically. But 'to be named analogically' is a *nomen intentionis*, like 'genus', 'species' and 'syllogism', not a *nomen rei*, like 'effect', 'wise' and 'substance'."[1] On this point of the purely logical nature of analogy, McInerny's view is very different from mine; he claims for it that it makes St. Thomas fully consistent and exempts him from vacillation or development. "St. Thomas did change his mind on several points and thought this important enough to bring to his reader's attention. In the matter of the analogy of names, there is no such warning nor is there any evidence that his thought underwent any significant change."[2]

In contrast to both these writers, Bernard Montagnes, in his very original work *La Doctrine de l'Analogie de l'Être d'après Saint Thomas d'Aquin* (1963), maintains that in the course of his life St. Thomas's thought underwent not merely a development but also an oscillation: in the *Commentary on the Sentences* he adopted analogy of attribution for the relation between creatures and God; in the *De Veritate*, fearing the danger of univocity, he adopted analogy of proportionality and wrote in terms of *form* and exemplarity; finally, in the *Contra Gentes*, the *De Potentia* and the *Summa Theologiae*, he lost this fear, returned to attribution and, recognizing the misleading character of the notion of a "distance" between God and creatures, wrote in terms of *act* and efficacity. While Cajetan held that only analogy of proportionality could be intrinsic, St. Thomas, according to Montagnes, held that attribution could be intrinsic too. Cajetan founds his doctrine of analogy on the real distinction between essence and *esse* in creatures, St. Thomas founds his on degrees of being. For Cajetan, "essence is defined as that of which *esse* is the act and not as that by which the being (*l'étant*) possesses *esse*."[3] Incidentally, in reading Montagnes it is important to notice that he substitutes the terms "relation" (*rapport*) and "proportion" for the usual "proportion" and "proportionality" respectively.

[1] Op. cit., p. 167.　　[2] Ibid., p. vi.　　[3] Op. cit., p. 156.

Battista Mondin's book *The Principle of Analogy in Protestant and Catholic Theology* (1963) was written too soon for him to have access to the work of Montagnes, but his own views are strikingly similar; thus he holds that attribution is primary, that it can be intrinsic and that St. Thomas returned to attribution in his latter thought. His main contribution to the discussion, however, is provided by his thesis that St. Thomas's somewhat baffling variety of classification of types of analogy can be made coherent and intelligible if the basic division of analogy is not into attribution and proportionality but into intrinsic and extrinsic analogy. Thus he proposes the following fourfold scheme:

(1) Analogy according to intrinsic denomination:
    (a) formally based on the relation of efficient causality between the analogates (intrinsic attribution);
    (b) based on similarity of relations (proper proportionality).

(2) Analogy according to extrinsic denomination:
    (a) according to proper signification (extrinsic attribution);
    (b) according to improper (metaphorical) signification (improper proportionality or metaphor).[1]

He then argues that the only form of analogy that provides a satisfactory way of speaking formally about God is (1) (a), namely intrinsic attribution: "In his doctrine of analogy of intrinsic attribution, Aquinas has elaborated an adequate tool for the interpretation of the God-creature relationship, and consequently, an adequate tool for theological language."[2] I have argued to a similar, though not identical effect in *Existence and Analogy*, where I have maintained that analogy of proportionality can be validly used in speaking about God only if it is combined with analogy of attribution *unius ad alterum*, this latter being based on the fact that God is the creator of the finite being from which the analogy is drawn.[3] It may further be remarked that Sylvester of Ferrara, in his commentary on the *Contra Gentes*, asserted the primacy of attribution; so too did Suarez and his school, but with these last the matter was complicated by the conceptualist bias of their epistemology.

The discussion of Thomism is, however, only part of Fr. Mondin's task, and is in some respects the less valuable as being the more common. What he has to say about analogy in Protestant theology is specially interesting. In spite of their many differences,

[1] Op. cit., p. 52.   [2] Ibid., p. 102.   [3] Op. cit., pp. 109 ff.

both Luther and Calvin, he tells us, held that God can be validly
known only by revelation and in faith, both of them denying the
possibility of a natural knowledge of God by man in his present
fallen situation. Furthermore, for both of them the knowledge
of God that man has by faith is only a knowledge by analogy
of extrinsic attribution:

> For both Luther and Calvin the image of God in man is so
> corrupted by sin that a natural knowledge of God becomes
> impossible forever. After the Fall true knowledge of God can be
> achieved only in so far as our words are taken from his Word.
> Neither in Luther nor in Calvin do we find trace of *analogia entis*
> after the Fall. They both assert that an analogy is established by
> Revelation (*analogia fidei*) but it is an analogy chosen by God him-
> self. Even after Revelation our theological language remains
> closed within the domain of extrinsic attribution. Both Calvin
> and Luther consider God's essence as wholly inscrutable. The
> idea of *Deus absconditus* is as native to Calvin's theology as to
> Luther's, with whom it is generally associated.[1]

Quenstedt, it is remarked, ascribed to Luther the view of intrinsic
attribution, but Mondin agrees with Karl Barth in thinking him
mistaken about this. Kierkegaard, too, must be understood as
holding that the *analogia fidei* is only one of extrinsic attribution.

Mondin passes on to consider the two famous contemporary
figures of Paul Tillich and Karl Barth. The obvious question to
pose about Tillich is whether his doctrine of symbolism is, as he
has repeatedly asserted, substantially the same as the Thomist
doctrine of analogy. After a careful examination Mondin comes
to the conclusion that it is not:

> Symbolism and analogy do not solve the problem of theological
> language in the same way. According to the symbolical theory of
> theological language everything can be predicated of God
> symbolically and only symbolically. According to the analogical
> theory some names are predicated literally, some symbolically and
> some neither literally nor symbolically.[2]

However:

> Both analogy and symbolism seek, on the one hand, to prevent
> any segment of creation from making itself God and, on the other
> hand, to shut out no segment or aspect of the creation from being
> a pointer to God; they both war against everything that usurps the
> place of God and everything that mutilates man and the sub-
> human order.[3]

[1] Op. cit., p. 110.   [2] Ibid., p. 144.   [3] Ibid., p. 146.

Turning to Barth, Mondin first points out that it is not true, as is often thought, that Barth repudiates the whole notion of analogy. What is true is that, like Luther and Calvin, he accepts only *analogia fidei* and this only as an analogy of extrinsic attribution. Nor is it even for faith to decide what language it can validly use about God; it is God alone who decides that. "God creates language first for himself . . . Man can extend his language to God because God has already used human language for himself."[1]

> [Barth's] solution may be summarised in three propositions: (*a*) human reason alone is unable to conceive any true concept of God; (*b*) analogous concepts of God are made possible only by Revelation; (*c*) analogous concepts do not express God openly but only hiddenly.[2]

As Mondin remarks, Barth has repudiated the whole doctrine of *analogia entis* with extreme emphasis; he calls it "the invention of Antichrist". But the grounds on which he alleges this, namely that *analogia entis* reduces the infinite qualitative difference between God and man by reducing it to a quantitative difference, and that it turns the divine–human relation upside down by starting with man in order to ascend to God are easily shown to rest on a misunderstanding, at any rate so far as Aquinas is concerned. "It is not in the infinite qualitative difference that one should look for a differentiation between Aquinas and Barth." Is it, then, in their difference about the relation between nature and grace? "Barth is understood to give such priority to grace as to make nature just an instrument of grace. Apart from grace, nature is meaningless . . . Aquinas, on the other hand, is understood to stress the consistency of creature and its self-sufficiency in such a fashion that its relation to grace is purely accidental. Nature has ontological priority over grace, it can exist and be known apart from grace."[3] However, in Mondin's opinion this is an over-simplification:

> Actually neither Aquinas nor Barth maintains the rigid views described above. Barth knows that such an extreme supernatural-ism is impossible. He knows that without some connection between nature and grace, man would not be able to recognise that grace has any meaning for him. . . As to Aquinas, he knows that in the present historical situation, nature and grace are inseparable.

[1] Ibid., pp. 156 ff. [2] Ibid., p. 159. [3] Ibid.

He knows that nature is not an end in itself, but is subordinated to grace as to its superior end. He knows that true knowledge of nature comes from grace.[1]

While recognizing that Barth and St. Thomas differ in emphasis, Mondin concludes that "instead of maintaining two conflicting doctrines, Aquinas and Barth simply emphasize different aspects of the same reality . . . In the description of the God–creature relationship Aquinas's and Barth's views are much closer than in the interpretation of the meaning of theological language."[2]

This is a remarkably irenical conclusion. I shall only add that Fr. Herbert McCabe, in one of the appendices that he has contributed to the new English edition of the *Summa Theologiae*, has told us that in his opinion, "too much has been made of St. Thomas's alleged teaching on analogy"![3]

In concluding this Essay I will only add a few words to supplement the remarks about St. Gregory Palamas which are to be found in this book and, at greater length, in my other books *Existence and Analogy* and *Via Media*. Now that we have the splendid works of John Meyendorff (*Gregory Palamas*, 1959, E.T. 1964) and Vladimir Lossky (*The Mystical Theology of the Eastern Church*, (1944, E.T. 1957); *The Vision of God* (E.T. 1963)) it seems clear that there was little in common between Gregory's doctrine of the divine energies and the sophiology of the Bulgakovian school. What stands out most prominently in Gregory's thought is, on the theological side, its unshakeable biblicism and incarnationalism and, on the philosophical side, its avoidance of both the Scylla of nominalism and the Charybdis of extreme Platonism, by both of which the Orthodoxy of his day was menaced. If he and St. Thomas could have met they would have found a great deal in common. It would not, I think, have surpassed Thomas's ingenuity to reconcile Gregory's doctrine of the divine energies with his own conviction of the divine simplicity. Unfortunately St. Thomas was a Latin of the thirteenth century while St. Gregory was a Greek of the fourteenth. We can only hope that they have enjoyed in heaven the conversation that was denied them on the earth. Unless, of course, they have found there some better thing to do, in comparison with which both their systems are, to use St. Thomas's own phrase, "like straw".

E.L.M.

King's College, London, 1966

---

[1] Ibid., p. 171.   [2] Ibid., pp. 172 ff.   [3] Op. cit., vol. III, p. 106.

CHAPTER I

INTRODUCTION

LOGICALLY and essentially, the doctrine of God is the fundamental doctrine of the Christian Religion, for, according to
its teaching, everything other than God depends upon him and
exists for his glory. "The Catholic Faith is this," declares the
Athanasian Creed, "that we worship one God in Trinity and
Trinity in Unity." This does not mean, however, that the truth
of the triune being of God is the first thing of which most of us
become conscious in our life as Christians. One of the drawbacks
of being a mere creature is that you see everything the wrong way
round; you look at things from man's standpoint and not from
God's. The order in which things ultimately exist, the *ordo essendi*,
is usually the precise opposite of the order in which we come to
know them, the *ordo cognoscendi*;[1] and this is specially true of that
which is of all beings the most fundamental, namely God himself.
If we were brought up in a Christian home, our first religious
contact was with the practices and objects of Christian devotion:
the crucifix or picture above our bed, the prayers which were first
said for us and which later on we learnt to say for ourselves, the
structure and furniture of our parish church. Then we learnt
about the events of our Lord's life and about his teaching, and
only—if ever—when we began to study the Catechism were we
given any systematic instruction about the nature of God. That
is to say, we passed from the practice of Christian devotion to the
study of the person of Christ, from that to some understanding of
God. The logical order is the reverse of this: God comes first; then
Christ, who is God incarnate in human flesh; and last of all, the
faith and devotion of the Church which Christ founded. And this
is, in fact, the order adopted by both the Apostles' and the Nicene
Creed, which begin with God the Father, then summarize the
facts of the Incarnation and of Redemption, and only at the end
mention the inspired Scriptures, the Church and Baptism. As
Karl Barth says, the order is not *genetical* but *essential*.[2] In saying,

[1] Professor Whitehead remarks that the "identification of priority in logic with
priority in practice has vitiated thought and procedure from the first discovery of
mathematics and logic by the Greeks." (*Process and Reality*, p. 75.)
[2] *Credo*, p. 40.

then, that the doctrine of God is the fundamental doctrine of the Christian Religion, we are not suggesting that it is what comes chronologically first in the normal education of the Christian soul; it must, however, be put in the first place if we are trying to make a systematic study of the Christian Faith and to see how its various parts fit together in a coherent and articulated whole.

The doctrine of God is thus of the most immense and basic importance. It has also, at any rate in this country, been most shamefully neglected. It has only too often been assumed that, however much English people may differ about the Church and the Sacraments and even about the person of Christ, they all (with the exception of a few avowed atheists) inherit, as by a kind of birthright, at least the essential elements of the Christian doctrine of God. The consequence is that we find ourselves trying to persuade people that Christ is God when their knowledge of God is practically non-existent, and that Christ is present in the Blessed Sacrament when they have only the haziest knowledge of what the Church believes about Christ.

There may have been some excuse for making this assumption in the last century, when the secularization of life and thought was less advanced than it is now; there is very little excuse for it to-day. And even in the last century it was a dangerous assumption to make, for it cannot be taken for granted that any doctrine of God claiming the name of Christian will form a satisfactory basis on which to erect the superstructure of the Church's sacramental life and practice. That is to say, there is not just one uniform doctrine of God held without variation by all who profess and call themselves Christians, upon which Catholic Christology and sacramental doctrine can be superimposed in successive layers. On the contrary, while it is a matter for gratitude that much truth is held in common by Christians of all denominations, there is a specific Catholic doctrine of God, which differs in important ways from the doctrine taught by liberal Christianity and even more from the vague sentiment of a shadowy and beneficent power behind the visible and tangible universe which is all that the ordinary Englishman has in mind when he admits, with considerable embarrassment, that of course he does really believe in God. And since, as we have seen, the doctrine of God is the basis upon which all other Christian doctrine rests, any error that has been allowed to creep into a man's belief about God will distort his understanding of every other Christian truth. If his idea of God is wrong, his idea of Christ will be wrong, since Christ is God incarnate; and his ideas of the Church and the Sacraments will be wrong, since the Church is Christ's Body and the Sacraments are the instruments of his action upon the human soul. It is a common experience of those engaged in Christian apologetics that the difficulties that trouble people concerning Christian belief and practice turn out, on careful investigation, in the great majority of cases to rest upon a misunderstanding of some element in the Christian doctrine of God. If English people are ever to be won back to the Faith of historic Christendom, it will very largely be as the result of an apologetic based upon a clear and reasoned exposition of the fundamental Fact of the triune and creative God. For, as Dr. W. G. Peck has said, "You cannot have a valid human meaning in a universe which is meaningless; and you cannot maintain the Christian respect for persons when you have dismissed the Christian doctrine of God."[1]

It was said a few lines back that the ordinary Englishman has some sort of vague sentiment which he would on occasions describe as his belief in God, and indeed one of the most universal characteristics of human beings is the possession of such a belief. It is a fairly safe generalization that all human beings, unless they are blinded by prejudice or sophistication, have a conviction, though often a very obscure conviction, of the existence of something which as a matter of fact is God, even though they may not themselves know what it is and even though they may express this conviction in a self-contradictory or ridiculous way. This may be illustrated by one or two examples which are none the less typical for probably being apocryphal. The farmer who complained that that there dratted providence had given him a bad harvest and no mistake, but thanked heaven that there was one above who would see justice done in the end; the Member of Parliament who, having supported the admission of Jews to the House, opposed the admission of atheists on the ground that we all of us believe in some sort of a something somewhere; and the Hyde Park orator who ended his recital of the crimes of organized religion with the words, "Well, if that's Christianity, thank God I'm an atheist"—all these were testifying to their belief in the existence of a being to whom a Christian would have to attribute the name of God even if they were not ready to do so themselves. And this belief is as common in so-called polytheistic primitive tribes as in civilized nations.

[1] *The Salvation of Modern Man*, p. 83.

After his very full discussion of this question in his book, *Religions of Mankind*, Otto Karrer writes: "Our conclusion must be the following: There is a 'consensus generis humani,' an *agreement* of mankind so far as our present knowledge extends, in the belief that there exists an absolute and supreme Being above ourselves which has ordered the universe and human life in particular. Mankind as a whole is conscious of being bound in return . . . by a power which is above all and mightier than itself."[1] And again, "in this widest sense it is true to say that history knows of no people godless and devoid of religion, though here and there particular groups, schools of thought or governments may combat religion."[2] And Fr. W. Schmidt has argued that the primitive religion is the "religion of the High God" and that nature-myths, fetichism, ghost-worship, animism, totemism and magic are absent, or almost absent, among the earliest peoples.[3] Among both savages and the civilized this one God tends to be kept very much in the background and the conception of his nature is often vague to the point of nebulosity; nevertheless, the belief is there, and, while Christian theologians might well hesitate to make it the basis of a formal argument for the existence of God, the universality of its occurrence is impressive.[4]

Historically speaking, the Christian doctrine of God arises from two main sources: Jewish religion, with its culmination in Jesus of Nazareth, and the philosophy of the Græco-Roman world. For the Christian Church emerged from the self-contained *milieu* of Judaism, with its rigid, and indeed almost fanatical monotheism, into the syncretistic culture of the Roman Empire with its Gods many and Lords many. And the history of the Christian controversies of the first five centuries is very largely the story of the adaptation of the categories of Greek thought to the Christian revelation and of the successful resistance on the part of the Church to all attempts to distort her Gospel in the process.

The contrast between the Jewish and Greek approaches to the

[1] Op. cit., E.T., p. 80.   [2] Ibid., p. 81.
[3] *The Origin and Growth of Religion*, E.T., *passim*. A short summary of W. Schmidt's views will be found in his two essays on "The Religion of Earliest Man" and "The Religion of Later Primitive Peoples" in *Studies in Comparative Religion*, Vol. I. He maintains that the essential monotheism of the most primitive peoples degenerates into an Earth-mother and moon religion in the matriarchal-agrarian culture, while remaining substantially itself in the large-family cattle-raising culture. In the later cultures, formed by the fusion of these three primary cultures, the religious conceptions and observances become correspondingly mixed. Cf. Mr. G. K. Chesterton's amusing stories of the experiences of missionaries given in *The Everlasting Man*, p. 101 f. Cf. E. Bevan, *Symbolism and Belief*, ch. ii.
[4] Cf. St. Thomas Aquinas, *S. Theol.*, I, ii, 1 ad 1; *S.c.G.*, III, xxxviii.

problem of existence is very largely the contrast between effective and formal causality. We might perhaps say that, while the Greeks were interested to know what sort of thing the world was, the Jews wanted to know what was the power behind it. But even to say "the Jews wanted to know" is to attribute to them an interest in philosophy which was, except where they became hellenized, foreign to their character. For the Jews were quite certain that they did know, since God had revealed himself to them. In his mighty redemptive acts, when he had delivered them, first from slavery in Egypt and then, centuries later, from captivity in Babylon, and in his disclosure of himself in the teaching of the great line of prophets—of Moses, Elijah, Amos, Hosea, Isaiah, Jeremiah, Ezekiel and the rest—he was manifested, not as a mere principle of philosophic explanation, nor as just the basis of man's moral aspirations, but as the Living God, who had made heaven and earth out of nothing, who had chosen the Jews out of all the nations of the earth to be his own peculiar people, who was righteous and faithful and who demanded righteousness and faithfulness from his servants, who scourged them for their sins and pardoned them on their repentance, who rode upon the thunderclouds and yet dwelt in the hearts of men, and whose throne upon earth was the Holy of Holies in the Temple of Jerusalem. And to those Jews who were Christians the climax of the revelation and the fulfilment of the prophecies had come in the person of Jesus of Nazareth, who by his death and resurrection had overcome death and wrought the supreme deliverance, and had sent his Church into the world filled with the Spirit—the very breath—of the Living God.

The God of the Jews was living, personal and creative; he was supreme Being and transcendent Act. And his claims were inescapable and paramount. "Hear, O Israel, the Lord our God is one Lord, and thou shalt love the Lord thy God with all thine heart and with all thy soul and with all thy might." "Before me there was no God, neither shall there be any after me. I, even I, am the Lord, and beside me there is no saviour. . . . I am the first and the last, and beside me there is no God." The revelation of God's true name and nature had been made to Moses at the burning bush, in words which became the basic text of the Christian doctrine of God—of what M. Gilson has called "the metaphysic of Exodus." His name is Jehovah—"I am that I am" or "I will be that I will be." "Thus shalt thou say to the children of Israel, I AM hath sent me unto you . . . I am Jehovah, and I appeared unto Abraham, unto Isaac and unto Jacob as God Almighty, but by my name I AM I was not known unto them."

In contrast to the Jews, the Greeks were almost devoid of any historical sense, and the Jewish conception of a Great Day at the end of time when the Living God would finally vindicate his supremacy over his creation and destroy the powers of evil was entirely alien to them. Their interest was not in what was happening in the course of history but in what was going on around them. How was the multiplicity of the world to be explained? What was its principle of unity? Who could solve the problem of the many and the one? What was the world's formal cause, its unifying principle? The answers given to these questions were many and diverse, and there were almost as many philosophies as philosophers, but perhaps we shall not be giving too inaccurate a picture of the attitude of Greek philosophy if we say that, when it believed in God at all, it tended to conceive of him as the principle of form and beauty rather than as a creative living being.[1] Whether he was personal, and if so in what sense, was at least doubtful; he could hardly be supposed to be interested in the world, and he influenced it probably through the attraction which his perfection had for it rather than through any deliberate effect exercised by him upon it. God and the prime matter of which the world was composed were very probably co-eternal, and his effect upon it was to impose form and order upon this pre-existent matter; or perhaps it was some kind of emanation from him. Anyhow, there was no question of creation, in the sense of making the world out of nothing—that would be a most unphilosophical idea! To the Greeks God was the great Thought behind the universe; not as to the Jews, the great Act. For nothing ever really changed, or perhaps nothing ever really stood still; in either case there was a complete absence of the Jewish insistence on the contrast between the changing, dependent and yet real world and the changeless, sovereign and creative God.

There had, of course, been some contact between Greek and Jewish thought, especially in the neighbourhood of the city of Alexandria, with its large colony of Jews and its extraordinarily cosmopolitan setting. Indeed, this provided Christian thought

---

[1] The preoccupation of the Greeks with the *nature* of the universe rather than with the *cause* of its existence becomes very clear from the reading of such an account as that given by M. Maritain in his *Introduction to Philosophy*, Part I, ch. ii–iv.

with at least one of the ideas that it needed for the proper formulation of its doctrine.[1] But in spite of this the clash of the Jewish religion of Christianity with the world of Greek thought was like the impact of flint upon steel—and fire was kindled by it.

Notwithstanding the work of the great Christian apologists and Fathers, the final synthesis did not appear until the thirteenth century, and then in the west of Europe. The immediate cause was the production at various times in the previous two centuries of some of the works of Aristotle in inaccurate double or triple translations from the Arabic, often through the medium of Hebrew.[2] The first reaction to this resurrected pagan on the part of Western Christendom was one of fear; in 1215 his works were condemned by the statutes of the University of Paris. But, largely through the labours of one supremely great and saintly intellect, Aristotle's thought was saved for the Christian Church. St. Thomas Aquinas, with his clear delimitation of the spheres of philosophy and theology and his doctrine of an ordered and organic relation between them, achieved the final synthesis of the Judæo-Christian revelation with Greek philosophical thought. It is a little ironical that it was the irreligious Aristotle who became for Christians the Philosopher *par excellence* rather than the much more devoutly minded Plato, to whom the majority of the Fathers had leaned. The answer is really very simple. It is that Aristotle had no religion to speak of, and therefore could be given one, while Plato had one, and it was largely false.[3] In the "baptism" of Aristotle by St. Thomas, Greek philosophy found its culmination and its true home. As Professor Gilbert Murray has remarked, "The religious side of Plato's thought was not revealed in its full power till the time of Plotinus in the third century A.D.; that of Aristotle, one might say without undue paradox, not till its exposition by Aquinas in the thirteenth."[4] And the Aristotelian arguments for a God who drew the world to him by the sheer force of his beauty without, in all probability, any consciousness that the world even existed were transformed, in the hands of the Angelic Doctor, into the Five Proofs of the existence of a living and loving eternal Creator and Preserver of heaven and earth.

[1] Namely, the idea of *Logos* or "Word."

[2] Cf. W. Turner, *History of Philosophy*, p. 320.

[3] Nevertheless there is a much greater Platonic element in St. Thomas than is always acknowledged, especially in his doctrine of the divine ideas (*S. Theol.*, I, xiv, xv; *S.c.G.*, I, xlix–liv. Cf. an article by V. White, O.P., in *E.C.Q.*, Jan.–Apr. 1941, p. 213 f.

[4] *Five Stages of Greek Religion*, p. 17.

*fundamental thing about God is that we
believe that he is.*

CHAPTER II

THE MEANING OF "GOD"

THE first of the Thirty-nine Articles of the Church of England
sums up the Christian doctrine of God in the following words:

> There is but one living and true God (*unus est vivus et verus
> Deus*), everlasting, without body, parts or passions, of infinite
> power, wisdom, and goodness, the Maker and Preserver of all
> things both visible and invisible. And in unity of this Godhead
> there be three Persons, of one substance, power, and eternity;
> the Father, the Son, and the Holy Ghost.

This article deals first with the unity and then with the trinity of
God, in the two sentences of which it is composed. The second
of these falls outside the scope of this book, the first is its primary
concern.

It is immediately clear that this sentence, and the similar statements which we might find in other confessions, gives us a description rather than a definition of God. It catalogues the most
important truths about God which the Christian religion holds,
but it makes no attempt to show that they are consistent with one
another or that all of them are logical consequences of some one
more fundamental truth. And, indeed, in the strictest sense of the
word "definition"—what is technically called "logical definition"
—it is impossible to give a definition of God. For logical definition
proceeds by the method of genus and differentia; it singles out the
being (or beings) with which it is concerned from some larger
class by attributing to it some specific character which is felt to
belong peculiarly to it. Thus, when we define man as a rational
animal, we single him out from the class of animals by means of
the differentiæ "rational"; if we define King George IV as the
first gentleman of Europe, we single him out from the class of
European gentlemen by means of the differentia "first." Some
differentiæ, of course, express the real nature of a being far more
intimately than others; there is a certain arbitrariness about the
definition just given of King George IV that does not attach to
that just given of man. Some philosophers have held that there is
for every being some definition—the *essential* definition—that does

8

not merely enable us to pick it out from the whole aggregate of beings of all kinds, but also expresses its essential nature as a specific entity, though they would add that the task of framing such a definition is usually impossible since the inner essence of things is not in general accessible to the human mind. "Rational animal," they would say, is what we *mean* by "man," but no one would say that "the first gentleman in Europe" is what we mean by "King George IV," even if the definition is accurate and adequate. We are not, however, concerned with this distinction here, but simply with the fact that God cannot be defined by genus and differentia in any way.

But, it may be objected, is this true? Has not God been described by such phrases as "the Supreme Being" and "the Heavenly Father," and does not this imply that he can be singled out from the genus "being" by the differentia "supreme" or from the genus "father" by the differentia "heavenly"? As a mere matter of verbal logic this might seem to be so, but we must not be led astray by words. We cannot lump together in one genus God and everything else, as if the word "being" applied to them all in precisely the same sense, and then pick out God as the supreme one. For if God is the Supreme Being, in the sense in which Christian theology uses the term, "being" as applied to him is not just one more instance of what "being" means when applied to anything else. So far from being just one item, albeit the supreme one, in a class of beings, he is the source from which their being is derived; he is not *in* their class but *above* it. Nor, to take the other example, can we lump together in one class God and all other fathers, and then pick out God from among them as the one who happens to be heavenly. So far from being one item in the class of fathers, he is, as St. Paul told the Ephesians, the Father from whom every fatherhood in heaven and on earth is named.[1] In the technical phrase, when we apply to God a term which is normally used of other beings, we are using it not univocally but analogically; for he is not just one member of a class with them, but their ground and archetype. St. Thomas puts this point more strictly philosophically by first remarking that if God were in any genus it would be that of being, and then showing that being cannot be a genus. For, he argues, following Aristotle, the differences which determine a genus to the species contained in it cannot themselves be members of the genus.

[1] Eph. iii, 15.

analogical language in referring to God.

(For example, when we define man as a rational animal, the difference "rational" must be distinct from the generic essence "animality," otherwise it could not differentiate it.) But every difference must be an instance of being, or else it would be simply non-existent. Therefore, being cannot be a genus.[1] This conclusion has, of course, very far-reaching consequences. It is the basis of the doctrine of the analogy of being, which permeates the whole of the Thomist metaphysics. It involves, for example, that, since being is not a genus that could be determined to its instances by the addition of differentiæ, it must be determined to them by its own inner dynamism. As M. Maritain has written, " It is being which is first known. . . . But nothing can be added to it from outside in order to differentiate it. Everything which differentiates it comes from within it, as one of its modes."[2]

If, however, we cannot, in the strict sense, give a definition of God, can we find some nominal or quasi-definition, that is to say, some form of words which will apply to God and to God alone; and, if more than one such form of words is available, is there one that expresses more fully than any other what God really is? What, that is to say, is the *meaning* of "God"? Or, in more accurate philosophical language, what is the formal constituent of deity? What is God's metaphysical essence? What really makes God God?

This was the question that was exercising the mind of a fat and silent young Italian boy in the thirteenth century, who startled his teacher by suddenly bursting out with the question, "What is God?" Years after he gave his own answer in the assertion that the most proper name of God is *He who is*. But this is to anticipate.

Many of the Greek philosophers would no doubt have replied in effect that the formal constituent of God was thought, and St. Augustine is following in their footsteps when in his *Confessions* he rises to God as subsistent Truth. In the late thirteenth century the Franciscan Duns Scotus regarded infinity as the primary divine attribute; many have given priority to intelligence or to goodness; others, like the modern Russian, Nicolas Berdyaev, to freedom.[3] Many Christians would no doubt feel that, in view of the plain declaration of the Beloved Disciple, the fundamental

---

[1] *S. Theol.*, I, iii, 5. Cf. *S.c.G.*, I, xxv.   [2] *The Degrees of Knowledge*, E.T., p. 211.
[3] Cf. R. P. Phillips, *Modern Thomistic Philosophy*, II, p. 305 f.; M. C. D'Arcy, *Thomas Aquinas*, p. 165 f.: R. Garrigou-Lagrange, *Dieu, son existence et sa nature*, E.T., II, p. 3 f.

fact about God is that he is love, and it will be well to pause for a moment to ask whether this is so.

Certainly we must admit that, from the point of view of Christian devotion, the fact that God is Love is all-important. "God is Love," wrote St. John to his flock, "and he that dwelleth in love dwelleth in God and God in him"; and a whole host of mystics and saints—Augustine, Bernard, Bonaventure, John of the Cross, to mention but a few—have found this to be the basic and all-inclusive truth about their experience of their Creator and Redeemer. But the attribute that is primary from the point of view of devotion may not necessarily be primary from the point of view of theology or of philosophy. For God has other attributes, such as power, wisdom and justice, and it does not seem possible to derive these from the fact of his love. Is there not something even more fundamental, from which love and all these other attributes can be deduced? The Thomist tradition has answered this in the affirmative when it has asserted that the formal constituent of deity is Being.

But before we look more closely at this it will be worth while to consider how St. Anselm of Canterbury in the twelfth century dealt with the question. In the second chapter of his "Address to God concerning his Existence," to which he gave the title *Proslogion*, he gives the famous definition of God on which the whole of his subsequent discussion is based: "Of a truth we believe that thou art *something than which nothing greater can be thought, aliquid quo majus nihil cogitari potest*." We must see precisely what this means

First we must notice that the word is *cogitari*, "thought," not "imagined." St. Anselm does not limit his idea of God by the capacity of the human mind. A simple illustration may help here. If I shut my eyes and try very hard to picture a polygon with a large number of sides, there is a limit to my power of visualization. I may be able to distinguish between a heptagon and an octagon, but beyond that the images which I form will probably be vague. My visual imagination has a limit, depending, of course, upon my personal make-up; suppose it is reached when the number of sides is eight. The most multilateral polygon that I can *imagine* is then an octagon, but I can easily *think* of a polygon with nine sides or ten, or for the matter of that with ten thousand. In this particular sphere my powers of conception are unlimited, while my powers of imagination are certainly not. In a somewhat similar way, in St. Anselm's definition of God we are not concerned with what we can imagine but with what can be thought; God is not limited by the capacities of the human mind.[1]

Secondly, the words are "that than which nothing greater can be thought," not "that than which nothing greater actually exists." Again, a simple parallel may make this clear. Somewhere in the world (or, perhaps, somewhere in the remote depths of starry space) there is an elephant which is heavier than any other elephant now alive. I do not know where it is, nor how much it weighs; nor, I imagine, does anyone else. But its existence is indubitable, unless indeed there are several elephants of precisely the same weight, which is very unlikely. Suppose it weighs x tons. It is the elephant than which no heavier elephant exists. But it is not the elephant than which no heavier elephant can be thought, for I can easily conceive the existence of one whose weight is $x + 1$ tons, and that will be heavier. So, to return to St. Anselm, he is not simply applying the name of God to the greatest being that actually exists, for that might for all we know be finite. God, for him, means that than which no greater can be thought, and so the question immediately arises whether God, as so defined, exists or not.

In the third place, it may be asked whether, after all, the definition really means anything. God, St. Anselm has told us, means that than which nothing greater can be thought, but what does the word "greater" mean when applied to God in relation to creatures? It obviously does not mean "larger," in the sense of spatial extension, or "heavier" in the sense of physical mass; it obviously does mean "more wise" and "more powerful," and it presumably means an infinity of things besides, of which we have no idea. Now there is a real question as to whether the definition in fact has a meaning, and we shall consider it later when we come to deal with St. Anselm's attempt to prove that God exists; it is not, however, what we are concerned with here. The present

[1] The geometrical illustration used must not be taken to imply that we can form an *adequate* concept of God, as we can of the ten-thousand-sided polygon. It is the notion of God's existence rather than the conception of his nature with which we are concerned. Thus St. Anselm himself writes: "Therefore, O Lord, not only art thou that than which no greater can be conceived, but thou art something greater than can be conceived." (*Proslogion*, xv.) He continues: "For because there may be conceived to be something greater than can be conceived, if thou art not that something, there may be conceived to be something greater than thee; which is impossible." Clearly, in this passage "conceive" (*cogitare*) is used both of the notion of God's existence and of the conception of his nature. "There may be conceived to be something greater than can be conceived" means "We may have the notion of the existence of something greater than anything of whose nature we can form a concept." As St. Thomas says, we know *that* God is rather than *what* he is. We shall return to this point later.

difficulty disappears if we accept—as we must, if any statements
that we make about God mean anything—the scholastic doctrine
of analogical predication, according to which the terms of human
speech when applied to God neither mean precisely what they
mean when applied to finite beings nor are completely meaningless.

It will now be clear that St. Anselm's approach to God, like
that of the later theologian Duns Scotus, sees God's formal constituent as his infinity. St. Thomas, however, while he readily
accepts the Anselmian definition as giving a true description of
God,[1] sees God's fundamental attribute as that of self-subsistent
being.[2] And in this he is not merely philosophizing in the abstract.
His starting-point is the "metaphysic of Exodus," the revelation
of the name of God as "I am that I am." *Ego sum qui sum, ait:
sic dices filiis Israel, Qui est misit me ad vos.* And the conception of
God as *ipsum esse subsistens*, subsistent being itself, is fundamental to
his whole discussion of the divine nature.[3] It draws into a unity
all the other attributes and operations of God: simplicity, perfection, goodness, infinity, immutability, eternity, unity, his character
as Prime Mover, as Uncaused Cause, as Sufficient Reason, as
Perfect Pattern and as Final End of all things. It involves that, if
God does exist, his existence is identical with his essence. It means
that he is not merely the *ens maximum*, the greatest being that exists,
but the *maxime ens*, that which completely *is*. So far from being,
as might appear at first sight, an arid and lifeless philosophical
abstraction, St. Thomas's definition of God is fertile of all the
fullness of Catholic devotion. From it we derive the great truths
that God is Life and Love and Power, and if, as we shall see, the
full content of these truths only appears when the arguments of
philosophy are supplemented by the revelation which God has
given of himself in his Son Jesus Christ, it is none the less true that
natural theology, as St. Thomas develops it, is something much
more than a sterile philosophical speculation.

[1] *S.c.G.*, I, xi; *S. Theol.*, I, ii, 1 ad 2. We may add that the great seventeenth-century
Anglican divine, Thomas Jackson, while taking infinity as the primary attribute of
God, insists that it is *infinity in being* (*Works*, V, p. 22 f.). He goes on to assert the
absolute identity of the divine essence and attributes and then argues for the infinity
of the various attributes, immensity, eternity, wisdom, immutability, and so on.
[2] "The selfsame thing which God is, is his existence." (*S.c.G.*, I, xi.)
[3] It should be noted that St. Thomas does not *state* that self-existent being is the
formal constituent of deity. It is, however, widely held that this was his view.

CHAPTER III

EXPERIENCE AND REVELATION

WHY do we believe God exists? This is an extraordinarily difficult question to answer, for several reasons. In the first place, it depends very much upon *us*. It may quite well be the case that no two people have come to believe in God in precisely the same way, and that no two people would give exactly the same set of reasons to justify their belief. But this does not mean that their reasons are necessarily unsound, for there may be quite a number of different arguments leading to a particular conclusion and all of them may be perfectly valid. If, however, we try to set up a body of argument which we feel would convince a perfectly reasonable man, we shall probably lay ourselves open to the charge of artificiality. For the perfectly Reasonable Man is as much an abstraction as is the Economic Man or the Average Man, as Mr. A. P. Herbert has amusingly demonstrated in one of his "Misleading Cases." "Devoid, in short, of any human weakness, with not one saving vice, sans prejudice, procrastination, ill-nature, avarice, and absence of mind, as careful for his own safety as he is for that of others, this excellent but odious character," said Mr. Justice Marrow, "stands like a monument in our Courts of Justice, vainly appealing to his fellow-citizens to order their lives after his own example. . . . All solid virtues are his, save only that peculiar quality by which the affection of other men is won." And, in fact, he is a myth.

As a matter of experience, most Christians have acquired their belief in the existence of God in extremely elaborate ways, which have varied widely from case to case, and which it is most difficult to disentangle into their component parts in such a way as to display a logical and coherent argument. This is not, however, as discreditable to Christian belief as it might seem. For the same thing is true about almost all the beliefs by which our lives from day to day are governed. Very few married men, for example, could give a perfectly watertight answer to the question, "How do you know that your wife really loves you?" Presumably, in most instances, if he was really forced to it, a man could put up some sort of case for the fidelity of the lady in question, but it is very doubtful whether it would be sufficient to convince a court of law, still less a professional logician; and it would in all probability bear only the remotest resemblance to the process which had actually led up to the establishment of his home.

It is very much the same in regard to belief in the existence of God. The trouble is not that there are no reasons, but that there are so many, and that it is impossible to discuss all of them at once. Furthermore, many of them are of the practical type which we constantly use in the affairs of common life but which are difficult to state in a clear and logical form. Nevertheless, it is important to see what rational grounds can be alleged for belief in God, if only for the sake of rebutting the contrary arguments of unbelievers. First, however, it may be well to inquire why any arguments should be necessary.

For, to revert to the parallel which we have just used, there might be some point, on occasion, in asking a man for his reasons for believing in his wife's affection, but we should hardly ask him why he believed that she existed. If we did, and were able to convince him that our question was serious, he would presumably reply, "Why, there she is. Can't you see her?" And it is the existence of God, and not any of his attributes, that we are concerned with at the present moment. Why do we need to ask for arguments and proofs for this?

The answer pretty plainly is that, while we have certain natural faculties for perceiving material objects, such as trees and stones and wives, we have no natural faculty for perceiving spiritual beings.[1] It is indeed true that some naturally devout Christian thinkers have asserted the existence in man of what, by a rather distant analogy, they have sometimes called a "religious sense," but very few of them have claimed for it the immediacy of knowledge that is claimed for the physical senses. It is possible, we may admit, to assert that the bodily senses are open to error, but very few, even among philosophers, have claimed that sensible experience is always and entirely delusion. The fact is that it seems to be commonly accepted that, while the evidence of the bodily senses needs definite and convincing arguments for its rejection, the evidence of any alleged religious sense needs arguments for its justification. We might sum this up by saying that, whether there is a specific religious sense in man or not, it is certainly not as immediate and sure in its operation as are the senses of the body.

[1] The view that we have such a faculty is called "ontologism."

If you want to know whether there is a tree in the garden or not, you merely have to go there and look, and as often as you turn your eyes in the right direction you will see it. It is impossible to produce at will a similar direct apprehension of God.

Having made the foregoing provisos let us then see what grounds can be urged for belief in the existence of God. We may divide the spheres in which man has claimed a knowledge of divine realities into three, and each of them has been claimed as providing the main basis for belief in God's existence. These are religious experience, revelation and reason.

In recent years a number of Christian apologists have tried to find the main justification for belief in God in the sphere of "religious experience," which they have sometimes interpreted as meaning a man's whole experience of life as possessing a religious quality, and sometimes as meaning the experience of certain comparatively rare moments in which the soul is filled with a peculiar and almost indescribable feeling of the certainty of divine reality. As examples of discussions upon these lines we might instance Otto's famous book, *The Idea of the Holy*, with its characterization of the essential content of religious experience as that of a *mysterium fascinans et tremendum*, and Canon Lindsay Dewar's more recent work, *Man and God*.[1]

Now those who claim to have had religious experience are agreed in ascribing to it two qualities. The first is that it is uniquely intimate and convincing, the second is that it is, in its essence, ineffable. The consequence is that, while it is extremely impressive to the person who has it, it is impossible adequately to describe it to anyone else and so to make it the basis of an argument. Either the other person has had it, in which case its very intimacy will have convinced him already, or else he has not had it and its incommunicability will make it impossible to convince him of its genuineness. The most that could be done would be to try to persuade him to put himself in the frame of mind in which he might perhaps experience it for himself, but even this raises difficulties, for it is pretty certain that religious experience cannot be turned on at will. The result of this is that, while religious experience, especially in those higher mystical forms which are known as the spiritual betrothal and the spiritual marriage, may well carry such conviction to the experient that anything in the

---

[1] Cf. H. Balmforth, *Is Christian Experience an Illusion?* This appeal to religious experience is explicitly taken as fundamental in the series of works called "The Library of Constructive Theology." See the General Introduction to that series.

nature of arguments for the existence of God seems to be ludicrously unnecessary, it does not seem capable of forming the basis of arguments to convince the outsider. As Professor Gilson has said, with reference to the great philosopher of religious experience, "After reading W. James, I still want to know if my religious experience is an experience of God, or an experience of myself."[1] There is a good deal to suggest that all that can be communicated in words—and even this only with great difficulty —is some of the psychological concomitants of the experience— states of feeling and the like—and that these can be paralleled in certain conditions of mental exaltation which are anything but religious in their origin, and which may arise from sheer sensuality or from the administration of drugs. The so-called "anæsthetic experience" is well known.

Even those who claim to have had a convincing experience of divine reality themselves are often extremely reluctant to admit the authenticity of similar experiences in others. Dr. E. W. Barnes, in his Gifford Lectures on *Scientific Theory and Religion*, describes his own experience in the following words:

"Four or five times in life, the first time when I was a boy some fourteen years old and the last time at the age of thirty-three, I have felt, enjoyed and wondered at a sudden exaltation which seemed to carry with it an understanding of the innermost nature of things. So vivid has been the experience that I could to-day go to the exact spot in the street of the Oxfordshire village where the flash of revelation first came. Always such experience has occurred in sunshine and out-of-doors, never in church. Always it has been unexpected. Always I have been alone. There has never been ill-health as an exciting cause. On the last occasion, which still remains vivid, I sat down in the early afternoon on a piece of bare turf in a fern-covered moor near the sea. I remember that I was going to bathe from a stretch of shingle to which the few people who stayed in the village seldom went. Suddenly the noise of the insects was hushed. Time seemed to stop. A sense of infinite power and peace came upon me. I can best liken the combination of timelessness with amazing fullness of existence to the feeling one gets in watching the rim of a great silent fly-wheel or the unmoving surface of a deep, strongly flowing river. Nothing happened: yet existence was completely full. All was clear. I was in a world where the confusion and waste and loss inseparable from time had vanished. At the heart of the world

[1] *Reason and Revelation in the Middle Ages*, p. 97.

there was power and peace and eternal life. How long this blank
trance, so full and so empty, lasted I cannot say. Probably a very
short time indeed. It passed, leaving me neither tired in body nor
mentally irritable. The memory remains. And it is because an
inexplicable quality of supreme significance attaches to it that it
remains precious."[1]

Later on in the same chapter Dr. Barnes quotes from a letter
written by a church worker describing her experience in a convent
chapel where the Blessed Sacrament was reserved:

"Immediately I entered I was gripped by a sense of a Holy
presence, the Presence of God, so that I trembled as I knelt. Then
I had to go lower on my knees. I could not help myself falling on
my face. Then I was flooded with the love of God as well as awed
by his nearness. I could not move for a long time. When at
length I felt I must rise and leave the Chapel, I trembled so that
I could scarcely walk. From that time my happiest hours of
communion with our Lord were spent in that presence. I
approached it in fear and trembling each time. . . . I cannot say
that now I have such exceptional experience."[2]

And here is Dr. Barnes's comment:

"Of course, the crisis of the churchworker is easily explained as
the result of suggestion operating in the lower unconscious levels
of her mind. She had heard much argument as to the value of
'reservation'; and, unknown to herself, had in her unconscious
mind accepted the doctrine of a spiritual presence connected
with the consecrated elements. The sudden uprush of latent
convictions had a memorable splendour; but significantly there
was no repetition of the experience after the period of crisis had
passed. The new belief with its emotional atmosphere was
within a few days firmly established."[3]

[1] p. 620.   [2] p. 634.
[3] p. 634. With the above experiences we might compare the following: "I was not
more than eighteen when an inner and esoteric meaning began to come to me from
all the visible universe, and indefinable aspirations filled me. . . . There was a deeper
meaning everywhere. The sun burned with it, the broad front of morning beamed
with it; a deep feeling entered me while gazing at the sky in the azure noon and in the
star-lit evening." "I was aware of the grass blades, the flowers, the leaves on haw-
thorn and tree: I seemed to live more largely through them, as if each were a pore
through which I drank. . . . I was plunged deep in existence, and with all that
existence I prayed." (Richard Jefferies, The Story of My Heart, pp. 199, 14, 15, qu. by
E. I. Watkin, Philosophy of Mysticism, p. 376.) Cf. also the experience at a Procession
of the Blessed Sacrament described by Mr. Alfred Noyes in The Unknown God, p. 304 f.
As an experience of a very peculiar type, which raises the question of the subjective
element acutely, we might instance the three appearances of the Divine Sophia to
Vladimir Solovyev. (See Karl Pfleger, Wrestlers with Christ, p. 223 f.) Cf. again the
instances given by Maritain, Degrees of Knowledge, E.T., p. 279.

One is tempted to wonder what a sceptical psychologist might be able to do in the way of accounting for Dr. Barnes's own experience, but the above passages have been quoted simply in order to illustrate the fact already mentioned, that religious experience may be absolutely convincing to the experient and entirely unconvincing to somebody else.

One of the most trenchant criticisms of the argument from religious experience that has been given in recent years will be found in Dr. F. R. Tennant's great work, *Philosophical Theology*;[1] it is in substance repeated in his *Philosophy of the Sciences*.[2] In the argument from experience, he asserts,

> "the point that is of epistemological import, is the assertion that numinous Objectivity or Reality is cognized with *immediacy* like that of sensatio [*sc.* the *act* of sensation], and as distinct from objectivity of the imaginal or the ideal order. A distinct faculty, not included in such as are contemplated in the psychology of natural knowledge, is thus affirmed; for valuation and emotion are not cognition of existents. Now, in sensatio, the particular *quale* of the impression is given; but there seems to be no corresponding or quasi-impressional *quale* presented, in alleged apprehension of the numinous Reality in the numinous phenomenon or thing. . . . And certainly the clearer conceptions of the numinous, characteristic of more highly developed religion, owe their definiteness to discursive thought. The vague original suggests the imaginal or ideal, rather than the underived such as we encounter in the concrete percept. . . . The numinous Real is indeterminate enough to enter equally well into a multitude of diverse mythologies and religions; it therefore seems to partake of the nature of the vague generic idea, rather than to be comparable with an underived and 'perceptual' object."[3]

Again he writes:

> "The imaginal and the ideational are objective. And emotional attitude can be evoked by such objects as well as by the perceptual, the 'feelings' being as profound and intense in the one case as in the other. The numinous . . . must be objective, but it is a further question, whether it is not conceptual; whether it is also Real; or only ideal, imaginal, or even illusory."[4]

[1] I, ch. xii.   [2] p. 167 f.   [3] *Phil. Theol.*, I, p. 309.
[4] Ibid., I, p. 310. For Tennant, "objective" (with a small "o") means having the status of the object of a mental act, but not necessarily having existence outside the mind concerned in it.

"We may," he admits,

> "believe in the Beyond, or in God, on less direct grounds reached by more circuitous paths; and *then* reasonably interpret numinous or religious experience in terms of the theistic concept and world-view: on the way back, so to say, as distinguished from the way out. But the short cuts of 'immediacy,' often pursued since the downfall of rationalistic proofs, seem to owe their seductiveness and their appearance of being other than 'no thoroughfare,' to the prevalence of the two confusions that have just been mentioned,"[1]

namely, the assumption that what *seems* to be immediate is really so upon reflection and analysis, and the ignoring of the fact that the objective includes the imaginal, etc., as well as the Real.

In dealing with specifically mystical experiences Tennant distinguishes between those that are strictly ineffable and those that admit of translation, partly or wholly, into terms of ordinary imagery and knowledge. Of the former he remarks that, by their very nature, they cannot be made the basis of rational argument, while, in the case of the latter, the imagery adopted is almost invariably derived from the mystic's past history and beliefs and so cannot belong to the alleged exterior object of the experience. In neither instance, therefore, can we argue from the experience to the God who is asserted as its object; the heart of the experience is strictly ineffable and therefore cannot be discussed.

Tennant's conclusion, therefore, is as follows:

> "What is called 'the truth of religion' or 'the validity of religious experience,'cannot be established by the *ipse dixit* of that type of experience. If it is to be established, it must be as reasonable inference from discursive 'knowledge' about the world, human history, the soul with its faculties and capacities; and above all, from knowledge of the interconnexions between such items of knowledge. Thence alone are derived the notions of the numinous, the supersensible, the supernatural, and the theistic idea of God. . . . Knowledge of God, on this view, is in the same case with knowledge of the soul, of other selves, and of the Reality behind the sensible.'worlds' of individual experients."[2]

[1] *Phil. Theol.*, I, p. 311.

[2] Ibid., I, p. 325. One or two comments on Tennant's remarks on mysticism seem to be called for. One is that, in Catholic mystical theology, "revelations" are discouraged rather than sought after; it is supernatural charity, rather than revelations, that unites the soul to God, and in the spiritual marriage extraordinary mystical phenomena almost invariably cease. And the part played by the mystic's own mind in providing the imagery of revelations is recognized quite definitely; Poulain gives thirty-two cases of

As will be seen later on, we shall have some criticisms to past upon Tennant's own approach; but we are at one with him in his rejection of religious experience as providing the primary basis for a rational approach to the existence of God. We shall see in a later chapter that the argument from experience is not to be altogether excluded, and we may note in passing that it forms one of the strands of the "threefold cord" in Professor A. E. Taylor's essay on "The Vindication of Religion,"[1] but we shall maintain that religious experience can only be properly assessed against the background of a theology which has taken as its starting-point the existence of finite beings; then we shall be able to express approval of the statement of Fr. D'Arcy that the argument from experience may well turn out to be "nothing but the old argument from contingency looked at from inside instead of from outside."[2]

Before leaving this question it may be worth remarking that Catholic theology has been on the whole very reluctant to admit that, even in authentic religious experience, there is anything that could validly be described as a direct apprehension or an immediate knowledge of God. The only exception that it would make would be in the rare case of mystical union, properly so called, and then it would say that the soul was apprehended by God, that it was seized upon by him, rather than that he was apprehended by it. And even then it would hesitate to say that the soul saw him in his essence, for it is separated from him both by the gulf that divides the finite from the infinite and by its union with the body, from which, even in ecstasy, it cannot be altogether severed. And it would be even more emphatically insisted that in non-mystical states an immediate knowledge of God in this life is impossible, since our knowledge of God here on earth is always through his

---

effects.[1] This is not, however, to deny that we can really know him, for knowledge by effects is real knowledge, and God's effects upon the soul in which he dwells by grace can be amazingly intimate. "No man hath seen God at any time"—this is indeed true—but "he that dwelleth in love dwelleth in God and God in him," and the promise of the Incarnate Son is, "If any man love me, my Father will love him, and we will come unto him, and make our abode with him."

---

[1] Cf. *S. Theol.*, I, xii, 11; *S.c.G.*, III, xlvii. With the growth in recent years of the view that God gives to all human beings at least a remote and general vocation to contemplative prayer (see, e.g., Garrigou-Lagrange, *Perfection chrétienne et contemplation*) a tendency has appeared in some theologians to admit that in this life it is possible without any *extraordinary* grace to have a direct, though obscure, knowledge of God by pure species and not by the intermediation of sensible things. Dom John Chapman outlines such a theory in the paper, "What is Mysticism?" printed at the end of his *Spiritual Letters*. He argues (1) that the human soul is radically capable of the angelic mode of cognition "by intelligible effects" and (2) that this mode of knowledge of God, which was possessed by Adam before the Fall but lost as a result of the Fall, can be so far restored by grace as to deliver us at least partially and on occasion from the tyranny of sense. It must be noted, however, that it is very obscure and so could hardly form the material for a rational argument for the existence of God and that, in any case, it depends upon the healing power of divine grace and does not inhere in human nature as fallen. Chapman claims to find support for his view in St. Thomas. Cf. the essay by Mr. Christopher Dawson, "On Spiritual Intuition in Christian Philosophy," in *Enquiries into Religion and Culture*.

It is worth noting that, while the approach to God by reason gives solid grounds for belief in a God who is personal, it is much more difficult to derive this conviction from "religious experience." A *mysterium fascinans et tremendum* is not obviously personal, nor indeed is the "power and peace and life" that Dr. Barnes experienced in the village street; still less obviously personal is the object of Richard Jefferies's experience quoted in the footnote on p. 18. And in mystical experience in the strict sense there does not seem to be any direct apprehension of God as personal, except possibly in the ultimate degree of the spiritual marriage. The Christian mystics, of course, know that God is personal, and this, combined with the fact that they are living in intimate moral and sacramental union with Christ, leads them to apprehend their experience as that of a personal God. But psychologically considered there does not seem to be for the most part a direct awareness of personality, as the impersonalistic theology of most non-Christian mystics shows. The Christian explanation of this is, of course, that God so exceeds the capacity of the human mind that the more the soul is brought face to face with God the less it is able to distinguish his features; it is "blinded with excess of light." Hence the phenomenon of the "Dark Night," which only ceases in the completely integrated state of the spiritual marriage in which the soul attains a kind of foretaste of the Beatific Vision. Mr. Aldous Huxley has the ingenious, but perverse, theory that the reason for the Dark Night is that God is really impersonal, and that it takes the soul a long time to get used to this; he claims support for his view from the fact that Hindu mystics, who have never really believed in a really personal God, do not experience the Dark Night. The obvious reply is that the Hindu mystics do not normally achieve a real mystical union with God at all; most Hindu mysticism—perhaps *bhakti* is an exception—is an egocentric psychological technique. (*See* p. 134, n. 1, *infra*.) And, in any case, the Dark Night can take very atypical forms. In the case of certain Islamic mystics, such as al-Hallâj, the authentic features of personalistic mysticism seem to be present. (Cf. A. Huxley, *Ends and Means*, ch. xiii, and *Grey Eminence*, ch. iii and x; J. Maritain, *Degrees of Knowledge*, Part II; E. I. Watkin, *Philosophy of Mysticism*, *passim*, especially ch. xiv; J. Maréchal, *Studies in the Psychology of the Mystics*, E.T., *passim*; Fr. Gabriel of St. Mary Magdalene, *St. John of the Cross*; V. Elwin, *Christian Dhyana*.)

We will now pass on to consider whether the sole significant source of our knowledge of God is to be found in divine revelation. It must first of all be made clear that we are here using the word "revelation" in the strict and proper sense which it has borne in Christian theology, of the unique self-disclosure of himself given by God to the Jewish people and culminating in his personal incarnation in the figure of Jesus of Nazareth, that revelation whose record is found in the Scriptures of the Old and New Testaments and which is preserved and mediated to the world by the Christian Church. If God in fact exists, there is no doubt a secondary sense which the word may bear as indicating the part which is played by the action of God in all man's experience of him and his works, for obviously he will not display himself merely as a lifeless object before the gaze of men. But it is not this "general revelation" that we are concerned with here.

Now certain theologians, particularly of the present-day neo-Protestant school, have maintained with considerable vehemence that the only knowledge of God that man can have—or, at any rate, the only knowledge of him that will not be hopelessly perverted and distorted—is given to us by the deliberate and unilateral action of God in Jesus Christ, and that man is an entirely passive recipient of it, accepting it by a pure act of faith as something which his own powers are totally inadequate to approach. Thus Professor Karl Barth in his Gifford Lectures on *The Knowledge of God and the Service of God* explicitly declares himself as "an avowed opponent of all natural theology."[1] "God," he writes,

> "is the one and only One and proves himself to be such by his being both the Author of his own Being and the source of all knowledge of himself. In both these respects he differs from everything in the world. A God who could be known otherwise than through himself, i.e. otherwise than through his revelation of himself, would have already betrayed, eo ipso, that he was not the one and only One and so was not God. He would have betrayed himself to be one of those principles underlying human systems and finally identical with man himself."[2]

And that this "revelation" to which Barth refers is not general revelation is shown when he goes on to say:

> "True knowledge of the one and only God . . . is based on the fact that the one and only God makes himself known. Every-

[1] p. 6.   [2] p. 19.

thing is through him himself or is not at all. He makes himself
known through himself by distinguishing himself *in* the world
from the world. Otherwise he cannot be known at all. He can
be known because he arises—'Arise, O Lord'—in human form
and therefore in a way that is visible and audible for us, i.e. as
the eternal Son of God in the flesh, the one and only God in
whom we have been called to believe, Jesus Christ. . . . Because
he manifests himself thus, he makes himself knowable to us not
through revelation of some sort or other, but through the fact
of his self-revelation."[1]

We may indeed be grateful for so definite a reaction against the
position of Liberal Protestantism, which tended—and frequently
more than tended—to view Christianity and the non-Christian
religions as so many human activities upon the same level, as a
number of parallel efforts upon the part of man to attain to the
ultimate truth of things. And we are in the whole tradition of
Christendom in recognizing that the things that the human
reason can find out about God look very small and pale by the
side of the tremendous truths that God has revealed about himself
in Christ. Where this tradition, however, parts company with
Barth is in its insistence that, however small and pale they appear,
the deliverances of reason are none the less true in their sphere,
and that they form a necessary base upon which the structure of
revelation is erected. Barth himself is—or was at one time—
prepared to recognize the occurrence of truth outside the sphere
of revelation in the strict sense, and even to concede to it, in a
secondary application, the name of revelation. But he has nothing
but contempt to offer it. "The discussion as to whether there is
not revelation also in 'other religions' is," he writes, "superfluous.
We need not hesitate to grant this to them, for revelation to them
clearly means something very different."[2] With all that he has
written about the uniqueness and supreme importance of the
Revelation that is in Christ we can heartily agree. But we cannot
conclude, as he does, that truth about God acquired in other ways
is therefore irrelevant and to be despised. For all truth is ultimately from God, and something more needs to be said than that,
in comparison with the act of God, the acts of man are as nothing.
It is that, man and his natural powers being themselves the work

[1] p. 20.
[2] From Barth's essay in the symposium *Revelation*, p. 45. A more temperate expression of this point of view is to be found in Emil Brunner. See, e.g., *The Mediator*, E.T.,
Book I, ch. i.

of God, there must be an organic relation between what man can find out about God and what only God can make known to him.

It is for this reason that Catholic theology has distinguished between the sciences of natural and revealed theology, and has also maintained that the two are intimately connected. The problem of their exact relation has received a good deal of attention in recent years, especially from the two distinguished French writers, M. Maritain and M. Gilson.[1] The precise question with which they have been concerned is how, if philosophy (of which natural theology is a part) is simply a work of human reason, there can be such a thing as a specifically Christian philosophy. How are we to account for the difference between the natural theology of an Aristotle and an Aquinas? If natural theology is the work of reason and not of revelation, how can it make any difference whether the natural theologian is a Christian or not? The essence of the answer that is given lies in the fact that, according to the Christian Faith, man's natural powers are themselves weakened by sin, and so his natural knowledge of God is, even in its own order, clouded and distorted; one need not be a Calvinist to recognize that man is not only *spoliatus gratuitis* but also *vulneratus in naturalibus*.[2] The answers given by Maritain and Gilson are, when shorn of technicalities, substantially the same. It is that grace not only supplies perfections that lie above the level of nature, but also restores nature to its own proper integrity; *gratia* is not only *elevans* but *sanans* too. Hence, while in principle there is a certain limited knowledge of God which is accessible to the human reason as such, in practice it is only in the light of revelation that the human reason can function adequately and obtain, even within its own proper limits, a knowledge of God which is free from error. Natural and revealed theology are thus in the abstract autonomous, being concerned respectively with the sphere of reason and nature and with the sphere of revelation and grace, but in the concrete a true natural theology can only be developed in the light of the Christian revelation. Thus Gilson speaks of "those rational truths . . . which did not enter philosophy by way of reason."[3] The relation between natural and revealed theology was described with force and humour by the late Abbot

[1] J. Maritain, *De la Philosophie Chrétienne*; E. Gilson, *Christianisme et Philosophie*, also *Spirit of Medieval Philosophy*, ch. i, ii. Cf. the discussion of "La Croyance et l'Autonomie de la Philosophie" given by Sertillanges in *Le Christianisme et les Philosophies*, I, p. 21 f.
[2] Cf. *S. Theol.*, II i, cix, 2c.   [3] *Spirit of Med. Phil.*, E.T., p. 47.

Chapman in one of his letters. "It is obviously not possible *in practice*," he wrote, "to disentangle the Supernatural from the Natural. The two are warp and woof from which our whole experience is woven. But it *is* possible to do so *in theory*, and SCHOLASTIC PHILOSOPHY deals ONLY with the Natural, and therefore not with life in all its complexity as we know it, but with the world as it would be without revelation and without grace (of all kinds), which are disturbing factors." Again: "The crucial instance of this abstract nature of pure philosophy is in *Natural Theology*, which is a *part* of philosophy; its subject-matter is what man can know of God *without revelation and without grace*; whereas it is (really) OF FAITH that it is within the power of every man to have divine faith (of some kind) and that no one is ever without 'sufficient grace.' ... Consequently, there is not and never has been in the world such a monster as a professor of purely natural religion. A human being falls lower or rises higher, but is never a simply *natural* man."[1]

This has been a digression, but a necessary one. Its purpose has been to justify the position that not by revelation alone, but also by reason, man is able to attain a true but limited knowledge of God. The traditional position maintains that by reason man can become convinced of the existence of God and of certain of his attributes, but that the truth of his threefold nature as Father, Son and Spirit is, while not in itself contrary to reason, beyond the power of reason to discover. It is assumed by the Anglican Bishop Butler in his famous *Analogy of Religion*, and we shall assume it here. It will follow that in discussing the existence of God we shall be relying primarily upon arguments based upon human reason. Nevertheless, in view of the close connection which we have seen to exist between natural and revealed theology, we shall, even in discussing the existence of God, make frequent reference to the Christian revelation; that is to say, we shall follow the line of Aquinas rather than that of Aristotle.

One last remark must be made before we leave this matter of revelation and reason. One of the grounds on which traditional theism has refused to base belief in God simply upon the fact of revelation is that revelation itself needs rational justification. To accept something on the authority of revelation is to accept it because one is convinced that God has said it; and this involves a previous conviction of the existence of God. On what can this

[1] *Spiritual Letters of Dom John Chapman*, p. 192 f.

conviction rest? If it is alleged to be due to an immediate experience of God, that experience itself must be vindicated as authentic and not illusory by the use of reason, unless indeed we were to accept the position, which we have seen reason to reject, that man has a natural faculty by which he can directly perceive God. If, on the other hand, it is not due to such an experience, it must be due to rational conviction. In either case, therefore, reason has to be appealed to, in one way or another, before we can base anything upon revelation. This is why St. Thomas says that "the existence of God and other like truths about God, which can be known by natural reason, are not articles of faith, but are preambles to the articles; for faith presupposes natural knowledge, even as grace presupposes nature. . . . Nevertheless," he adds, no doubt having in mind the ordinary believer who has not succeeded in disentangling the various strands which have gone to produce conviction of the existence of God, "there is nothing to prevent a man, who cannot grasp a proof, accepting, as a matter of faith, something which in itself is capable of being scientifically known and demonstrated."[1] To say that a man's conviction of the existence of God is based upon reason is not to say that he must be capable of setting it out in the form of a technical theological argument; it does, however, mean that before he can accept anything upon the authority of God, he must first of all have been convinced that there is a God and that God has spoken.[2]

[1] *S. Theol.*, I, ii, 2 ad 1.

[2] St. Thomas shows a very pleasing sympathy with the ordinary busy, and not always over-intelligent, man or woman in his insistence that "the truth about divine things which is attainable by reason is fittingly proposed to man as an object of belief." (*S.c.G.*, I, iv.) "Three disadvantages," he claims, "would result if this truth were left solely to the inquiry of reason. One is that few men would have knowledge of God, . . . for three reasons. Some indeed on account of an indisposition of temperament, by reason of which many are naturally indisposed to knowledge. . . . Some are hindered by the needs of household affairs. . . . And some are hindered by laziness. . . . The second disadvantage is that those who would arrive at the discovery of the aforesaid truth would scarcely succeed in doing so after a long time. . . . First, because this truth is so profound. . . . Secondly, because many things are required beforehand. . . . Thirdly, because at the time of youth, the mind, when tossed about by the various movements of the passions, is not fit for the knowledge of so sublime a truth. . . . The third disadvantage is that much falsehood is mingled with the investigations of human reason, on account of the weakness of our intellect in forming its judgments, and by reason of the admixture of phantasms." (Cf. *S. Theol.*, II II, ii, 4*c*.)

Cf. Lancelot Andrewes: "If by knowledge only and reason we could come to God, then none should come but they that are learned and have good wits, and so the way to God should be as if many should go one journey, and because some can climb over hedges and thorns, therefore the way should be made over hedges and thorns; but God hath made his way *viam regiam*, 'the king's highway.' Many are weak natured, and cannot take the pains that is needful to come to knowledge; and many are detained by the affairs of the commonwealth. Many are cut off before they come to

Those who reject this position fall into one of two opposite kinds of irrationalism. On the one hand there are the neo-Calvinists, who rely upon the self-evidencing authority of the Word of God. Against them there lies the criticism which M. Maritain has made of the most eminent of them, Professor Barth. Barth, he says, "wishes to hearken only to God and he wishes only to hearken to God. . . . Yet when he speaks, and most of all when he speaks in order to proclaim that man must only listen to God, it is he himself that speaks, he himself that is heard, and it is his personality which moves and stirs his listeners."[1] On the other hand, there is the attitude, which has been all too common in England in recent years, according to which any real certainty in matters of religion would deprive faith of all its merit. For this school of thought, "believing where we cannot prove" becomes the essence of religion, and sometimes the suggestion is even made that God has deliberately concealed himself from us in order that we may exercise the virtue of believing on insufficient evidence—a view which is somewhat reminiscent of the famous theory of Mr. Philip Gosse that God created the world in the year 4004 B.C. with fossils ready made beneath the surface of the earth as a test of our faith in the historicity of *Genesis*. To it we may reply that, whether or not the existence of God is capable of proof, the merit of faith lies not in the mere intellectual recognition of the fact that there is a God, but in one's readiness to accept its implications. Mere *fides informis* can only increase one's damnation; it is in *fides caritate formata* alone that any merit is to be found. There is no particular

---

age to understand reason and to attain knowledge. . . . If they should in any matter be driven to prove everything by reason, it would drive them into madness. No man can make demonstration of every thing, no not in matters of the world." (*Pattern of Catechistical Doctrine*, ch. ii.)

And Joseph Butler: "It is impossible to say, who would have been able to have reasoned out that whole system, which we call natural religion, in its genuine simplicity, clear of superstition: but there is certainly no ground to affirm that the generality could. If they could, there is no sort of probability that they would. Admitting there were, they would highly want a standing admonition to remind them of it, and inculcate it upon them. And further still, were they as much disposed to attend to religion, as the better sort of men are: yet even upon this supposition, there would be various occasions for supernatural instruction and assistance, and the greatest advantages might be afforded by them." (*Analogy of Religion*, II, i, 1.)

Compare also the definition of the Vatican Council: "*Huic divinæ revelationi tribuendum quidem est, ut ea, quæ in rebus divinis humanæ rationi per se impervia non sunt, in præsenti quoque generis humani conditione ab omnibus expedite, firma certitudine et nullo admixto errore cognosci possint.*" (Sess. III, cap. ii; Denzinger, *Enchiridion*, 1786.)

[1] *True Humanism*, E.T., p. 63. Cf. E. Gilson: "God speaks, says Karl Barth, and man listens and repeats what God has said. But unfortunately, as is inevitable as soon as a man makes himself God's interpreter, God speaks and the Barthian listens and repeats what Barth has said." (*Christianisme et Philosophie*, p. 151.)

connection between charity and uncertainty; and faith will not be of less value if it is a leap not into the dark but into the light.

To summarize the position that has been reached. We have considered briefly two of the grounds that have been urged for belief in God—experience and revelation. The former has been seen to possess the disadvantage, from an apologetic point of view, that, while it may be completely convincing to those who have it, it is incommunicable to those who have not. The latter raises the question as to how its own authenticity is to be vindicated. This does not by any means deprive them of all value. For it may very well be the case that a conviction of God's existence is not to be obtained solely by the construction of formal rational arguments. It may rest not upon one or two logically displayed "proofs," but upon a whole body of considerations, made very largely unconsciously and only with great difficulty disentangled and systematized. Belief that there is a God may be acquired, not in the way in which we deduce from the principles of Euclidean geometry that the angles at the base of an isosceles triangle are equal, but rather in the way—whatever that may be—in which a man is convinced that his wife is faithful to him, that the beer which he is just going to drink is not poisoned, or that there is such a place as Australia. This possibility should not, however, deter us from investigating whether or not reason is capable of demonstrating the existence of God; and in any case, as we have seen, it is impossible to base belief upon experience or upon revelation without questions arising which require the exercise of reason for their answer. Leaving experience and revelation, therefore, we will go on to the main task of this book and inquire what can be asserted about the existence of God from the standpoint of human reason.

CHAPTER IV

THE TRADITIONAL APPROACH

(1) SELF-EVIDENCE OR PROOF?

W E now pass on to consider what can be learnt as to the existence of God by the exercise of the human reason. As we have already seen, even in the discussion of religious experience and of revelation the rational element cannot be altogether excluded. But it was there involved in a different way from that with which we are now concerned. There it came in simply in order to decide whether the claims which were made for religious experience and for revelation were justified; here, in contrast, it is itself the instrument by the use of which the problem of God's existence is to be investigated.

St. Thomas Aquinas divides his discussion of the existence of God in the *Summa Theologica*[1] into three articles: Whether the existence of God is self-evident? Whether it is demonstrable? And, lastly, whether in fact God exists? And he discusses the same three points in greater detail in chapters x to xiii of the First Book of the *Summa contra Gentiles*.

Under the first heading he first of all explains what is meant by self-evidence. "Those things," he tells us, "are said to be self-evident which are known as soon as the terms are known,"[2] and he gives as an example the truth that the whole is greater than the part, which, he says, is known immediately as soon as it is known what is meant by whole and part. This would seem at first sight to exclude any possibility of argument whatsoever. If the existence of God was self-evident in this sense, we should only have to make certain that we understood what was meant by the definition of God in order to see immediately that he existed. And, indeed, M. Gilson has suggested that St. Thomas's great Franciscan contemporary, St. Bonaventure, actually held this position. "For St. Anselm," he writes, "the definition of God implied a content which our thought had to unfold in order to get at the conclusion involved in it," but "for St. Bonaventure, the same definition becomes an immediate evidence, because it participates in the

[1] I, ii. [2] *S. Theol.*, I, ii, 1 obj. 2.

necessity of its content. . . . Since the assertion of God's existence is founded upon the intrinsic evidence of the idea of God, it should suffice to place this idea before our eyes to ensure our perceiving its necessity: if God is God, God exists; and since the antecedent is evident, the conclusion is evident likewise."[1] St. Thomas, however, extends the meaning of self-evidence to include the case in which a certain amount of reasoning is needed in order to render explicit the content which the definition contains. And he is hence led to consider under this heading the famous Ontological Argument expounded by St. Anselm in the second and third chapters of the *Proslogion*.

St. Anselm, as we have already seen, takes as his definition of God "something than which nothing greater can be thought," and he states his argument in the following words:

"It is one thing for a thing to be in the understanding, and another to understand that the thing really exists. For when a painter considers the work which he is to make, he has it indeed in his understanding; but he doth not yet understand that really to exist which as yet he has not made. But when he has painted his picture, then he both has the picture in his understanding, and also understands it really to exist. . . . And surely *that than which no greater can be conceived* cannot exist *only* in the understanding. For if it exist indeed in the understanding only, it can be thought to exist also in reality: and real existence is more than existence in the understanding only. If then *that than which no greater can be conceived* exists in the understanding only, then *that than which no greater can be conceived* is something a greater than which *can* be conceived: but this is impossible. Therefore it is certain that something *than which no greater can be conceived* exists both in the understanding and also in reality."[2]

St. Thomas states the same argument more succinctly without any change in its substance, as follows:

"By this word [*sc.* "God"] is signified that thing than which nothing greater can be conceived. But that which exists actually and mentally is greater than that which exists only mentally. Therefore, since as soon as the word 'God' is understood it exists mentally, it also follows that it exists actually. Therefore the proposition 'God exists' is self-evident."[3]

[1] *Philosophy of St. Bonaventure*, E.T., p. 127.
[2] *Proslogion*, ii. In this and the following extract I have allowed the translation "conceived" to stand and have not substituted the reading used elsewhere in this book, viz. "thought."   [3] *S. Theol.*, I, ii, 1 obj. 2.

The reaction that most people feel when they are first confronted with this example of the *reductio ad absurdum* is very similar
to that which they feel when they see a conjurer extract a rabbit
from an apparently empty hat. They cannot explain how the
rabbit got there, but they are pretty certain that the conjurer
introduced it somehow.[1] The transition that St. Anselm makes
from the realm of verbal definition to that of concrete existence
seems too good to be true, and yet it is not at all easy to see exactly
what is wrong with it. It has been attacked by philosophers of
very different schools, of whom we may instance St. Anselm's
contemporary Gaunilo, St. Thomas Aquinas and Kant; it has also
been many times recast and restated, as for example by Descartes
and Leibniz.[2] Gaunilo objected that if the argument proved anything at all it could equally well be used to prove the existence of a
perfect island, by simply substituting in the definition of God the
word "island" for "something" and the words "more perfect"
for "greater," but to this it could be replied that the very idea of
an island than which none more perfect can be conceived is a
contradiction in terms, whereas this is not evident of God as
St. Anselm defines him. The objection does, however, at least
raise the *possibility* that the definition is self-contradictory; "to
show that the affirmation of necessary existence is analytically
implied in the idea of God," remarks Gilson, "would be, as
Gaunilo remarked, to show that God is necessary if he exists, but
would not prove that he does exist."[3] It was presumably the
recognition of this that prompted Duns Scotus to re-word the
Anselmian definition in the form "*quo cogitato sine contradictione
majus cogitari non potest sine contradictione*: that which can be thought
without a contradiction but than which nothing greater can be
thought without a contradiction," and then to assert that when
and only when God as thus defined has been shown to be "thinkable" the ontological argument is valid.[4]

In fact, the objections that may be brought against the argument are of three types:

It may, in the first place, be suggested as above that for all we
know the definition may be meaningless, it may be as inherently
self-contradictory as would be the idea of a round square. The

---

[1] Cf. C. D. Broad, *Examination of McTaggart's Philosophy*, II, p. 313.
[2] Cf. A. E. Taylor, *E.R.E.*, XII, p. 268.
[3] *Spirit of Med. Phil.*, E.T., p. 62.
[4] *Op. Ox.*, I, d. ii, q. 2, n. 32 (Ed. Vivès, VIII, p. 479). Cf. Harris, *Duns Scotus*,
II, p. 168: A. E. Taylor, *E.R.E.*, XII, p. 270, *s.v.* "Theism."

fact that, whereas we can immediately see the self-contradictoriness of this latter idea, we cannot immediately see any self-
contradiction in the Anselmian definition of God is irrelevant, for
it appears to be the case that there are various self-contradictory
ideas whose self-contradictoriness is not immediately apparent.
Many mathematical logicians believe that the notion of a class
composed of all non-reflexive classes is self-contradictory, but this
self-contradictoriness is not evident from the definition. It is
suspected only because a certain argument based upon the notion
leads in practice to an absurdity. A similar contradiction arises
with the adjective "heterological."[1] May not the Anselmian
definition of God be just as absurd? The suspicion receives some
support from the fact that there is a very similar notion to which
it is known that nothing can correspond: that is, the "schoolboy"
notion of "infinity." If we define "infinity" as a number than
which no greater can be conceived, we are simply using a meaningless set of words, for however large a number we like to conceive
we can always conceive a greater; for example, by adding the
number "one" to it. And there is at least sufficient similarity
between this definition and the definition of God given by St.
Anselm to make us wonder whether perhaps that too may really
be meaningless.[2]

Professor C. D. Broad has followed up this point in much detail.
He first points out an ambiguity in the definition itself. It could
mean either "a being such that nothing more perfect than it is
logically possible" (the comparative interpretation) or "a being
which has all positive powers and qualities to the highest possible
degree" (the positive interpretation). Now, unless all positive
characteristics are mutually compatible, the positive interpreta-

[1] A class is said to be "reflexive" if it fulfils its own defining characteristic. Thus the
class of mathematical ideas is reflexive because it is a mathematical idea; while the
class of cabbages is not reflexive, because it is not a cabbage. The question is then put:
"Is the class of non-reflexive classes reflexive or not?" Either of the answers, Yes or
No, is easily seen to lead to a contradiction.
  A predicate is said to be homological or heterological according as it can or cannot
be predicated of itself. Thus the predicate "verbal" is homological, because it is itself
verbal; while the predicate "pink" is heterological, because it is not itself pink. The
question is asked: "Is the predicate 'heterological' heterological or not?" As before,
either of the answers, Yes or No, leads to a contradiction.
  A discussion of this antinomy is given in F. Gonseth's *Fondements des Mathématiques*,
ch. x. Cf. B. Russell, *Intro. to Math. Phil.*, ch. xiii; M. Black, *Nature of Mathematics*,
p. 97 f.; P. P. Ushenko, *Problems of Logic*, ch. ii.
[2] This possibility is seized upon as the weak point in the Anselmian argument by
Professor A. E. Taylor in his discussion of St. Anselm in the article on "Theism" in
E.R.E., XII, p. 268. As a verbally similar, but obviously meaningless notion, he
instances that of a "line so crooked than none crookeder can be conceived."

tion becomes meaningless.[1] And unless the same condition is
fulfilled the comparative interpretation is inapplicable. For, supposing that A and B are incompatible characteristics, how can we
decide whether the combination ACDEF . . . , from which B is excluded, is more or less perfect than the combination BCDEF . . . ,
from which A is excluded? Furthermore, the positive interpretation will be meaningless unless every positive characteristic
has an *intrinsic* maximum; and unfortunately there are some
characteristics in our experience, such as length or temperature,
which have none. If any such fall within the meaning of
"positive powers and qualities" in the definition, the definition
will then be meaningless. And, lastly, if there is nothing that
answers to the positive interpretation, it is clear that nothing could
answer to the comparative one.[2]

The second objection, and it is the one which St. Thomas puts
forward, is that all that the argument proves is that, if you define
God as St. Anselm does, you are bound to think of him as existing,
but that this does not prove that he exists. That is to say, the idea
of a necessarily existent being does not necessitate its existence.
As Dr. R. P. Phillips writes, "The fact that we conceive, and must
conceive, of God in a certain way, namely as existing of himself,
in no way shows that in fact there is a Being which exists of itself,
but merely that if there is a Being to whose concept existence
attaches necessarily, he will, if he exists at all, exist necessarily."[3]

In the third place, it may be urged that existence is not a quality
like other qualities, the possession of which adds to the perfection
of a being. Ought we to say that a being which exists is more
perfect than a precisely similar being which does not exist? Is
existence a quality that can be added to other qualities, and not
rather something entirely different from qualities, which, in any
actually existing being, underlies them all? Modern logicians

---

[1] It is, we may remark, very far from obvious that, for example, infinite justice and
infinite mercy are compatible. Cf. Garrigou-Lagrange, *Dieu*, E.T., II, p. 108 f.
Leibnitz argued that all positive simple predicates are compossible in a single subject,
since if two predicates are incompossible one must deny what the other affirms and
so one of them must be negative. He previously asserts that all complex predicates
can be resolved into simple ones. See Taylor, *E.R.E.*, XII, p. 272.

[2] *J.T.S.*, Jan. 1939, p. 19 f. I have slightly altered Professor Broad's wording, but
have left the argument unchanged except to question by implication his assumption
that temperature, length, etc., as we know them must be included among the positive
powers and qualities of the definition. To assume this is to deny the principle of
analogy, and Broad presumably does deny it. But even if we accept it, his objection
holds, at any rate as a possibility.

[3] *Modern Thomistic Philosophy*, II, p. 266.

have with considerable cogency criticized Aristotle for treating existence as a predicate; and is this not precisely what St. Anselm was doing in his argument?

Professor Broad has stated this difficulty very forcefully in the following words:

"The Ontological Argument professes to make a *categorical* comparison between a non-existent and an existent in respect of the presence or absence of *existence*. The objection is twofold. (i) No comparison can be made between a non-existent term and anything else except on the hypothesis that it exists. And (ii) on this hypothesis it is meaningless to compare it with anything in respect of the presence or absence of *existence*."[1]

We may, then, not unreasonably share St. Thomas's hesitation to admit the Anselmian argument, much as we may admire its ingenuity. Before we leave the question, however, it will be worth while to make one observation. This is, that the mere occurrence of the argument shows how firmly, by the time of St. Anselm, the concept of God in terms of being had become rooted in Christian thought. M. Gilson has put this with his usual directness and clarity:

"That no trace of it [*sc.* the Ontological Argument] exists in Greek thought is quite undisputed, but it does not seem to have occurred to anyone to ask either why the Greeks never dreamt of it, or why, on the contrary, it was perfectly natural that Christians should be the first to conceive it.

"Once the question is asked the answer is obvious. Thinkers like Plato and Aristotle, who do not identify God and being, could never dream of deducing God's existence from his idea; but when a Christian thinker like St. Anselm asks himself whether God exists he asks, in fact, whether Being exists, and to deny God is to affirm that Being does not exist. That is why the mind of St. Anselm was so long filled with the desire of finding a direct proof of the existence of God which should depend on nothing but the principle of contradiction. . . . The inconceivability of the non-existence of God could have no meaning at all save in a Christian outlook where God is identified with being, and where, consequently, it becomes contradictory to suppose that we think of him and think of him as non-existent."[2]

If now, following the example of St. Thomas, we reject the Ontological Argument for the reasons that have been given, what

[1] *J.T.S.*, Jan. 1939, p. 22. [2] *Spirit of Med. Phil.*, E.T., p. 59.

grounds can we find for believing in the existence of God? How
does St. Thomas himself go about the matter?

We must remind ourselves that the definition of God which he
assumes is somewhat different from St. Anselm's. He thinks of
God, not primarily as *aliquid quo majus nihil cogitari potest*, but as
God revealed himself to Moses in *Exodus*, as *ipsum esse subsistens*.
But this is equally a definition in terms of being, and indeed it is
not difficult to argue that the two notions have really the same
content, and that either of them implies the other. If, then, we
have grounds to suspect that St. Anselm's notion may conceivably
be self-contradictory, will not the same objection apply to St.
Thomas's? The answer to this is that St. Thomas's arguments
are not ontological. They claim, not from the mere content of the
idea, but on quite other and extraneous grounds, to show that a
being corresponding to the idea does in fact exist, and therefore,
by implication, that the idea is not self-contradictory. If he were
not conscious of the necessity of this indirect approach, St. Thomas
could base an ontological argument for the existence of God on his
notion of God just as well as St. Anselm could on his. For no more
than St. Anselm will he admit that God's existence is a mere
accident. "A thing," he writes,

> "can be self-evident in either of two ways; on the one hand,
> self-evident in itself, though not to us; on the other, self-evident in
> itself, and to us. A proposition is self-evident because the
> predicate is included in the essence of the subject, as 'Man is an
> animal,' for animal is contained in the essence of man. If, there-
> fore, the essence of the predicate and subject be known to all, the
> proposition will be self-evident to all . . . If, however, there are
> some to whom the essence of the predicate and subject is unknown,
> the proposition will be self-evident in itself, but not to those who
> do not know the meaning of the predicate and subject of the
> proposition. . . . Therefore I say that this proposition, 'God
> exists,' of itself is self-evident, for the predicate is the same as the
> subject; because God is his own existence as will be hereafter
> shown. Now because we do not know the essence of God, the
> proposition is not self-evident to us; but needs to be demonstrated
> by things that are more known to us, though less known in their
> nature—namely, by effects."[1]

In short, if we knew God in his essence, we should see that his
existence was necessary, but if we did so know him we should not

[1] *S. Theol.*, I, ii, 1c.

need to prove it. We may therefore agree with Professor Broad when he writes:

"St. Thomas Aquinas, I think, would have held that it is necessary that there is something that exists, but that only God or angels can see the necessity of this fact. Men can see only that the existence of God is a necessary consequence of certain facts which, so far as we can see, are contingent, e.g., the fact that there is motion and qualitative change."[1]

The arguments that St. Thomas himself puts forward for the existence of God are the famous *Quinque Viæ*, which are stated in the third article of the second question of the First Book of the *Summa Theologica*. They are, in a general way, based upon Aristotle, though they are completely transformed by the conception of God in terms of being, which we have seen is entirely due to Christianity.[3] They are all of them arguments to the existence of God from the existence and nature of his effects; therefore their scope is considerably limited. Sensible things, says the Angelic Doctor,

"cannot lead our intellect to see in them what God is, because they are effects unequal to the power of their cause. And yet our intellect is led by sensibles to the divine knowledge so as to know about God that he is, and other such truths, which need to be ascribed to the first principle. Accordingly some divine truths are attainable by human reason, while others altogether surpass the power of human reason."[2]

And, so far from being remote and "highbrow" arguments, they are, as Fr. Garrigou-Lagrange has pointed out, nothing more than philosophical refinements of one broad general proof that is used, largely unreflectively, by quite untrained people. He writes as follows:

"The principle of this general proof, 'The greater cannot arise from the less,' condenses in effect into one single formula the principles on which our five typical proofs rest: becoming can emerge only from determinate being; caused being only from uncaused being; the contingent only from the necessary; the imperfect, composite and multiple only from the perfect, simple and one; order only from an intelligence. The principles of the

---

[1] *Examination of McTaggart's Philosophy*, I, p. 23.   [2] *S.c.G.*, I, iii.
[3] There is an interesting discussion of "The Historical Aspect of the *Quinque Viæ*," by Fr. Hilary Carpenter, O.P., in the volume *God*.

first three proofs place in relief especially the dependence of the world upon a *cause*, the principles of the last two insist on the *superiority* and *perfection* of this cause; all of them can be summed up in this formula: 'The greater does not arise from the less; only the higher explains the lower.'

"This general proof needs to be made scientifically precise by the five others; but, while by itself it remains rather confused, it possesses the strength of all the others put together. In it we see realized what theologians teach about natural knowledge of God. 'Although the existence of God needs demonstrating,' says Scheeben (*Dogmatics*, II, 29), 'it does not follow that its certitude is only the result of a reflective and conscious scientific proof, based on our own investigations or the teaching of someone else, nor that its certitude depends on the scientific perfection of the proof. On the contrary, the proof which is necessary for every man in order to attain full certitude is so easy and so clear that one hardly notices the logical procedure which it implies, and that the scientifically developed proofs, so far from giving man his first certitude of the existence of God, only illuminate and con-solidate that which already exists. Moreover, since the proof, in its original form, presents itself as a sort of demonstration *ad oculos* and finds an echo in the deepest recesses of the rational nature of man, it provides the foundation of a conviction stronger and more unshakable than any conviction artificially obtained, and it can-not be shaken by any scientific objection.' "[1]

Garrigou-Lagrange goes on to expound this proof as follows:

"We know beings and facts of different orders: an inanimate physical order (minerals), an order of vegetative life (plants), an order of sensitive life (animals), an order of intellectual and moral life (man). All these beings come into existence and afterwards disappear, they are born and die, their activity has a beginning and an end; thus, they do not exist of themselves. What is their cause?

"If there are beings to-day, then there must always have been something; 'if for one single moment, there is nothing, then there will be nothing for evermore' (*ex nihilo nihil fit*, non-existence cannot be the reason or the cause of being; this is the principle of causality). And it makes no difference whether the series of corruptible beings had or had not a beginning; if it is eternal, it is eternally insufficient: the corruptible beings of the past were as indigent as those of to-day and were no more self-sufficient than

---

[1] *Dieu, son existence et sa nature*, E.T., I, p. 252 f. The English translation of this work is rather free, so I have given, in all extracts from it, a literal translation of my own. The references are to the English edition.

they. How could any one of them, which cannot even explain itself, explain those that come after it? That would be to make the greater arise from the less. There must therefore be, above corruptible beings, a *First Being* which owes its existence to itself alone and which can give existence to others."[1]

It is then successively argued that because the world contains living beings, the First Being must have life; because there are intelligent beings, It must be intelligent; because there are principles of reason, It must be a first and immutable truth; because there are morality, justice, charity and holiness, It must be moral, just, good and holy Itself. Thus, Garrigou-Lagrange concludes, by the principle that "the greater cannot arise from the less" (which is only one form of the principle of causality) we have demonstrated, starting from the world of our experience, that there is a First Being who is at the same time supreme Life, Intelligence, and Truth, perfect Justice and Holiness, and sovereign Good.

[1] *Dieu, son existence et sa nature*, E.T., I, p. 252 f.

CHAPTER V

THE TRADITIONAL APPROACH

(2) The Five Ways

IT must be admitted that St. Thomas himself does not explicitly
state the very general argument which has been outlined in the
last chapter, or claim that his Five Ways are only different forms of
one more ultimate proof. On the other hand, there is one of the
Ways to which he obviously ascribes very special importance, so
much so that in the *Summa contra Gentiles* he lays almost exclusive
emphasis on it. This is the Kinetological Argument, or Argument
from Motion, which he collects out of Books V to VIII of the
Physics of Aristotle; it occurs in substance also in Books XI and
XII of the *Metaphysics*. In his later work, the *Summa Theologica*,
St. Thomas stated the Argument from Motion, not in practical
isolation, but merely as the first of the Five Ways, and moreover
gave it a much shorter and less closely Aristotelian form.[1] This
may show some change in the Angelic Doctor's estimate of the
argument, but there are two other factors that may have been
responsible for it. The first is that the *Contra Gentiles* sets out to be
a primarily philosophical work, whereas the *Summa Theologica*, as
its name implies, is primarily theological; the second is that the
Contra Gentiles was written to refute the teaching of the Muslim
philosophers Averroes and Avicenna and hence naturally meets
them on their own Aristotelian ground.

In its full form the Argument from Motion is of very considerable complexity. It can be stated in either a direct or an indirect
way and is highly technical. It will perhaps be sufficient to give
the main points of the former in the text, and to relegate a summary of the full argument to a footnote.[2] The starting-point of the

[1] Cf. J. Rickaby, *Studies in God and his Creatures*, p. 33 f. A shorter form is also given
in the *Compendium Theologiæ*, I, iii and iv (qu. by Wicksteed, *Dogma and Philosophy*,
p. 281 f.), but it is not quite so compressed as in the *Summa Theologica*.
[2] The Argument from Motion is stated by St. Thomas in ch. xiii of the First Book
of the *Summa contra Gentiles*. A full discussion is given in Gilson's *Christian Philosophy
of St. Thomas Aquinas*. ch. iii.
N.B.—"Movement" means any kind of change.
  "Move" is always a transitive verb.
  "Being moved" does not necessarily mean "being moved by something else,"
  but simply "being in motion."

argument is the existence in the world of our experience of what is called "motion," by which is meant not merely change of position in space but any kind of change. Basing his thought upon the Aristotelian distinction between potentiality and act, δύναμις and ἐνέργεια, the Angelic Doctor asserts the truth of two propositions. The first is that everything which is in motion must be put in motion by something else, since change means the realization in actuality by a being of some property which previously existed in it only in a potential state, and the being cannot itself possess the power of actualizing this potentiality or it would have done so from the start. The second is that we cannot go back to infinity in this series of beings which are in motion and beings which move them. If A is moved by B, and B by C, and C by D, and so on, somewhere we must come to a being—let us call it Z—which is the first in the series, and which both causes the movement of all the others and is itself unmoved and so requires no antecedent being to move it. "It is necessary," writes St. Thomas, "to arrive at a First Mover,

---

I. DIRECT PROOF.
    From two propositions:
       1. *Everything set in motion is so moved by something else.*
          Three proofs of this:
            i. For a thing to be in motion of itself:
               a. It must have the principle of its movement in itself.
               b. It must be moved primarily, i.e. by its whole and not by any part.
               c. It must be divisible and have parts.
               Now, since it is moved primarily, if one part were at rest the whole would be at rest. For if one part were moved while another were at rest, not the whole but a part would be moved primarily. But if the quiescence of the whole depends on the quiescence of a part, the movement of the whole would depend on the movement of the part. Hence the whole is not moved by itself. And this is a contradiction.
            ii. By induction. Things are moved either accidentally or *per se*.
               a. If accidentally, they are not moved by themselves.
               b. If *per se*, then either:
                  α. By force, and so not by themselves. Or
                  β. By nature, and so either
                     aa. By something in them (as animals). Or
                     bb. By something not in them (as heavy bodies).
             Ergo
            iii. Nothing is at the same time and in the same respect both in act and in potency.
       2. *It is impossible to proceed to infinity in the series of movers and things moved.*
          Three proofs of this:
             i. All the members would move at the same time as any one of them. But one, being finite, is moved in a finite time. Therefore, so are the infinite number of them. Which is impossible.
            ii. There would be no first mover, and so nothing would be moved.
            iii. All would be instrumental movers. Which is impossible.
    From 1 and 2 the existence of an immobile First Mover follows.

put into motion by no other; and this everyone understands to be God."[1]

It is interesting to note that, while to the Middle Ages this argument seemed to be the strongest of the five, to the modern mind it is perhaps the least convincing. This may be due to the habit of thought engendered by modern science, of assuming that change, especially change of local position (which is what the word "motion" most readily suggests), is something ultimate which we can take for granted without demanding an explanation. The fact that, whereas the pre-Newtonian astronomers felt the necessity of postulating some force to keep the planets moving at all, Newton stated as his First Law of Motion that any body continues in a state of rest *or of uniform motion in a straight line* except in so far as it is acted upon by a force, is symptomatic of this. And the tendency has gone so far that, in the present century, it is possible for philosophers like Bergson and Whitehead to conceive of change as fundamentally inherent in the category of existence.

II. INDIRECT PROOF.

    Suppose "Whatever moves is moved" is true. It is then true either *per accidens* or *per se.*

      1. Suppose it is true *per accidens.*
        Then:
          i. "Whatever moves is moved" is true. But
          "Nothing that moves is moved" is possible.
          Therefore "There is no motion at all" is possible.
          But it is impossible that there should ever be no motion at all.
          Therefore the proposition is not true *per accidens.*
          ii. Alternatively:
          If *moving* and *being moved* occur together *per accidens,*
          And, as we know, *being moved* sometimes occurs without *moving*;
          Then probably, *moving* sometimes occurs without *being moved.*
        Thus the proposition is not true *per accidens.*
      2. Suppose it is true *per se.*
        Then either:
          i. A mover receives a movement of the same kind as it imparts, which is contrary to experience. Or
          ii. It receives a different kind, and either
            a. We get an infinite regress, which is impossible, since the number of different kinds of movement is clearly finite. Or
            b. After a finite number of steps we get to the same kind, and so the case is reduced to case i.
        Thus the proposition is not true *per se.*
Therefore it is not true at all.

But: we have only proved that the First Mover is unmoved by anything outside itself.

However: if it moved itself, then either:
    i. The whole moves the whole, and it is in potentiality and in act at the same time and in the same respect, which is impossible. Or
    ii. Part of it moves another part, and so again we have an immobile First Mover.

Therefore: there exists an absolutely immobile First Mover.

[1] *S. Theol.*, I, ii, 3c.

Largely as a result of this, though perhaps for other reasons as well, the Aristotelian notions of potentiality and act have become quite unfamiliar to the modern mind, as indeed has the whole process of metaphysical argument. It must, in consequence, be emphasized that we are concerned here with metaphysical and not with purely physical and mathematical concepts. "Physics, beware metaphysics" may have been a very necessary warning in the days of Newton, but "Metaphysics, beware physics" is not less necessary to-day. And, in spite of the difficulties to which it gives rise, the distinction of potentiality and act, or at least some modern equivalent for it, seems to be unavoidable if we are to discuss the extremely mysterious fact of change without subtly substituting something else for it. For unless we are prepared to say that, if X changes into Y, Y was potentially in X before the change, we shall not be recognizing that X *has changed* at all. We shall, instead, be assuming that X has been annihilated and that Y has been created to take its place, and we shall be substituting for the rich complexity of a universe which, with all its processes of generation and corruption, of life and death, persists through time a succession of discrete states without any real continuity. But it must be admitted that, like most of the concepts that Thomism has adopted, the notions of potentiality and act do not ultimately *explain* anything; they do, however, make it certain that we are stating the problem that really has to be solved and are not substituting for it an easier problem having no reference to concrete reality.

Nevertheless, we must be prepared to recognize that, if the modern world finds the notions of potentiality and act difficult to assimilate, the First Way of St. Thomas will make less appeal to it than some of the others will. That is only to be expected.

Something must now be said about the second proposition which St. Thomas asserts, namely, that it is impossible to go to infinity in the succession of movers and moved, and that we must finally arrive at an unmoved First Mover. If this is true, it might be objected, we only arrive at a first mover which is itself a member of the series, and therefore is nothing like the Christian idea of God. It would bear the same relation to the other members of the series as the integer "one" bears to the succeeding members of the series of integers, "two," "three" and the rest. Its status is essentially the same as theirs, except that it happens to have no predecessor. It would appear that here St. Thomas has followed

Aristotle in his wording of the argument in a way that does not
really express his own convictions, for the whole essence of his
position is that God is of an entirely different nature from all
other beings, that he belongs to an infinitely higher order of reality.
Garrigou-Lagrange's remark, which we have already quoted, to
the effect that an eternal series of corruptible beings would be
eternally insufficient, suggests the clarification that is necessary,
and indeed he develops it explicitly in his discussion of the First
Way. The point is not really that we cannot have an infinite
regress in the order of nature, but that such an infinite regress in
the series of moved movers would necessitate an unmoved First
Mover not *in* the order of nature but *above* it. Garrigou-Lagrange
writes as follows:

> "The second proposition, 'We cannot go to infinity in the series
> of movers which are actually and essentially subordinate,' rests on
> the very notion of causality and not on the impossibility of an
> infinite and innumerable multitude. With Aristotle, St. Thomas,
> Leibniz and Kant, we do not see that an infinite series of accident-
> ally subordinate movers in the past would be contradictory. . . .
> What is repugnant is that a movement which exists in fact should
> have its *sufficient reason*, its *actualizing raison d'être*, in a series of
> movers *which have only the status of moved movers*: if all the movers
> receive the influx which they transmit, if there is no first one which
> gives without receiving, the movement could never take place, for
> there would never be a cause for it. . . .
>
> "But there can be no need to come to a halt in the series of *past*
> movers, since they exert no influence on the actual movement
> which is to be explained; they are causes *per accidens*. The
> principle of sufficient reason (*principe de raison d'être*) does not
> oblige us to *terminate* this series of accidental causes, but only to
> *leave* it, to rise up to a mover of another order, *not itself moved,
> and in this sense motionless*, not with the immobility of potentiality
> which is anterior to movement but with the immobility of the
> act which has no need to become because it already is (*immotus
> in se permanens*)."[1]

And, as is well known, St. Thomas caused something of a scandal
in his time by maintaining against contemporaries of the eminence
of St. Bonaventure that it is impossible to prove by reason alone
that the world had a beginning in time.[2]

A further point that calls for comment is St. Thomas's identification of the Prime Mover with God. "This everyone understands

[1] *Dieu*, E.T., I. p. 264 f.   [2] Cf. *S. Theol.*, I, xlvi, 2c; *S.c.G.*, II, xxxviii.

to be God." But has he any right to? As this same point arises in connection with each of the Five Ways, it will be convenient to defer it until our outline of them is complete.

The Second Way is the Proof from Efficient Causality, or, as it is sometimes called, the Ætiological Argument. In the *Summa Theologica* it is given equal prominence with the argument from Motion; in the *Contra Gentiles* it forms a kind of appendage to it. It is important to notice that the idea of efficient causality is somewhat different from what is suggested by the words "cause" and "causation" as they are used in modern physical science. It is sometimes asserted that modern science has no use for efficient causality and, if that means that efficient causality does not fall within its sphere of interest, that assertion may be admitted, at any rate as regards the sciences of physics and chemistry (it is rather less certain in the cases of biology and psychology). But this is quite different from admitting that efficient causality is an unnecessary or discredited notion; the fact is that the method of investigation of the world which physical science adopts—observation of measurable phenomena and their correlation and prediction by general statements—is such as to exclude efficient causality from its purview, and hence renders it quite incompetent to decide whether there is efficient causality or not. Efficient causality is not a physical concept but a metaphysical one, and it is only because the physical scientists of the eighteenth and nineteenth centuries insisted on illicitly talking physics in terms of efficient causality that their successors, having discovered that efficient causality is not what physics is as a matter of fact concerned with, have only too often assumed that it is non-existent.

The notion of efficient causality is inevitable as soon as we inquire not merely *how* things happen, but *why*. Events are caused by other events, things have effects upon one another. And the Second Way proceeds by two steps which are closely similar to those in the First. It begins from the assertion that in the world there is an order of efficient causality, an interrelation, sometimes simple, sometimes very complex, of causes and effects. And it then argues that we cannot proceed to infinity in the sequence of efficient causes; there must be a First Cause, which is itself uncaused but is, directly or indirectly, the cause of everything except itself. And to this, concludes St. Thomas, "everyone gives the name of God."

All that was said in discussing the question of an infinite regress in connection with the First Way will, with obvious verbal changes, apply here. But one or two remarks may be added. We are, it must be noted, not primarily concerned with causes *in fieri*, but with causes *in esse*, that is, not with the causes which bring things into existence but with those that keep them in being. It must be stressed that a cause is needed for the continued existence of a being just as much as for its original production. If the question "Why did it begin?" needs answering, so does the question "Why does it go on?", and just as it would be maintained that unless something had produced it it could not have begun to be, so also it must be maintained that unless something was preserving it it would collapse into non-existence. It was the neglect of this consideration that led the eighteenth-century deists to be satisfied with the idea of a God who had created the world at some date in the remote past but had been since then nothing but an "absentee landlord." We are not, therefore, arguing about a chain of causes stretching back into the past, but about a chain of causes existing in the present and each depending on the one beyond. And, just as with the First Mover, so here with the First Efficient Cause we are not arguing to a first member of the series having the same status as all succeeding members except for the fact of being the first; if the number of beings in the world be admitted to be infinite (though this is a supposition that St. Thomas would have been reluctant to concede[1]), so that the causal chain might have an infinite number of members, it will still be necessary to postulate a Cause outside the series for the existence of the series itself.[2] For an infinite number of insufficient beings will still be insufficient; you cannot get sufficiency out of insufficiency by multiplying by infinity. The argument in its essence is simply this: that in the world we find any number of causes of things, but they all demand causes for themselves. We must therefore either give up philosophizing altogether or admit the existence of a Cause which does not require a cause for itself. And to this, in the words of St. Thomas, "everyone gives the name of God."

The Third Way is frequently called the Cosmological Argument, though that name may quite reasonably be applied to all the five or, at any rate, to the first three, since they all start from a consideration of the *cosmos*, the world of which we ourselves are

[1] Cf. *S. Theol.*, I, vii, 4c.
[2] St. Thomas himself makes this point. Cf. *S. Theol.*, I, xlvi, 2 ad 7.

part. In the *Summa Theologica* it immediately follows the Ætio-logical Argument; in the *Contra Gentiles* it does not appear in the chapter on the existence of God, but, in a simpler and more satisfactory form than in the *Summa Theologica*, in the chapters "That God is eternal" (I, xv) and "That God is to all things the cause of being" (II, xv). It holds a similar position in the *Compendium Theologiæ* in the chapter "*Quod Deum esse per se est necessarium*" (I, vi), where it occurs, as an alternative to an argument from God's immutability, to prove that God's being is necessary. It is generally called the argument *e contingentia mundi*. Its general form is very similar to that of the preceding two, but it raises some special questions.

It first establishes as a preliminary thesis the existence of some necessary being or beings. In the world, it asserts, there are clearly many beings whose existence is possible but not necessary. This is shown by the fact that they are subject to generation and corruption, they come into existence and then pass away, so there cannot be in the nature of things any necessity for them to exist; of any one of them it is true that, since at one moment it exists and at another it does not, it can either be or not be. Now, it is argued, it is impossible for the totality of existent being to be of this type. For, if it were, we should merely have to go back far enough in time to come to a moment when nothing existed. But, if at any moment there had existed absolutely nothing, it is clear that nothing could have subsequently come into existence, and therefore nothing would exist to-day. This would contradict the fact of experience from which we began. Therefore the hypothesis which we assumed must be false. That is to say, at any moment the existence of some being or beings is necessary.[1]

---

[1] The exact nature of the argument in the Third Way is to some degree a matter of uncertainty. I assume that the true reading of a crucial sentence in the proof as stated in *S. Theol.*, I, ii, 3, is *Impossibile est autem omnia quæ sunt, talia [sc. possibilia esse et non esse] esse*, as in the best uncials, and not *Impossibile est autem omnia quæ sunt talia, semper esse*, as in most of the printed editions (I am indebted to Fr. Victor White, O.P., for this information). The latter reading involves a complete *non sequitur*; Fr. Garrigou-Lagrange is reduced to mistranslating it by "*S'il n'y a que des êtres contingents, il est impossible qu'ils existent depuis toujours*" (*Dieu*, p. 270; cf. E.T., I, pp. 293–4). Gilson also takes the second reading when he writes, "*Il est impossible que toutes les choses de ce genre existent toujours*" (*Le Thomisme*, p. 104); the E.T. reads, "It is impossible that everything of this kind should always exist" (*Christian Phil. of St. Thomas Aquinas*, p. 69. Dr. R. L. Patterson ignores the word *omnia*, when he writes, "It is impossible that such things should always exist." (*Conception of God in the Philosophy of Aquinas*, p. 51.) Sertillanges, in the edition of *S. Theol.* edited by him with a French translation gives the longer Latin reading but translates it by "*Il est impossible que tout soit de telle nature*," in agreement with the shorter. Again in *Saint Thomas d'Aquin* he

Having established this fact, the argument proceeds as follows. Such a necessary being either has its necessity caused by another or it has not. Now, if the former alternative holds, we shall have an infinite regress similar to those previously considered. Therefore, there must be some necessary thing whose existence is not caused by another, but which, while it causes the necessity of others, has its own necessity in itself; that is, in other words, something whose existence is involved in its essence. And "this all men speak of as God."

The presentation of the argument in terms of time is not really necessary to it; in the form given in the *Contra Gentiles* and the *Compendium Theologiæ* no reference to time occurs and the two steps are telescoped into one. Dr. R. P. Phillips states it in this shorter form, as follows:

> "It is clear that any existing being which can cease to exist does not contain in itself the reason of its own existence; and must therefore derive its reason of being from something else; and, in

writes "*Peut on penser que tout soit ainsi? Non.*" (I, p. 151.) Maquart (*Elem. Phil.* III, II, p. 304) takes the shorter reading.

It must further be noted that the argument does not assert that, if *every individual existent* comes into being and passes away, there must have been a moment when none of them existed. If we admit the possibility of an actually infinite manifold of things (though, as we have seen, St. Thomas would have been reluctant to do this; cf. *S. Theol.*, I, vii, 4), and suppose that No. 1 has existed for one year, No.2 for two years and generally No. *n* for *n* years, then each of them will have had a beginning and yet there will never have been a moment when none of them existed. What is asserted is that, if existent-being-as-a-whole came into being and passed away, there must have been a moment when nothing existed; this will still be true if we suppose existent-being-as-a-whole to have different compositions at different times. The upshot is thus that, at any moment, the existence of *something* is necessary, and the argument goes on from this.

It is also important to notice the force of the second step in the argument. Having decided that at any moment the existence of *some* thing is necessary, we want to know whether this particular thing exists just because something must exist and this happens to be the thing that does, or whether it exists because its existence is intrinsically necessary. The former alternative, by the regress-argument, involves the existence of some other being whose existence *is* intrinsically necessary; the second alternative furnishes such a being at the start. Therefore, in any case an intrinsically necessary being must exist.

Professor A. E. Taylor, in his long article on "Theism" in *E.R.E.*, Vol. XII, gives a rather different interpretation of the argument. Presumably taking the second of the above readings of the text, he apparently falls into the fallacy mentioned in the second paragraph of this footnote and asserts as the conclusion of the first step of the argument that "There must be 'something in things' which is *necessary*, i.e. INCAPABLE OF NOT EXISTING" (op. cit., p. 270, n. 2, small capitals not in original). He then takes the second step as serving simply to prove that there is *one* ultimately necessary being.

It may be added that the question as to the possibility of an actually infinite manifold is not the out-of-date medieval subtlety that it might appear. The theory of infinite number as developed by Bertrand Russell depends upon the axiom that the number of things in the world is infinite (cf. *Intro. to Math. Phil.*, ch. xiii), an axiom which logicians are by no means unanimous in accepting. (Cf. M. Black, *Nature of Mathematics*, p. 104 f.)

the long run, from a being which exists of itself; for we cannot proceed to infinity in a series of beings which derive their reason of being from some other. To suppose that some contingent being, or the series of such beings, is eternal, does not in any way account for their existence, or relieve us of the necessity of demanding a necessary being as the cause of such eternal existence. Even if the series is eternal, it is eternally insufficient."[1]

Before we go on to consider the last two of the Five Ways, it may be as well to see just where we have got already. The similarity of the three arguments which we have considered will be evident. Each of them argues from some characteristic of beings such as we experience to the existence of a First Being possessing a corresponding attribute. The first one argues from the occurrence of motion (i.e. change) to a First Unmoved Mover, the second from the dependence of finite things to a First Cause, the third from their contingency to a First Necessary Being. Furthermore, each of them establishes its case by denying the possibility of an infinite regress. But, however similar, they are not identical, for they concentrate upon different elements in finite being. Dr. Phillips, in the manual from which we have just quoted, remarks that "though both the first and second ways argue from causation, the first applies it to the transition from potency to act in the becoming of things, while the second applies it to the being of things which demands a cause for its preservation and continuance." Again, while "the second way starts from the observation of causes which continuously bestow on things a certain kind of being," the third starts from "the observation of things which do not possess being of any kind of themselves, and so must receive being simply speaking, and not only a particular kind of being." Thus, he says, the third way "has a wider basis than the second, for it starts with all finite being, not only with those that are causes *per se*. Similarly, the basis of this second way is wider than that of the first, which deals only with causes *secundum fieri*, while the second deals also with causes *secundum esse*."[2]

---

[1] *Modern Thomistic Philosophy*, II, p. 285. Dr. Phillips goes on to state, as a subsidiary consideration, the argument in the form in which we have rejected it in the last note. He assumes the usual reading of the disputed sentence, and then argues that if all beings individually came into being and passed away, there must have been a moment when none of them existed. This involves a transition from the distributive to the collective sense of *omnia* and is a subtle form of the fallacy of composition. Neither he nor Garrigou-Lagrange nor Gilson apparently sees the flaw which the argument contains when it is stated in this way.   [2] Ibid., II, pp. 294, 295.

One difficulty which will be felt by many to the form in which the arguments are stated is that the notion of causation as a simple linear sequence is very much over-simplified. Even in the Middle Ages it must have been obvious that no event ever has only one efficient cause, and the view of the universe that modern science has disclosed to us shows it as a vast system of interconnected operations and entities in which linear causal sequences are rarely to be discerned and, when they can be disentangled, are abstract and rough approximations to the real causal nexus. The criticism may be admitted, but it does not really affect the argument. Indeed, one may suspect that St. Thomas—and perhaps also Aristotle—was merely presenting a simplified picture for the sake of clearness, leaving his readers to see that this simplification did not make any substantial difference to the argument. For a network, however complicated it may be, of entities which are in themselves insufficient is just as insufficient as an infinite linear sequence of them would be; and just as in this latter case, sufficiency cannot be obtained from insufficiency by adding complexity to it. Professor A. E. Taylor has expounded this point very adequately in a well-known essay. He writes as follows:

"I can explain the point best, perhaps, by an absurdly simplified example. Let us suppose that Nature consists of just four constituents, A, B, C, D. We are supposed to 'explain' the behaviour of A by the structure of B, C, and D, and the interaction of B, C, and D with A, and similarly with each of the other three constituents. Obviously enough, with a set of 'general laws' of some kind we can 'explain' why A behaves as it does, if we know all about its structure and the structures of B, C, and D. But it still remains entirely unexplained why A should be there at all, or why, if it is there, it should have B, C, and D as its neighbours rather than others with a totally different structure of their own. That this is so has to be accepted as a 'brute' fact which is not explained nor yet self-explanatory. Thus no amount of knowledge of 'natural laws' will explain the present actual state of Nature unless we also assume it as a brute fact that the distribution of 'matter' and 'energy' (or whatever else we take as the ultimates of our system of physics) a hundred millions of years ago was such and such. . . . As M. Meyerson puts it, we only get rid of the 'inexplicable' at one point at the price of introducing it again somewhere else. Now any attempt to treat the complex of facts we call Nature as something which will be found to be more nearly self-explanatory the more of them we know, and would become quite self-explanatory if we only knew them all, amounts to an attempt to eliminate 'bare fact' altogether, and reduce Nature simply to a complex of 'laws.' In other words, it is an attempt to manufacture particular existents out of mere universals, and therefore must end in failure."[1]

It must be admitted that not all modern scientists would agree to Professor Taylor's further remark that "the actual progress of science bears witness to this." Professor Eddington, in particular, has made a very valiant effort to demonstrate that the whole physical universe, including such apparently contingent characteristics as the number of ultimate particles that it contains, is an inevitable outcome of the way in which the human mind is bound to arrange and classify any impacts that it receives through the medium of sensory stimulation. He has expounded this philosophy of "selective subjectivism" in his Tarner Lectures on *The Philosophy of Physical Science*. But it may be doubted whether what he presents as a demonstration of the entire inevitability of the physical universe really amounts to more than an inverted exposition, illustrated in the most fascinating way from the extraordinarily beautiful theories of modern mathematical physics, of the Aristotelian doctrine of the intelligibility of being. And it may be seriously doubted whether, as a matter of fact, he has succeeded in eliminating the factor of "brute fact" from the universe. The ordinary reader of the work just mentioned receives from it somewhat the same impression of baffled but unconvinced mystification that is produced by the Ontological Argument, with the difference that, whereas St. Anselm produces an apparently previously non-existent rabbit out of an empty hat, Professor Eddington uses his hat in order to reduce a very substantial rabbit to non-existence. And a very acute critic of the lectures referred to has pointed out that there is, in fact, a considerable element of the purely empirical in Eddington's treatment which is obscured by an equivocal use of terms and by a pseudo-Kantian epistemology for which there seems no sound basis.[2]

[1] "The Vindication of Religion," in *Essays Catholic and Critical*, p. 53.
[2] E. F. Caldin on "Eddington, Physics and Philosophy" in *Blackfriars*, March 1940. Professor Whitehead remarks that "the four dimensions of the spatio-temporal continuum, the geometrical axioms, even the mere dimensional character of the continuum—apart from the particular number of dimensions—and the fact of measurability . . . are additional to the more basic fact of extensiveness." (*Process and Reality*, p. 127; cf. Part II, ch. iii, sec. iv; and *Modes of Thought*, p. 212.) See the criticisms of Eddington's earlier expositions (which he does not answer in *The Philosophy*

We will therefore pass on to the consideration of St. Thomas's Fourth Way, leaving one or two further important points raised by the first Three Ways for later discussion when the exposition of the Five Ways is complete.

The Fourth Way is the Argument from Degrees of Being or from Multiplicity; it is also known as the Henological Argument. In the *Contra Gentiles* it is stated with extreme brevity, relying upon two places in Aristotle, as follows.[1] Those things which excel as true excel as beings. But there is something supremely true, because, of two false things, one is falser than the other and therefore one is truer than the other, and this is by approximation[2] to that which is simply and supremely true. Hence there is something that is supremely being. And this we call God.

The presentation in the *Summa Theologica* is rather more elaborate. Among beings, some are more and some are less good, true, noble, and so on. But more and less have a meaning only in so far as things approximate in the quality under consideration to that which possesses the quality in the supreme degree, which "has all of it that there is," as we might say. And this being that possesses the quality in the supreme degree must be the cause of its occurrence in other beings in lesser degrees; as for instance fire, which is the supreme degree of heat, causes all other heat. Therefore, concludes St. Thomas, "there must also be something which is to all beings the cause of their being, goodness, and every other perfection: and this we call God."[3]

Several comments seem to be called for. In the first place, the rather trivial illustration from heat and fire must not be taken too seriously. If it was intended to be more than a remote parallel, St. Thomas would presumably conclude that God was not only perfectly true, good and the rest, but also perfectly hot. It is only to such qualities as truth, goodness and nobility, which of their nature demand something directly akin to them as their cause, that the argument applies, in distinction from those impure perfec-

of Physical Science) by Professor L. Susan Stebbing in *Philosophy and the Physicists*, especially ch. iv. See also the important and very critical review of *The Philosophy of Physical Science* by R. B. Braithwaite in *Mind*, Oct. 1940, and Eddington's reply in *Mind*, July 1941. Cf. Professor C. D. Broad's remark, in criticism of Eddington on this point, that "no valid argument can derive a *singular* conclusion from premises which are all *universal*." (*Philosophy*, July 1940, p. 312.)

   [1] *S.c.G.*, I, xiii. The references are to *Metaphysics* II and IV.
   [2] i.e. "nearness." The truer thing is the nearer to the supremely true.
   [3] *S. Theol.* I, ii, 3.

tions whose nature prevents them from applying directly to God,[1] such as this very instance of heat. Goodness, so the argument claims, demands as its cause a God who is good; while heat, though it necessarily demands a God whose knowledge of possible being includes an idea of heat, does not demand a God who is hot as its cause, but only a God who can create. And this leads on to a further observation.

The question is sometimes raised whether the argument, assuming it is valid at all, proves the existence of an absolute good, truth and the like or only a relative one. That is to say, does it prove a good than which no greater good can be conceived, or only a good than which no greater good exists? And are we not, in either case, confronted with a difficulty? For if the argument asserts an absolute maximum, are we not subtly falling into the Ontological Argument, which we have seen reason to reject? And if it asserts a relative maximum, is not that merely a finite being of a very high degree of perfection and so something less than God? The second alternative must obviously be rejected if the argument is an argument for the existence of God, as it claims to be, but it does not appear that the first alternative is necessarily equivalent to the Ontological Argument. For that argument claimed to deduce the existence of God from the mere concept of him, whereas the argument now under review does not claim to deduce the existence of maximum good from the mere concept of goodness. On the contrary, its starting-point was the concrete existence of things which, albeit imperfectly, are good. There is no transition from the order of concepts to that of existence. The only question is whether the argument can in fact prove what it claims to; whether the concrete existence of finite good necessarily implies the concrete existence of an absolute maximum good. (And similarly, of course, with the other types of perfection.) It is here that the addition which the form of the argument in the *Summa Theologica* makes to that in the *Contra Gentiles* is of importance, for it asserts the existence of a supreme degree of each perfection not merely as the pattern or exemplar of the lesser degrees, but as their creative cause. And because it is creative, that is because it is capable of bestowing *being*, it must, so it is implied, be self-existent

[1] Cf. *S. Theol.*, I, xlv, 7c: "Some effects represent only the causality of the cause, but not its form; as smoke represents fire. Such a representation is called a *trace* (*vestigium*). . . . Other effects represent the cause as regards the similitude of its form, as fire generated represents fire generating; and a statue of Mercury represents Mercury; and this is called the representation of *image*."

being itself. It is not merely that the *idea* of finite perfection implies the existence (or even the idea) of infinite perfection as its *model*, but that the *existence* of finite perfection implies the existence of infinite perfection as its *cause*.[1] There will be more to say about this later on,[2] but we will leave it here for the present.

It is perhaps just worth while to add that, although St. Thomas does not include beauty among the perfections enumerated, the argument will obviously apply to it too. It is therefore not true to suggest, as is sometimes suggested, that St. Thomas has no place for æsthetic considerations in his conception of God. The reason for his omission is far more probably that he did not consider beauty as a distinct perfection from those which he instances. "The beautiful is the same as the good," he says elsewhere, "and they differ in aspect only."[3] "Beauty," writes a modern Dominican, "is the good known and the known loved," and he quotes Eric Gill to the effect that beauty is "a union of the true and the good, and the faculty which has beauty for its object is the whole and undivided mind."[4] St. Thomas, then, will agree with St. Augustine's acclamation of God as *pulchritudo tam antiqua et tam nova*,[5] as the eternal beauty which is the cause of all beauty in created things.

The Fifth Way is the Argument from Design, or, as it is also called, the Teleological Argument, though it is, at least in the form given to it in the *Summa Theologica*, very substantially different from the arguments to which that name has been given since St. Thomas's time. It does not start, as Paley did, from the appearance of design manifested in living organisms, nor, as many present-day writers do, from a similar appearance alleged to be evident in the course of nature as a whole or in processes, either organic or inorganic, extending over centuries or millennia. It simply asserts that, when we are confronted with any being, however insignificant, the question, "What is its purpose?" is just as valid and necessary as the question, "What began it?" or "Why does it go on?" In other words, the very existence of a being, as an ontological fact, necessitates the existence of a final cause for it just as much as that of an efficient cause. If there were only efficient causes and no final causes, nothing could come into

---

[1] Cf. Descartes' Third Meditation.
[2] Cf. the discussion of Professor Broad's objections, p. 57 *infra*.
[3] *S. Theol.*, II I, xxvii, 1 ad 3; cf. I, v, 4 ad 1.
[4] Kenelm Foster, O.P., on "Created Holiness," in *Blackfriars*, Feb. 1941.
[5] *Confessions*, X, xxvii.

existence. Final and efficient causality are equally involved in the production of being. (Incidentally, we may note that the Fourth Way asserted that *formal* causality is involved as well.[1]) Now, in some cases, as in that of intelligent beings, it might be alleged that the internal nature of the being itself provided the final cause; conceivably I myself decide what my actions are *for*, and so I have no need to postulate God as my final cause. But, whether this is true or not of some beings—and the admission need not in any case be too readily made, since we are concerned with the final cause not merely of *actions* but of *being*—it certainly is not true of all. "We see," writes St. Thomas, "that things which lack intelligence, such as natural bodies, act for an end, and this is evident from their acting always, or nearly always, in the same way, so as to obtain the best result. Hence it is plain that not fortuitously, but designedly, do they achieve their end. Now whatever lacks intelligence cannot move towards an end, unless it be directed by some being endowed with knowledge and intelligence; as the arrow is shot to its mark by the archer. Therefore some intelligent being exists by whom all natural things are directed to their end; and this being we call God."[2]

It is fairly clear that, if it is taken in isolation, this argument is insufficient to put the existence of God beyond all shadow of doubt. The teleological nature of beings in their separate particularity, the purposiveness which they show in simply going on existing and operating as the sort of beings that they are, might conceivably be accounted for by supposing that each of them was provided with a spiritual guardian or angel to direct its operations. In the *Contra Gentiles* the argument is put in a rather less strictly metaphysical and superficially more "modern" form; though this last adjective might be questioned, since the reasoning is based upon that of the great eighth-century Greek theologian, St. John of Damascus. "We see," it tells us, "that in the world things of different natures accord in one order, not seldom and fortuitously, but always or

[1] The Aristotelian distinction of the four kinds of cause is thus explained by Dr. Phillips:
"There are . . . four ways in which the cause may pass into the effect; for it may be that *by* which the effect is produced, and we have an efficient cause; or that *for whose sake* the effect is produced, and we have a final cause; or that *out of which* it is produced, and we have a material cause; or that which makes the effect to be *of a particular kind*, and we have a formal cause.
"A man building a house is its efficient cause; it is built to afford protection from the weather, and this is its final cause; it is made of bricks and mortar, its material cause; and it is a building, and a building of a particular kind, which is its formal cause." (*Modern Thomistic Philosophy*, II, p. 234.) [2] *S. Theol.*, I, ii, 3.

for the most part. Therefore it follows that there is *someone by whose providence the world is governed*. And this we call God."[1]

In this form the argument evades the objection we have just mentioned, but it has its own particular difficulties. For, in the first place, is a governor of the world's processes necessarily God? It is not immediately evident that to direct the world and to be the source of its being are necessarily properties of the same being. And, secondly, does the argument face the problem of evil? What sort of governor is the world seen to have? We shall come back to both these points later.

---

[1] I, xiii. Cf. John Dam., *De Fide Orth.*, i, 3.

CHAPTER VI

THE TRADITIONAL APPROACH

(3) Its Significance and Validity

BEFORE we gather up the results of this discussion of the *Quinque Viæ* in order to see exactly where it has led us, it may be well to see what objections can be brought against them as a whole. Kant, it is well known, brought against the Third Way in particular the charge that it made an implicit and illicit appeal to the Ontological Argument in identifying necessary being with *ens realissimum*. Professor W. R. Sorley has pointed out that Kant's criticisms were really directed against theology as such; "We see," he writes, "that they are directed not simply against the old forms of argument, but against any possible arguments for a knowledge of the ultimate nature, or of the whole, of things."[1] Much discussion has ranged round them, and it need not be reproduced here. It will perhaps be more profitable to consider the criticisms recently made by a present-day philosopher, Professor C. D. Broad, who has stated the case against all forms of argument from the existence of the world to the existence of God with consummate clearness. And this task will be all the more

---

[1] *Moral Values and the Idea of God*, p. 299. A very thorough refutation of the Kantian objections is given by Professor A. E. Taylor in *E.R.E.*, XII, p. 276 f., *s.v.* "Theism"; cf., for a more scholastic discussion, H. S. Box, *The World and God*, ch. xxi, or the very long treatment by Garrigou-Lagrange in *Dieu*, E.T., I, p. 61 f. Prebendary R. Hanson writes as follows: "Since the time of Kant they [*sc.* the scholastic arguments for the existence of God] have been very generally held to be invalid, to which it may be sufficient to reply that on the Kantian theory of knowledge they certainly are, but not necessarily so on a different theory of knowledge, and not at all so on the Scholastic and Aristotelian theory of knowledge." ("Dogma in Medieval Scholasticism" in *Dogma in History and Thought*, p. 103.) Cf. Taylor: "It is one question whether Kant has proved that the demonstration of theism is impossible on the assumption that the special doctrine of his *Critique* as to the limits of human knowledge is true, but quite another question whether that doctrine *is* true, and consequently whether Kant has proved the fallaciousness of natural theology unconditionally." (art. cit., p. 276.) Again, Dr. R. L. Patterson, while very critical of St. Thomas in many respects, refuses to admit the validity of the Kantian objections; he points out that St. Thomas did not merely *assume* that necessary being was *ens realissimum*, but argued at length to prove this. (*Conception of God in the Philosophy of Aquinas*, p. 96 f.) Cf. also Maritain, *Degrees of Knowledge*, E.T., p. 224.

It is not always realized that it was only in late middle-age that Kant developed his hostility to natural theology and that in his earlier works he argued vigorously in support of it.

worth while, because in performing it we shall elucidate more thoroughly the nature of the argument itself.

Broad includes under the title of the Cosmological Argument all types of reasoning which assert that because there exist particular things, persons and events possessing certain characteristics there must be some necessary being which is the cause of their existence but requires no cause for its own. His discussion thus covers the first four, if not all, of the Thomist "Ways." He agrees that the coming into existence of certain things and persons and the occurrence of certain events are felt by us to need explanation. "The first move," he says,

> "is to try to explain it by reference to previously existing things or persons . . . and by reference to earlier events. . . . Now this kind of explanation is, in one respect, never completely satisfactory. . . . This is for two reasons. The first is that such explanations always involve a reference to *general laws* as well as to particular things, persons, and events. Now the general laws are themselves just brute facts, with no trace of self-evidence or intrinsic necessity about them. The second and more obvious reason is the following. The earlier things, persons, and events, to which you are referred by explanation in terms of ordinary causation, stand in precisely the same need of explanation as the thing or person or event which you set out to explain."

"It is alleged," Broad continues,

> "that we can conclude, from the negative facts already stated, that there must be a substance which is neither a part of nature nor nature as a collective whole. And we can conclude that there is another kind of dependence, which is not the ordinary dependence of a later state of affairs on an earlier one in accordance with *de facto* rules of sequence. The existence of this nonnatural substance must be intrinsically necessary. And the existence of all natural events and substances must be dependent upon the existence of this non-natural substance by this nonnatural kind of dependence."

This is, of course, simply the argument of Professor Taylor which was quoted a few pages back. But here is Broad's criticism of it. "The human intellect," he says,

> "is completely satisfied with a proposition when either (*a*) the proposition is seen to be intrinsically necessary by direct inspection of its terms, or (*b*) it is seen to follow by steps, each of which is

seen to be intrinsically necessary, from premises which are all seen to be intrinsically necessary. . . . Now it is logically possible that complete intellectual satisfaction should be obtained about natural events and substances if and only if the following conditions were fulfilled. (*a*) If there were one or more existential propositions which are intrinsically necessary. . . . And (*b*) if all other true existential propositions followed with strict logical necessity from these, combined, perhaps, with certain intrinsically necessary universal premises. . . . And I admit that, if the universe is such that this kind of intellectual satisfaction is theoretically obtainable about nature, then its structure must be very much as philosophic Theism says that it is."

However, there is, according to Broad, a suppressed assumption in the argument, namely that the universe is such as to give this kind of intellectual satisfaction. And Broad sees no reason why it should be.

For, he says, "whenever we have this kind of completely satisfactory insight we are dealing with the formal relations of abstract entities, such as numbers or propositions, and not with the existence or the non-formal properties of particulars. There is no reason whatever to think that this kind of rational insight is possible in the latter case."

But this is not the only objection. It has been shown, Broad urges, that for the argument to hold there must be some intrinsically necessary existential propositions. But such a proposition would be of the form, "There *must be* something which has the characteristics x, y, z, etc.," where this set of characteristics constitutes the definition or description of a certain possible object. However, necessary propositions are always of the form, "If anything had the attribute x, it would necessarily have the attribute y," or "*If* p were true, *then* q would be true," that is, they are always conditional. Hence the conclusion of the argument is not only unproven but false.

Furthermore, even supposing there were an existent or existents whose existence was intrinsically necessary, this would not make nature intelligible in the sense required.

"The difficulty is as follows. Anything whose existence was a necessary consequence of its nature would be a *timeless* existent. If a certain set of attributes is such that it *must* belong to something, it is nonsensical to talk of its beginning to belong to some-

thing at any date, however far back in the past. . . . Now
nature is composed of things and persons and processes which
begin at certain dates, last for so long, and then cease. But how
could a *temporal* fact, such as the fact that there began to be a
person having the characteristics of Julius Cæsar at a certain
date, follow logically from facts all of which are *non-temporal*?
Surely it is perfectly obvious that the necessary consequences of
facts which are necessary are themselves necessary, and that the
necessary consequences of facts which have no reference to any
particular time can themselves have no reference to any
particular time."[1]

Let us consider Broad's objections in succession. The first was
that we have no reason to suppose that the universe is such as to
give a certain kind of intellectual satisfaction, a kind which, we
may observe, he says is reached in pure mathematics and hardly
anywhere else. It is the satisfaction obtained when a particular
existential proposition is seen to be the necessary logical consequence of existential propositions which are themselves intrinsically necessary. That is to say, we should obtain this kind of
satisfaction if the proposition, "A world having the characteristics
of the world of our experience exists," was a necessary logical
consequence of the proposition, "God exists," supposing that this
latter proposition was intrinsically necessary. And Broad rightly
says that no such necessary logical implication of the one proposition by the other obtains.

Now we may certainly concede his point. Indeed we may go
further and say that if such a logical implication did hold it would
be exceedingly embarrassing for the Christian, for it would mean
that the existence of the world followed necessarily from the
existence of God; that, to use the terminology of creation, God was
bound to create a world and, indeed, precisely this world and no
other. A Christian would receive very little intellectual satisfaction from a demonstration that the existence of the world
followed from the existence of God in the same way that the
proposition that the angles at the base of an isosceles triangle are
equal follows from the axioms and postulates of Euclidean
geometry.[2] St. Thomas Aquinas, in fact, devotes three chapters
of the *Contra Gentiles* to arguing that God does not necessarily will

[1] *J.T.S.*, Jan. 1939, p. 25 f.
[2] It is usual to take this instance as an example of an indisputable logical deduction,
but anyone who has studied the philosophy of mathematics knows how questionable
even this assumption is. Cf. Gonseth, *Fondements des Mathématiques*, ch. i, ii.

anything other than himself.[1] The Christian theist gets his satisfaction—if that is the word to use—not by convincing himself that
if there is a God there must be a world, but by convincing himself
that since there is a world there must be a God. The world proceeds from God, according to Christian theism, not by a logical
necessity, but by an unnecessitated act of creative will. This may
not give us the same kind of intellectual satisfaction as is given
by a mathematical argument, but Broad has nowhere demonstrated that no other kind of intellectual satisfaction is possible. His
mistake is to have interpreted as an argument in deductive logic
what is in fact an argument in metaphysics.

A similar reply can be made to his second objection, namely
that necessary propositions are always conditional. In logic, of
course, they always are, because logic is always concerned with
the relations between propositions and never with being as such.
Metaphysics, in contrast, is concerned with the inner constitutive
nature of being. If a necessary being exists, it does so not in
obedience to a logical demonstration, but because its very nature
is such as to maintain it in existence, because, if we may venture
to use the expression, it keeps going under its own ontological
steam. And the argument that if beings exist that are not self-
sufficient they derive their being from a being that *is* self-sufficient
is not merely the deduction of one proposition from another by
the rules of logic; it results from an understanding of the very
nature of non-self-sufficient being. We shall return to this point
when we consider precisely what it is that the arguments profess
to do.

The third objection, that temporal facts cannot follow logically
from non-temporal facts, becomes largely irrelevant once we have
recognized that the relation between God and the world is not
merely one of logical dependence. But even so, there is a sheer
confusion of language. For facts in the sense of true propositions
(which is the sense adopted by Broad when he speaks of "the fact
that there began to be a person having the characteristics of
Julius Cæsar at a certain date") can hardly be described as
temporal at all, though the persons or events which they are about
may be temporal.[2] The *fact* that Julius Cæsar was born on a
certain date is true in the twentieth century and was true ten

---

[1] I, lxxxi–lxxxiii. Cf. *S. Theol.*, I, xix, 3.
[2] It is surprising to find Broad falling into this ambiguity, for elsewhere he has
written very convincingly against it. Cf. *Examination of McTaggart's Philosophy*,
ch. xxxv.

thousand years before the great Roman general was born. What Broad presumably means is that a fact involving temporal beings or events cannot follow *as a mere logical consequence* from a fact involving only non-temporal ones, and this we may readily admit. But, as we have said, creation is not an operation of logic but of will. The Christian tradition has consistently maintained that creation is a non-temporal act of the divine will by which the whole temporal created order is maintained in existence, and that the creation and conservation of the universe is one timeless act. The whole of the eleventh book of the *Confessions* of St. Augustine is really an exposition and a development of the theme that the timeless and eternal God has posited the world not *in tempore* but *cum tempore*, by bestowing upon it its whole being. St. Thomas echoes this repeatedly. "The duration of God which is eternity has no parts but is utterly simple. . . . Wherefore there is no comparison between the beginning of the whole creature and any various signate parts of an already existing measure . . . so that there need be a reason in the agent why he should have produced the creature at this particular point of that duration. . . . But God brought into being both the creature and time together."[1] "Newness of movement is consequent upon the ordinance of the eternal will to the effect that movement be not always."[2] "Creation in the creature is only a certain relation to the Creator as to the principle of its being."[3] "The preservation of things by God is a continuation of that action whereby he gives existence, which action is without either motion or time."[4] "God's will to create the world was eternal; not that the world should exist from eternity, but that it should be made when he actually did make it."[5]

We conclude, therefore, that Professor Broad has failed to make good his charges against the validity of arguments from the existence of the world to the existence of God. We may, therefore, go on to consider what, when we look back upon them, we see that the arguments have actually told us.

In looking back upon the Five Ways of St. Thomas, we must first observe that each of them takes its starting-point in finite being, and that, at any rate as regards the first three of them, any finite being will do. In contrast with the favourite modern argu-

---

[1] *S.c.G.*, II, xxxv.　[2] Ibid., II, xxxvi.　[3] *S. Theol.*, I, xlv, 3*c*.　[4] Ibid., I, civ, 1 ad 4.
[5] *De Pot.*, I, iii, 17 ad 9.

ment which, in a rather different sense from that in which the name has been given to St. Thomas's Fifth Way, is usually known as the teleological, they do not ask us to consider the boundless depths of space or the unfathomable ages of past time, they do not argue from any characteristics of the universe as a whole or even of that part of it which is open to our investigation, but from any finite being, of whatever type and however humble it may be. It is not from the properties of this, that or the other finite being that the argument starts, but from the very nature of finite being itself. It calls attention to some aspect of finitude and argues to the existence of a being with some corresponding aspect of infinitude as its ground. It is entirely free from the transatlantic snobbery of size; all finite beings are so poor in comparison with God that the least of them is as adequate as the greatest to lead us to him. "It is enough that things exist for God to be unavoidable," writes M. Maritain. " Let us but grant to a bit of moss or the smallest ant its due nature as an ontological reality, and we can no longer escape the terrifying hand that made us."[1]

> "Two men looked out through prison bars;
>   The one saw mud, the other stars."

But for St. Thomas the mud will form just as firm a basis for belief in God as the stars will, for, in the words of a saint of later time, "All created things are but the crumbs which fall from the table of God."[2]

We may remark here that, while as we have seen, to St. Thomas the Argument from Motion was of primary importance, many later theologians have laid their main emphasis upon the Arguments from Causality and Contingency. Thus in the seventeenth century Dr. Thomas Jackson argues first from the maxim, "Whatsoever hath limits or bounds of being hath some distinct cause or author of being" in order to prove that the existence of the world implies the existence of a First Cause, and then from the maxim, "Whatsoever hath no cause of being can have no limits or bounds of being," in order to prove that this First Cause is infinite. He distinctly states that he is concerned with natural and not temporal precedence, and argues:

---

[1] *The Degrees of Knowledge*, E.T., p. 110.
[2] St. John of the Cross, *Ascent of Mount Carmel*, I, vi, 2. Cf. Robert Sanderson: "From the goodness of the least creature guess we at the excellent goodness of the great Creator. *Ex pede Herculem.*" (Sermon at Paul's Cross, 21st November 1624, quoted in *Anglicanism*, p. 227.)

"Whether we conceive effects and causes distinctly as they are in nature, or in gross, so long as we acknowledge them (this or that way conceived) to be finite and limited, we must acknowledge some cause of their limitation, which (as we suppose) cannot be distinct from the cause of their being. . . .

"The greatest fulness of finite existence conceivable cannot reach beyond all possibility of non-existence, nor can possibility of non-existence and perpetual actual existence be indissolubly wedded in any finite nature, save only by his infinite power who essentially is, or whose essence is to exist, or to be the inexhaustible fountain of all being. The necessary supposal or acknowledgment of such an infinite or essentially existent power cannot more strongly or more perspicuously be inferred, than by the reduction of known effects unto their causes, and of these causative entities (whose number and ranks are finite) into one prime essence, whence all of them are derived, itself being underivable from any cause or essence conceivable. In that this prime Essence hath no cause of being, it can have no beginning of being: and yet is beginning of being the first and prime limit of being, without whose precedence other bounds or limits of being cannot follow."[1]

And a century later Bishop Beveridge in his *Discourse on the Thirty-nine Articles* states the regress-argument for a First Cause in the classical form,[2] while in his *Thesaurus Theologicus* he outlines his first argument for the existence of God as follows:

"1. From the order of causes; for of every effect there must be a cause, till we come to the first and Universal cause of all things.
"Everything that is, was either made or not made; if made, it must be made by something that was not made."

and then adds in confirmation arguments from conscience, miracles, prophecy and universal consent.[3] In his *Private Thoughts* he gives the argument in a peculiar quasi-Cartesian form:

"The other articles of my faith I think to be true because they are so; this is true, because I think it so: for if there was no God, and so this article not true, I could not be, and so not think it true. But in that I think, I am sure I am; and in that I am, I am sure there is a God; for if there was no God, how came I to be?"

[1] *Works*, V, p. 12 f. First published in 1628–9.
[2] Ibid., VII, p. 5. First published posthumously in 1716.
[3] Ibid., IX, p. 49. No details of the arguments are given. The *Thesaurus* was first published in 1711, posthumously.

He adds that

> "the like may be said of all other created beings in the world.
> For there is no natural cause can give being to any thing, unless it
> has that being it gives in itself; for it is a received maxim in
> philosophy, that 'nothing can give what it has not.' And so,
> however the bodies of men, or brutes, or plants, may now in the
> ordinary course of nature be produced by generation, yet there
> must needs be some one Supreme Almighty Being in the world,
> that has the Being of all other beings in itself; who first created
> these several species, and endued them with this generative power
> to propagate their kind."[1]

The arguments, as we have seen, depend simply upon the brute
fact of the existence of being as being. The particular properties
of the beings under consideration are entirely irrelevant. As it has
somewhere been said, reduced to their bare essentials they are
equivalent to the unadorned assertion; "If anything exists, God
must exist; if God does not exist, nothing can exist." They do,
however, involve the recognition of the existence of finite being.
This might not seem a very startling assumption to make, in view
of the fact that we plainly perceive beings that exist, a fact that to
St. Thomas would be too obvious for question. Later philosophers have, however, so subtilized and idealized being away
that the point needs emphasis. It is a fundamental axiom of the
Thomist theory of knowledge that the human intellect is by its
very nature capable of apprehending beings, whatever may be at
times its misunderstanding of their nature. Against all sensationalist and conceptualist theories it insists that the impressions produced upon the senses and the concepts formed in the mind are not
the objects of perception but are the media through which external
objects are perceived; not the *quod* but the *quo* of the cognitive
act. And against all phenomenalist theories it makes the same
assertion about the qualities which we observe. Extra-mental
reality is the direct object of human perception; we *know* from
experience that *beings exist*. This is not something that can be
argued about; a man either admits it or he does not. But even if
he does not admit it in words he must behave as if he believed it,
if he is to go on living at all.[2]

---

[1] *Works*, VIII, p. 140. A similar argument is found in Locke's *Essay*, IV, x. It
goes back in some form at least to Augustine; cf. *De Civ. Dei*, XI, xxvi.
[2] A note may not be out of place on the more recent type of scepticism taught by the
logical positivists, who, following in the steps of Wittgenstein, deny the relevance of all
metaphysical arguments because, as they hold, all metaphysical statements are

But even if this realist theory of perception is rejected, the arguments do not lose all their weight, for it is in practice impossible to deny that something exists, unless you have attained a kind of philosophical Nirvana. If, with Mr. F. H. Bradley, you reduce

meaningless and therefore cannot apply to anything. The position is open to two main objections. (1) If it is true, no syntactical proposition can be significant, and hence its basic principle that "the meaning of a proposition is the method of its verification," which is a syntactical proposition, is nonsense. Hence, as Weinberg says, "logical positivism cannot eliminate metaphysics without destroying itself." (*Examination of Logical Positivism*, p. 199.) (2) It involves itself in a peculiar type of solipsism ("linguistic solipsism" or "solipsism without a subject" [Weinberg, op. cit., III, vii, and p. 68]), in which communication of the sense of propositions is impossible. There is also a very doubtful postulation of "empirical atomic facts" as the ultimate and exclusive referents of discourse. Carnap's logical syntax of language and the "radical physicalism" of Carnap and Neurath try to meet these objections, but apparently with doubtful success; they are briefly described in Carnap's two small books, *Philosophy and Logical Syntax* and *The Unity of Science*. Weinberg sees in Carnap the same linguistic solipsism that Carnap sees in Wittgenstein, and so produces his own theory of language, which he claims is less open to question. We may also refer to the very telling criticisms made by Bertrand Russell in *Meaning and Truth*, ch. x, xxii. Cf. Maritain's remarks in *Scholasticism and Politics*, p. 36 f., also the chapter on "Meaning and Implication," in Cohen's *Preface to Logic*.

It is interesting to note in the whole movement a transition from an earlier phase in which the rejection of metaphysics as meaningless is necessitated by the logical theory that has been adopted, to a later stage in which, the former logical theory having been largely abandoned, the meaninglessness of metaphysics is postulated as a dogma and a new logical and linguistic theory is constructed to conform to this. One is thus led to suspect that perhaps after all metaphysics has some validity. Weinberg himself rejects metaphysics on the ground that "it is plain that the only specifiable referent of a non-logical statement is the non-discursive realm of empirical reality" (op. cit., p. 290). But he apparently identifies metaphysics with the attempt to extract existential propositions from purely logical or ideal data. This would provide a valid argument against the ontological arguments of St. Anselm and Descartes or the Hegelian dialectic; indeed, it is the essence of the objection made by St. Thomas to St. Anselm. It does not, however, destroy the Thomist position, which takes its starting-point in concrete empirical beings. The Thomist position does, of course, assume the doctrine of analogy, which Wittgenstein's statement of the meaning of a proposition denies; but then, as has been remarked, it is not clear that Wittgenstein's approach is valid.

Mr. A. J. Ayer has tried in his recent work, *Language, Truth and Logic*, to save the situation by a considerably mitigated positivistic doctrine. He distinguishes practical verifiability from verifiability in principle, since we understand many propositions which we cannot verify, e.g. "There are mountains on the far side of the moon." Again, he distinguishes the "strong" sense of verifiability (when the truth could be conclusively established by experience) from the "weak" sense (when experience could only lead to a probability). He points out that the strong sense would rule out as meaningless such propositions as "Arsenic is poisonous" or "All men are mortal" (which such positivists as Schlick indeed describe as merely "important nonsense"). All that he demands for a proposition to have meaning is that an affirmative answer can be given to the question, "Would any observations be relevant to the determination of its truth or falsehood?" Having said this, he then goes on to argue that metaphysics, ethics and theology are all mere pseudo-sciences, since, as he alleges, the statements which they make are, even in the light of this mitigated doctrine, meaningless.

Three replies seem to be called for. (1) If "meaningfulness" *means* "verifiability," then the strongest form of the positivistic doctrine is necessary. If, on the other hand, a weaker form of the doctrine is adopted, then "meaningfulness" and "verifiability" are distinct, and the very basis of logical positivism is undermined. (2) In any case, whether significant statements are always verifiable or not, "meaningfulness" does not *mean* "verifiability" but "intelligibility." Metaphysical statements may "mean" something even if we cannot verify them or even if they are inherently unverifiable,

everything that the ordinary person assumes to be real to the
status of appearance, the question arises—appearance of what?
If, with Kant, you maintain that the *ding-an-sich* is unknowable,
at least you know that it exists. If, with Sir Will Spens, you define
objects as complexes of persisting opportunities of experience, it
may well be asked—experiences of what? For it will not get us
any further to say that we have opportunities of experiencing
complexes of opportunities of experience.[1] If you descend to the
depths of solipsism—that vice which, as Professor Broad has
remarked, is more often imputed than committed[2]—you presumably believe in your own existence, unless indeed you have
managed to attain the position of the character in Chekhov's
Three Sisters who toyed with the hypothesis that perhaps, after all,
we don't really exist but only think we do. If, again with Kant,
you maintain that the category of causality applies only within the
sphere of phenomena, the answer is that the sphere of phenomena

---

for we may know their meaning not by verifiability but, for example, by analogy.
(3) If moral and aesthetic judgments are rejected as mere expressions of feeling without
any meaning, it is difficult to see why judgments about the external world should not
be rejected in the same way. It may be added that, in spite of his seventh chapter,
Mr. Ayer does not succeed, as Professor Stebbing showed in her review in *Mind* of
July 1936, in avoiding linguistic solipsism, nor does he seem to do so in the discussion
of "the Egocentric Predicament" in ch. iii of his later work, *The Foundations of Empirical
Knowledge*.

The outcome would seem to be that, when it discards whole tracts of human thought
as meaningless, logical positivism is merely demonstrating the limitations it has placed
itself under by its initial assumption that meaningfulness is identical with verifiability.
If, as Mr. Ayer contends in opposition to the whole tradition of the *philosophia perennis*,
philosophy is purely linguistic in character and so is concerned with words and not
with things (*Language, Truth and Logic*, p. 62), the question of the relation between the
realm of logic and the realm of concrete reality, between words and things, remains
unanswered, for there is no other science that can answer it. And it is interesting to
note that, at the end of his recent *Inquiry into Meaning and Truth*, Bertrand Russell
concludes "that complete metaphysical agnosticism is not compatible with the main-
tenance of linguistic propositions" (p. 347). He previously expresses the opinions
that "'true' is a wider concept than 'verifiable,' and, in fact, cannot be defined in
terms of verifiability" (p. 227), and that "there is no reason why 'truth' should not
be a wider conception than 'knowledge'" (p. 246).

It is no doubt too early to pass a final judgment upon the various types and off-
shoots of logical positivism. But, for a short discussion which is both sympathetic and
discriminating, see the article by Mr. D. M. MacKinnon under the title "And the
son of man . . ." in *Christendom* for September and December 1938. The *philosophia
perennis* would at least agree with the logical positivists in rejecting a purely deductive
metaphysics having no basis in concrete fact, though it may be doubted whether they
have realized this. See also an article by F. L. Cross in *Theology*, Jan. 1939.

[1] See "The Eucharist" in *Essays Catholic and Critical* and cf. *Belief and Practice*,
lect. xi; also the discussion between Sir W. Spens and Canon Quick in *Theology*,
January to March and May 1929, following the publication of the latter's book, *The
Christian Sacraments*.

[2] *Examination of McTaggart's Philosophy*, II, p. 259. Cf. Bertrand Russell's amusing
story of the correspondent who said that solipsism was so reasonable a philosophy that
he could not understand why so few people held it. (*Outline of Philosophy*, p. 302.)

is precisely the sphere in which causality—not in the secondary, and for our purposes irrelevant, sense that the word bears in physics, as merely indicating the occurrence of regular sequences, but in the proper and philosophical sense of efficient causality—can be dispensed with.[1] Where it cannot be dispensed with is in the sphere of being. As soon as we have recognized that something really exists, then either it is necessary being and the argument is complete before it has begun, or it is contingent being and so necessarily implies the existence of necessary being.

A rather different objection might be brought against our position. We agreed in an earlier chapter with Professor Broad, when he found fault with the Ontological Argument on the ground that it professes to make a categorical comparison between a non-existent and an existent in respect of the presence or absence of existence, whereas no comparison can be made between a non-existent term and anything else except on the impossible hypothesis that it exists. Now, it might be said, does not our present argument contain just this flaw? In arguing that contingent being points to necessary being as the ground of its existence, are we not in effect comparing a contingent being that exists with a being that is precisely similar in every respect save that of existence and then postulating necessary being as the cause that confers existence in the one case and not in the other? A little consideration will show that, plausible as this accusation may appear, it is not true. According to the classical arguments God is not needed simply as the power which can confer existence on essences which dwell independently of him in an ideal world, as in Professor Eddington's famous example of the uncocked snooks waiting in patient non-existence for somebody to cock them.[2] Such ultra-Platonism is entirely foreign to their outlook. They postulate God as the ground not of the mere existence, but of the total being, the essence-realized-in-existence, of the finite thing. They do not compare the existent essence with a non-existent essence, because they do not compare it with anything at all. They direct our thought, not to existence illicitly considered as one of the thing's

[1] At least a passing reference must be made to the vigorous defence of the realist doctrine of perception undertaken by M. Gilson in his *Réalisme Thomiste et Critique de la Connaissance,* and to the criticisms which he passes there on such attempts as those of Mgr. L. Noël, Fr. Picard, Fr. Roland-Gosselin and Fr. Maréchal to combine the essential features of Cartesian and post-Cartesian thought with those of Thomism. Chapters vii and viii of this book contain a very clear statement and defence of the realist position. Cf. Maritain, *Degrees of Knowledge,* E.T., ch. iii, sec. i.
[2] *The Philosophy of Physical Science,* p. 214.

properties, but to the contingency which is radically inherent in its very being, in all that it is and in all that it has. They are concerned with the thing itself in its concrete actuality; the universal is all the time *in re*.

The arguments are thus entirely general in their scope, and require as their starting-point nothing more than the real existence of something, no matter what. But, for this very reason, they can tell us very little about the nature of the ultimate being at which they arrive. Thus St. Thomas writes that:

> "from effects not proportionate to the cause no perfect knowledge of that cause can be obtained. Yet from every effect the existence of the cause can be clearly demonstrated, and so we can demonstrate the existence of God from his effects; though from them we cannot perfectly know God as he is in his essence."[1]

And again:

> "Our mind cannot be led by sense so far as to see the essence of God; because the sensible effects of God do not equal the power of God as their cause. Hence from the knowledge of sensible things the whole power of God cannot be known; nor therefore can his essence be seen But because they are his effects and depend on their cause, we can be led from them so far as to know of God *whether he exists*, and to know of him what must necessarily belong to him, as the first cause of all things, exceeding all things caused by him."[2]

We cannot, therefore, discover by argument either *why* God is or *what* he is, but only *whether* he is and what he is *not*. Our arguments are *demonstrationes quia*, not *propter quid*. They answer the question *an sit*, not *quid est*. This might seem to deprive them of all value. What, it might be said, is the use of knowing that there is a God, if we know nothing about him except that he is the cause of finite beings? Is not our knowledge of him as scanty as would have been Robinson Crusoe's of Man Friday if when he saw the footprint on the sand he had had no previous knowledge whatever of human beings or their feet? This is a question that can only be answered by experiment. And it is, in fact, surprising how many attributes of God St. Thomas sees to be implied in the fact that he is the cause of finite being. The reason—so far as we can expect a reason—would seem to lie in the amazingly full and

---

[1] *S. Theol.*, I, ii, 2 ad 3.   [2] Ibid., I, xii, 12*c*.

fertile content of the idea of being itself.[1] Little, indeed, can be
deduced about a being from the mere knowledge that it must be
such as to be able to leave an impression of a certain form; but
much can be deduced about it from the knowledge that it must
be such as to be able to impart not only form but being. And it is
almost amusing to see how much St. Thomas tells us about the
First Being after he has informed us that we have really proved
nothing about him except that he exists. Even so, we can acquire
by the use of reason no information as to the inner constitution of
his being. We know that God is supremely intelligent, but not
that this intelligence is the eternal generation of a Son; we know
that he is good, but not that he raises us to a share in his own
nature. All such truths as this come to us by revelation alone.

We saw that each of the Five Ways ends with the words, "And
this everyone understands to be God" or their equivalent. A very
natural reaction to this assertion would be to say, "But why?"
St. Thomas has not at this stage very clearly even committed
himself to a definition of what he means by God, though he has
admitted that St. Anselm's *quo majus nihil* is a true description of
God if he exists[2] and has just quoted the Mosaic text, *Ego sum qui
sum*.[3] The Five Ways have each led us to admit the existence of a
being (or, we might wonder, should it be "beings"?) with a determinate character: First Mover, First Efficient Cause, First Necessary Being, First and Supreme Perfection, Ultimate Final Cause.
But must all these be the same being? Is it, for example, certain
that the First Mover is also the First Efficient Cause? Might not
the universe be governed by a Supreme Council of Five?

One way of meeting this objection is to try to show that each
of the five attributes can only belong to self-existent being. Dr.
Phillips summarizes this reply in the book from which we have
already quoted. He argues that (1) the First Mover is always in
act and contains no element of potentiality, hence it is not merely
capable of existing, and so exists essentially; (2) the First Cause,

---

[1] Cf. Maritain: "*Scire an sit* or *quia est* (knowing in the range of or within the perspective of fact) is not at all limited to knowing of an inductive type, for in a general
way (in opposition to *scire quid est* or *propter quid est*, knowing in the range or perspective
of a reason for being) this expression designates any knowledge that does not succeed
in laying hold of the essence itself in all its intelligible constitution." (*Degrees of
Knowledge*, E.T., p. 33, n. 1.). He remarks that " all knowledge which does not attain
the essence *in itself* belongs to *scire quia est*." (Ibid., p. 230. Cf. Appendix II.) Dr.
R. L. Patterson has indeed gone so far as to argue from this that the distinction
between knowledge *quia Deus est* and *quid est* is invalid. (*Conc. of God in Phil. of Aquinas*,
p. 257.) See also Garrigou-Lagrange, *Dieu*, p. 212.   [2] *S. Theol.*, I, ii, 1 ad 2.
[3] Ibid., I, ii, 3, *sed contra*.

being uncaused, cannot receive existence from another, and hence must itself *be* existence; (3) Necessary Being is incapable of not existing, and hence must have existence as an essential predicate; (4) the Supreme Being cannot be composite, and so cannot have a share of existence, but must *be* existence; (5) although the Supreme Intelligence has not been strictly demonstrated to be infinite, there is no reason to disassociate this argument from the others, and furthermore such an intelligence must be Pure Act, for if it were essentially related to an object of intelligence, such a relation would, in virtue of the Teleological Argument itself, have to be produced by a higher intelligence.[1]

It is doubtful whether such arguments as those just quoted are really conclusive, however probable they may seem. It might be suggested, for example, that "self-existent" does not mean precisely the same in each case; that in the first it merely means "receiving *motion* from no other being," in the second "being efficiently caused by no other being," and so on. Have all the five First Beings been shown to be self-existent purely and simply, or only in five closely similar but not necessarily identical senses? No doubt this question could be argued interminably, but it is noteworthy that St. Thomas himself does not follow this line. He simply says, "This all men speak of as God," and he seems much more interested to deduce the attributes of God from the Argument from Motion, which, as we have seen, is given the place of priority, than to demonstrate that the Five Ways all lead to the same Supreme Being. In the *Compendium Theologiæ*, having briefly stated the Argument from Motion, he develops in turn the attributes of immobility, eternity, necessity, aseity, unity, and so on.[2] He follows a similar course in the *Contra Gentiles*, and, while it is true that in the *Summa Theologica* he expounds the Five Ways *en bloc*, it is also true that he hastens to establish, as the core of his thesis, that God is his own essence and that therefore in him essence and existence are the same. But perhaps we may see in the very phrase, "This all men speak of as God," the clue that we are seeking. For, as we saw earlier, the Five Ways are, if Fr. Garrigou-Lagrange is correct, simply five scientifically stated analytical formulations of different aspects of one fundamental inclusive argument addressed precisely to the "all men" to whom St. Thomas appeals. They are, that is, not really independent of one another, but are related as different aspects of one whole.

[1] *Modern Thomistic Philosophy*, II, p. 292.   [2] I, iii *seq.*

But perhaps we shall find even a fuller answer when we go on to examine more thoroughly the evidential value of the Five Ways.

We may begin this examination by observing that, in effect, each of the ways is in the form of a hypothetical constructive syllogism (*modus ponens*). It proceeds as follows:

> If there exists a being that is finite in such-and-such a respect, then there exists a being that is infinite in such-and-such a corresponding respect.
> But there does exist such a finite being.
> Therefore, there exists the corresponding infinite being.

Then there is the appeal to universal agreement: this infinite being must be what we mean by God.

For instance, the third way argues thus:

> If there exists a contingent being, there must exist a Necessary Being.
> But there does exist a contingent being (e.g. Cleopatra's Needle, or Dr. Goebbels, or the oxygen in the atmosphere).
> Therefore, there exists a Necessary Being.
> And "this all men speak of as God."[1]

But, it may be asked, how do we know that the major or hypothetical premiss is true? Presumably because we have come across contingent beings, such as Cleopatra's Needle, Dr. Goebbels or the oxygen in the atmosphere, and have seen from a thoughtful consideration of them that they do not provide the reason for their own existence. If, *per impossibile*, I have never met with a contingent being—and the hypothesis is strictly impossible, since it supposes that I had never met with myself—or if, as is more likely, I had never seriously thought about one—I shall certainly never have been led to the assertion that, if a contingent being exists, a Necessary Being must exist as well. This is a good Thomist argument, for one of the basic principles of Thomist philosophy is that our abstract knowledge is always derived ultimately from acts of sensible experience; *nihil in intellectu quod non prius in sensu*. In other words, although we may be convinced of the truth of the major premiss as a necessity of reason, and although we may be convinced that, from a purely formal standpoint, the syllogism is a valid logical inference, in the concrete our postulation of both the major

---

[1] I have here stated the argument in its simplest form, not in the two steps as in the *Summa Theologica*.

and the minor premiss has been derived from the same basis in our experience, namely, our acquaintance with contingent beings. In practice, it is impossible for us to have been led to accept the major premiss without having been led to accept the minor as well, and, unless we are quite extraordinarily devoid of powers of inference, without having been led to accept the conclusion too. That is to say, in practice the argument is either accepted or rejected as a whole according as we have or have not come to know the things of this world as being what they really are. And this contention is strengthened by the fact that, as we have seen, in the hands of St. Thomas the argument does not simply assert that the proposition "Necessary Being exists" is a logical consequence of the proposition "Contingent being exists," but maintains that contingent being derives its own existence from Necessary Being; in other words, that we are not concerned just with logical relations between propositions, but with metaphysical or ontological relations between existent beings.

What is necessary, in short, if we are to pass from a belief in the existence of finite beings to a belief in the existence of God is not so much that we should thoroughly instruct ourselves in the laws and procedures of formal logic as that we should thoroughly acquaint ourselves with finite beings and learn to know them as they really are.

This is not, it must be stressed, a lapse into ontologism; it is not here maintained that we can, by the use of our natural powers directly apprehend God, that God is the terminal object of all or any of our acts of perception, or that finite beings are only the instruments or media through which we perceive him. On the contrary, our acts of perception terminate in the finite beings, which are the *quod* and not the *quo* of the acts; and it is only too possible for us to apprehend them in their bare particularity and to derive from them no notion of a Creator. Since, however, the human mind, just because it *is* a mind, is essentially adapted for the understanding of being as such (however much that understanding may be limited by the fact that the mind is united to a body and experiences external beings through the bodily senses, and however much it may be obscured by the mind's own frailty and opacity), it remains true that the mind is not only able to apprehend the mere existence of finite beings and their external properties, but is also capable in some degree of comprehending them, of entering into their inner essence and making them its own, of recognizing not only their finitude but also whereon that finitude rests. If we perceive finite beings as they actually are, we shall perceive them as the creatures of God. And if we do so perceive them *sub ratione creaturarum*, we shall in perceiving them recognize the existence of the God whom we cannot perceive. We cannot, at any rate in this life, know God under the aspect of his deity, but we can know him under the aspect of his Creatorship, in recognizing his creatures for what they are.

Mr. C. E. Faithfull has said that "it would seem that St. Thomas can only escape the charge of ontologism in some form or other if we may, with some Neo-scholastics, see implied in all his system the activity of intuitive as well as of discursive reason." He recognizes that St. Thomas denies to man the type of intuition that the angels possess; that is to say, a pure intuition of the essence of beings unmixed with any discursive mental act or any intervention of the senses; but he points out that the intuitive powers of the human mind function only in the closest co-operation with the discursive reason. "The recognition of contingent being, and the argument from the contingent to the necessary," he says, "illustrates the force with which the principle of causation can be recognized apparently spontaneously. In view of the modern awareness of the hidden activity of the discursive reason that can be involved in such an experience, and that unconsciously but unremittingly tests it by the light of other experience, it could hardly be maintained that St. Thomas would be forced by his rejection of intuition to deny the identity of this approach to God with his own. . . . Granted the possibility of the illumination of experience by some form of intuition, there is no great difficulty of allowing that the existence of various degrees of being may be perceived as a fact, and that the existence of the standard, the absolute, may be not a presupposition nor yet a corollary, but perceived in the same intuitive act."[1] It is, we must observe, not

---

[1] "The Proofs of the Existence of God in the Philosophy of St. Thomas Aquinas" in *Laudate*, September 1934, p. 160 f.

How real an appeal to intuition is hidden behind the axiomatic and deductive structure of even the most abstract of sciences, namely pure mathematics, is seen from such a work as Dr. F. Gonseth's *Fondements des Mathématiques*. "It is not only," he writes, "when he applies rigorously and impeccably the rules of logic that the mathematician can avoid contradiction, but when in addition, by an unconscious and profound divination, he applies them knowingly. . . . Thought, when it tries to find its support and its foundation in itself, can ultimately meet with nothing but a vacuum. . . . In its essence mathematics is only a collection of schematic views and processes of our mind, a conscious replica of the unconscious activity which creates in us an image of the world and a collection of norms according to which we act and react" (pp. 239, 240).

God himself that is perceived, but the fact of his existence; or, since the word "perceive" is usually restricted to our knowledge not of facts but of beings, it would perhaps be better to say not "perceived" but "apprehended."

If this account is true, it will follow that the knowledge of God to which the consideration of finite beings leads us is not merely probable but certain. Provided that we put ourselves in the right frame of mind for seeing things as they really are—and this, of course, in practice involves a real effort of moral and intellectual integrity—we can grasp the fact of God's existence as the ground of the existence of the beings under our consideration with just as much certainty as we perceive the beings themselves.[1] If we were merely arguing discursively from the fact of their existence our argument might indeed be only probable, and we should have to agree with many modern writers that the exercise of reason can lead us to no more than a probability that God exists; then, like Pascal, in his famous "wager argument," we should have to stake our lives upon that probability.[2] The various arguments for God's existence would then merely reinforce one another by increasing the probability, but we should never attain certainty, and our recognition of God would be a pure leap in the dark—an act, which, for some reason, is held by many people at the present day to be highly meritorious. This is not, however, the position that is being urged here; and we agree with St. Thomas that the various arguments do not increase the probability that God exists, but exhibit him to us under a number of different aspects, as First Mover, First Efficient Cause and so on. And here we must observe that in this particular respect the parallel that was drawn in the third chapter between our conviction of the existence of God and a man's conviction of his wife's fidelity breaks down. For this latter conviction, based as it is upon a vast number of indications most of which could only with extreme difficulty be put into words, can never lead to complete certainty; it can at most lead only to that moral certitude which is all that we demand for the practical ordering of our lives; even those husbands who were most sure of their wives' faithfulness have sometimes been deceived. And presumably even the most devoted and happily mated of husbands would, if he were a convinced believer in God, be ready to admit

[1] See Appended Note on "Certainty and Certitude," p. 93 *infra*.
[2] The "wager argument" is, of course, strictly *ad hominem* and does not represent adequately the basis of Pascal's own belief. It is stated in the *Thoughts*, E.T., No. 233.

that his certainty of God was of a higher order than his confidence in his wife. For what is being maintained here is that our conviction of God's existence is not merely of a high degree of probability or even of purely moral certitude; it is objectively certain. And, as has just been indicated, the purpose of the multiplication of proofs is not to increase our assurance of God's existence but the scope of our knowledge about him.[1]

We may admit that, to the modern mind, it will appear that in thus maintaining that the existence of God can be known with certainty we are depriving belief in him of all merit. What credit, it will be asked, can there be in recognizing a fact that is indisputable? We do not admire a man for admitting that seven nines are sixty-three. This objection might be countered by inquiring what merit there can be in acting as if things were certain when they are only probable. Is not this, we might say, simply intellectually dishonest? Is it not acting a lie? Admittedly we have to act either as if God existed or as if he did not, but, while it may be more prudent to base our lives on the more probable alternative, it is difficult to see that such a course is more creditable. And if we do not admire a man for admitting that seven nines are sixty-three, nor do we admire him for betting upon the crew which he thinks is more likely to win the Boat Race. Such a reply would, however, be merely *ad hominem*, and having made it we may, like St. Augustine in another connection, disclaim it with the observation, *Aliud est videre, aliud est ridere*. And, in fact, there is at least one respect in which some credit is due to a man for recognizing that God exists, even if his existence is absolutely certain.

We must notice first that the act of accepting any intellectual proposition involves the operation of the will. Its subject is not the intellect in isolation, but the whole man; and the will is one of his faculties just as much as the intellect is. I have to make an act of will in order to admit that seven nines are sixty-three just as I have to make an act of will in order to speak courteously to an unwelcome visitor. It is, of course, true that in most cases to admit that seven nines are sixty-three makes no moral demands on me; therefore the admission is in no way meritorious and I make it spontaneously. There are certain intellectual propositions, on the other hand, whose acceptance makes a real moral demand. I

[1] This apprehension of God's existence seems to be in essence identical with the knowledge of divine things by intellectual connaturality which M. Maritain describes in the tenth chapter of *Redeeming the Time* (p. 226), a natural contemplation which he distinguishes plainly from mystical experience of the natural order.

may refuse to admit—even to myself—that I owe a certain debt, not because there is any doubt about it, but because I am avaricious. I may refuse to accept a clear demonstration that I am suffering from an incurable disease because I am lacking in courage. And I may refuse to admit that finite being is really what it is because I am lacking in the humility necessary to accept my own finitude.[1] For, as we have seen, the arguments for the existence of God start from the recognition of finite being, and this involves the recognition that we are finite ourselves.[2] It must be observed that what is in question at the moment is not the previous acts of diligence necessary if we are to embark upon the consideration of the arguments, or the subsequent acts of obedience to God that are necessary if we are to put our belief into practice after we have acquired it. Those acts are indeed meritorious, but they do not impart merit to the acceptance of the proposition itself. The point is that, however clear the truth of the proposition "God exists" may be—and it has been asserted that our recognition of it can be so immediate as perhaps to deserve the name of intuition rather than of argument—unless we have the virtue of humility we shall simply be unable to see the data as they are and so we shall also be unable to see God's existence as implied in them. There is thus a threefold moral activity involved: diligence in investigating the question, humility in recognizing the data, and courage in acting upon the conviction when acquired. But it is the second of these that is involved in the actual intellectual acceptance of God's existence, and, if it is lacking, we shall simply hide God's evidence from ourselves by putting up a kind of intellectual smoke-screen.

One other condition is also necessary. If we are to recognize finite being as what it really is, it is not sufficient merely to recognize it as finite; we must also recognize it as *being*. This is, of course, where idealistic philosophies of the Bradleian type are so

---

[1] Cf. D. M. MacKinnon, *God, the Living and the True*, p. 73.

[2] We may recall the peculiar semi-Cartesian argument for the existence of God stated by Bishop Beveridge in his *Private Thoughts*, which is based upon his own existence as a thinking being. "The other articles of my faith," he wrote, "I think to be true because they are so; this [*sc.* that God exists] is true, because I think it so: for if there was no God, and so this article not true, I could not be, and so not think it true. But in that I think, I am sure that I am; and in that I am, I am sure there is a God; for if there was no God, how came I to be?" (*Works*, VIII, p. 140.) This particular form of statement is of hardly more than historical interest, but it exemplifies the point just under discussion, namely the finitude of the investigator himself. It is followed by a general statement of the argument from causality: "And the like may be said of all other created beings in the world. For there is no natural cause can give being to any thing, unless it has that being it gives in itself," etc. (p. 141).

unsatisfactory. In his famous work, *Appearance and Reality*, Mr.
F. H. Bradley claimed to have reduced to the status of appearances
everything that we normally recognize as being real: qualities,
relations, time, space, things and selves fall beneath his blows in a
remarkably small number of pages. Beneath all his arguments,
however, there lies one recurrent fallacious assumption: namely,
that anything that can be shown not to be infinite being is not
being at all, but only appearance. And as it is fairly easy to show
that none of the entities mentioned above is infinite being, it is
fairly easy to draw his conclusion. The consequence of his denial
of the analogy of being is that, instead of recognizing finite beings
as the creatures of God, he treats them as appearances of the
Absolute. But Christian theism insists that finite beings can be
directly apprehended as beings that are finite, and that this
recognition involves the immediate postulation of a Being that is
infinite as their ground.

If the nature of the classical arguments for the existence of God
is really as we have described it, one further point becomes clear.
That is, that the Five Ways do in fact lead to the same infinite
Being and not to five different beings infinite in five different
respects. It also solves such difficulties as that which may be
raised in connection with the Third and Fifth Ways, that it is not
clear that there is only one Necessary Being and only one ultimate
Final Cause. For though, considered simply as syllogistic arguments, the different Ways terminate in five different aspects of
infinite being and thus do not demonstrate their unity in one
Infinite Being, considered as intuitions (in the special sense that
we have given to this word) they all terminate in the same Being.
The different arguments are not obtained by syllogizing five
different kinds of act of inspection of finite beings; they are all
obtained from one kind of act, and indeed can all be obtained
from one single act. If we see any finite being as it really is—one
point of moss or the smallest ant, to use Maritain's illustration—
we shall see that God is implicated in it as First Mover, First
Efficient Cause and all the rest. We penetrate the nature not of
one particular being, but of being itself, in all its complexity and
fecundity, in all its analogical character and inner dynamism.[1]

---

[1] As Fr. Rousselot says, "Far from characterizing intelligence as the faculty of abstraction, we must, on the contrary, designate it the faculty of complete 'intussusception'."
(*The Intellectualism of St. Thomas*, E.T., p. 32.) He is, of course, at great pains to make
it clear that the human soul is the lowest of all intelligences.

For, to quote Maritain again, " a cherry between the teeth holds within it more mystery than the whole of idealistic metaphysics."[1]

When this has been said, however, it must not be concluded that the statement of the Ways in the form of syllogistic arguments is unnecessary or mistaken. The precise formulation which St. Thomas gave to them was of course adapted to the intellectual climate of his time; it was because philosophers (including himself) were interested in Aristotle and the syllogism that he put his arguments in the precise Aristotelian form. But some syllogistic or quasi-syllogistic form was necessary if they are to be stated as *arguments* at all, and even in the formation of an act of intuition such as we have described argument plays a very real part. The relation between argument and intuition may perhaps be made clearer by a simple parallel.

Anyone who has studied mathematics knows the difference between merely being convinced by a long chain of reasoning and getting a real and intimate grasp of a mathematical theorem. In the former case, if each step is seen to be valid, the student feels bound to admit the truth of the conclusion, but his acceptance of it remains disturbed and dissatisfied; he sees *that* the conclusion is true, but does not see *why* it is true; he does not see how premisses and conclusion are related as parts of a whole possessing a definite —one might even say, an *æsthetic*—form. From time to time, however, and very often after long and painful consideration of mere chains of reasoning, the form suddenly becomes evident in a flash; the theorem has been "got hold of" at last, it is, as it were, seen "in the solid," and the student feels that he is now not just assenting to an external fact but that he has penetrated to the nature of the object and made it part of himself. He sees the conclusion as involved in the premisses, and not only as derived from them by a chain of discursive reasoning. And the reason why some mathematical methods are disliked as being "messy," while others are described by such adjectives as "elegant" and "beautiful," is primarily because the latter, but not the former, stimulate precisely this kind of intuitive grasp of theorems as a whole. A fairly close parallel may be drawn between this and the case that we have been considering, though we must not forget the difference in the subject-matter of the two sciences, mathematics being concerned with entities of reason derived from concrete beings (*entia rationis cum fundamento in re*) and metaphysics with

[1] *The Degrees of Knowledge*, E.T., p. 335.

concrete beings (*entia realia*) as such. The arguments for the existence of God are not fallacious, and to anyone who understands what they are about and is capable of following them they can carry complete conviction. Nor are they unnecessary, for without them—or at least without some equivalent consideration such as Garrigou-Lagrange's one general proof—our belief will not be explicitly rational. But their real value is in stimulating the mind to examine finite beings with such attention and understanding that it grasps them in their true ontological nature as dependent upon God, and so grasps God's existence as their Creator.

This may provide the clue to the fact that at the present day people in general seem to find it extraordinarily difficult to see the necessity of the existence of God. Even if they can be got to listen to an exposition of the Five Ways and to follow the steps of the argument, they are frequently quite unmoved. This is, it may be suggested, mainly due to the fact that, under modern conditions of life, people very rarely give themselves the leisure and the quiet necessary for the straightforward consideration of finite being. They never really sit down and look at anything. This diagnosis is borne out by the common experience of people making their first retreat, that after the first day or so natural objects seem to acquire a peculiar character of transparency and vitality, so that they appear as only very thinly veiling the creative activity of God. But what is possible after a period of repose and silence in the atmosphere of a retreat-house is very difficult to achieve if one spends one's working life in a stockbroker's office or a steel foundry and one's leisure time at the pictures or dancing to the accompaniment of a saxophone-band. It is more easily achieved in the country or on the ocean, and it is well-known that country-folk and sailors have a sense of God as immanent in nature which town-dwellers rarely possess. The following story, related by Mr. Arnold Lunn, is very much to the point. After remarking that "materialism is a disease of the great cities and does not flourish among men who are in close touch with Nature," he writes: "I remember a night on an East Coast Convoy, when we were expecting an E-boat attack. I asked the Captain, as he peered out into the star-reflecting waters of a calm but sinister sea, whether he had ever met a sailor who was an atheist. 'No,' said the Captain, 'not one. Sailors have time to think.' "[1]

[1] *Blackfriars*, September 1942, p. 368.

We may add that, under modern conditions of life, our attention is almost always concentrated upon the form that man has imposed upon matter rather than upon the nature that God has given it; we are thus led rather to see what man has done with it than what God is doing with it. We do not consider copper and aluminium and indiarubber and ebonite in their nature as physical matter given them by God, but in their function as components of a wireless-set given them by man. It is not therefore surprising if we find it difficult to see the Creator at work in his creatures; for we seldom or never look honestly and calmly at the creatures themselves.

One of the essential prerequisites, therefore, for an acceptance of Christian theism is a contemplative and reverent attitude to finite beings. It has been pointed out by several recent writers that modern man's lack of reverence for Nature has led to some of the great economic evils of the day, the ruthless exploitation and exhaustion of the soil for financial gain, the heedless squandering of subterranean deposits, the almost irreparable destruction of forests and so on; it now appears that the same failing has largely been responsible for the loss of his belief in God. For it is hardly likely that we shall see things as the creatures of God if our primary attitude to them is as things for us to do something with. We have already seen that a certain moral integrity is needed for understanding the arguments for Christian theism; now we have seen reason to believe that a readiness simply to sit down and look at things in order to penetrate into their nature is no less indispensable.

There is one final point that calls for notice. It may seem that, when all is said and done, we are hardly within sight of anything of real value for religion. What, after all, is Self-existent Being in comparison with the God and Father of our Lord Jesus Christ? Is not Barth right in maintaining that the God whom natural reason discloses to us is so faint a reflection of the God of revelation that the natural reason, so far from providing a basis upon which revelation can build, merely misleads and deceives us? What can be deduced about God from natural theology will be discussed later on. We may, however, admit at once that natural theology is woefully insufficient to supply the religious needs of man; this is one of the reasons why it is supplemented by revelation. But when we look back, in the light of revelation, upon God as reason has shown him to us, we are able to see that *ipsum esse subsistens* is pregnant with all the fullness of Christian truth. Revelation, which is apprehended by faith, surpasses reason, but does not destroy its deliverances. And as revelation surpasses reason, so does the experimental knowledge of God that is granted to the mystics surpass revelation. With three sentences from M. Jacques Maritain we will conclude this chapter.

" In saying ' Subsistent Being itself,' or ' in Him there is no real distinction between essence and existence,' the metaphysician designates, without seeing it, the sacred abyss which makes the angels tremble with love and with awe."[1]   " If an ignorant shepherdess can be raised to such wisdom, it is true that she is ignorant of metaphysics and theology. But it is not true that she is an ignoramus. She has faith, and by faith she holds in their divine source all the truths that the theologian expounds in the sweat of his brow."[2] Of the Christian mystic it is true as of St. Augustine that " it is a matter of joining, within the heart's deepest recesses, the one who dwells there as in his own temple and in whom alone the heart can find its rest, not the God of philosophers and scholars—a God that can be reached without faith—not even the God of theologians—for he can be reached without charity—but the God of the saints, the Life of Life who offers himself to us in grace and love."[3]

---

[1] *Degrees of Knowledge*, E.T., p. 230.   [2] Ibid., p. 238.
[3] Ibid., p. 297. Cf. the words of a writer whose general attitude is widely different from that of Maritain: "The experience of the saints gives to us a deeper understanding of human personality than the whole of metaphysics and theology put together." (Berdyaev, *Freedom and the Spirit*, E.T., p. 39.)

CHAPTER VII

INTELLECT AND INTUITION

THE argument of the preceding pages has involved the assumption that our knowledge of the external world is essentially what scholasticism would call *adæquatio intellectus ad rem*, that the human mind, by its very constitution, is capable of penetrating beneath the phenomenal surface of finite beings and of grasping them, however imperfectly and partially, in their ontological nature and so apprehending them in their dependence upon an infinite Being which, as St. Thomas says, all men call God. A good deal has been said by the way in justification of this point of view; but it is so foreign to the habits of thought of most modern philosophers that it will be worth while spending a little more time in trying to make its truth more readily acceptable.

The prevailing trend in epistemology in recent years has been to deny both that extramental beings conceived as concrete substances or essences exist, and in consequence that the human mind is constitutionally capable of apprehending them. The fundamental elements of our experience are taken to be such mere particulars of sensory awareness as red patches, loud noises, hot feelings on the skin and the like, and the mind is alleged to construct from them, in one way or another, what it mistakenly believes to be external beings. The particulars may be described in many ways—as sense-data, sensa, sensibilia, or even opportunities of experience—and the operation of the mind may be conceived either as the building up these particulars into artificial complexes on the ground of accidental similarities, or as the addition to them of characteristics which they did not possess before, or in some other way. Dr. Tennant, for example, believes that our experience is inevitably contaminated by an interpretation which we impose on it in the very act of experiencing; his distinction between the "psychological" and the "psychic," though superficially it resembles the scholastic distinction between the *quod* and the *quo* of experience, is used in such a way as to deny that we can have any undistorted knowledge of the *quod*.[1] Bertrand Russell believes that "events" are strung together into

---

[1] *Phil. Theol.*, I, p. 255. See p. 165 *infra*.

objects by the action of the person who perceives them, but as this person is believed to be nothing more than a string of events himself it is rather difficult to make out who does the tying.[1] Both of them would agree that the only object of which we have direct knowledge is the particular sensum, and both would assert that the mental element in perception inevitably introduces error, which subsequent reflection may or may not be able to correct. All such views as these are in radical opposition to the Thomist doctrine that, in the very act of apprehension, the reception of the sensible species by the sense is accompanied by the abstraction of its intelligible content by the intellect, which, passing through the species, obtains a direct, though mediated, knowledge of the thing itself, so that any error which may be involved is due, not to some kind of demonic twist in the nature of intellect as such but to an accidental disordering of it in the particular case. To say this is not to assert that the human mind is capable of abstracting the fullness of the essence and knowing it in all its ontological richness as God, or even the angels, do. On the contrary, scholastic philosophy has always insisted that the human mind is the lowest of all intelligences, and indeed not worthy to be called an intelligence, but rather a mere intellect; Fr. Rousselot has shown most clearly how the human mind substitutes knowledge by concepts, science, systems and symbols for knowledge by the pure idea.[2] What we are concerned to maintain is that, with whatever limitations, it is the inherent function of the human intellect, as the very derivation of "intellect"—from *intus legere*—implies, not to *read into* its object qualities that are not really there, as all the Kantians and quasi-Kantians teach, but to *read that which is within* them, to extract from them, however partially and imperfectly, their intelligible content. The truth is not that the human mind is an instrument which in its normal functioning misinterprets the universe in such a way that only philosophers can disentangle the

[1] Cf. *The Analysis of Mind*, especially lect. xv. "Mind and matter alike are logical constructions; the particulars out of which they are constructed, or from which they are inferred, have various relations, some of which are studied by physics, others by psychology. Broadly speaking, physics group particulars by their active places, psychology by their passive places" (p. 307). "The causal laws of physics . . . differ from those of psychology only by the fact that they connect a particular with other appearances in the same piece of matter, rather than with other appearances in the same perspective " (p. 301).

[2] *The Intellectualism of St. Thomas*, E.T., Part II. Rousselot tends to a rather extreme view of the limitations of the human intellect through the union of the soul with the body, and it would be inaccurate to claim his support for all the details of the position maintained here. But he is as insistent as anyone upon the fact that the intellect is essentially the faculty of apprehending being.

real objects of its perception from the elaborate illusions which it has worked into them and discover their true nature; rather it is that the mind, while it is, like all human faculties, including the genius of the philosophers, subject to error, is nevertheless capable of apprehending truth and normally does so.[1]

The interpretation which we have given to the Five Ways of St. Thomas involves that just such a power as this is native to the human mind, though like other powers it may need training and developing. In rising to a conviction of God's existence from finite beings, we do not, it was asserted, merely perceive the existence of these beings by the senses and then, by a subsequent process of purely logical deduction, arrive at an intellectual acceptance of the proposition "God exists." On the contrary, if our mind is in a healthy and vigorous state and is able freely to fulfil its proper function of apprehending finite beings as they really are, it will, in the very act by which it apprehends them, be capable of penetrating to the ontological depths of their nature so as to know them as the creatures of God.

This doctrine, that the proper function of the intellect is not merely discursive ratiocination about the deliverances of the senses but the penetration of the inner essence of things, forms the main theme of one of the most remarkable books on the philosophy of religion of recent years, Fr. M. C. D'Arcy's *Nature of Belief*. It is, in principle, a restatement and an expansion of Cardinal Newman's teaching about the "Illative Sense," detached from the unfortunate philosophical background against which Newman

[1] A very thorough answer to the problem of error is given by M. Gilson in the course of ch. vii and ch. viii of his *Réalisme Thomiste et Critique de la Connaissance*. The main points of his argument, which is strictly Thomist, are as follows: (1) Concrete existence is always of singulars; universals occur only in them (and, intentionally, in the intellect which abstracts from them). (2) The apprehension of singulars is the function of sensation, the apprehension of universals is that of intellection; since it is the human being as a whole who has both intellect and senses, he thus knows the universals as they occur in the particulars. (3) If sensation is deranged, or temporarily latent, the criterion by which existence is judged no longer operates. "The problem of the judgment of existence . . . is linked up with the analogous problem of the apprehension of singulars. It must be so in a doctrine for which only singulars exist." (op. cit., p. 210.) "Since it is sensation that attests existences, we need no other existential index than the certitude with which sensation is accompanied. That a person who does not possess the criterion should be exposed to error is only natural. So long as he is asleep a dreamer cannot know that he is dreaming, but he knows that he has been dreaming as soon as he wakes up. It would indeed be tragic," he adds, "if philosophers philosophized in a dream; the realist at least tries to avoid that." (op. cit., p. 204.) Cf. the rather different discussion by Rousselot in *The Intellectualism of St. Thomas*, E.T., p. 73 f.; he writes: "The root-cause of all human error lies in the twofold multiplicity that characterizes human knowledge: St. Thomas says so explicitly. The cause of error is to be sought either in sense-knowledge, or else in that multiplicity which is implied in discursive reasoning." (Op. cit., p. 81.)

wrote. Newman's starting-point was the undeniable fact that many of the beliefs about which we are most certain—such as, for example, that Great Britain[1] is an island—have never been obtained by rational demonstration, and would moreover be practically impossible to demonstrate. Anyone who has argued with a supporter of the flat-earth theory will have realized how little we depend on clear logical demonstration for some of our most firmly held convictions. The fact is that the human mind is so constituted that it is able to extract from the whole body of fact with which it is confronted certain particular truths by a way quite different from those of scientific investigation or mathematical deduction; "given sufficient detail the mind has the power of interpreting what that detail signifies."[2] This may involve deriving from a number of instances of a particular truth the truth itself as a universal property, in spite of the fact that syllogistic reasoning could not attain it; this would be the case, for example, if, from the spectacle of a number of corpses we were led to assert that all men were mortal, not because the dead men we had seen actually comprised the whole human race, but because the contemplation of these spectacles of mortality had given us an understanding such as we had never had before of the inherent corruptibility of man and had made us see how frail and uncertain our own condition was. On the other hand, our certainty may be derived not from a number of instances of what we afterwards come to accept as a universal law, but from a multitude of varied, and possibly bewildering, facts, as in the case already mentioned of our conviction that Great Britain is an island. In the former case we have what traditional logic calls an "induction," in the latter case what has been called in recent years a "unity of indirect reference." But in either case we have the human mind going beyond what it knows by formal logical argumentation and exercising a kind of intuition.[3] This operation is given by Fr. D'Arcy the name of *interpretation*, and the main contention of his book is that, like other operations of the mind, it is a reliable, though, again like other operations, not an infallible, instrument of knowledge. "Just as the object of sense presents itself to us as

---

[1] D'Arcy actually says "England"!   [2] *Nature of Belief*, p. 180.
[3] The argument is in no way weakened if, with the modern logicians, we interpret universal propositions as not categorical but hypothetical. If "All men are mortal" really means "If x is a man, x is mortal," it can only be known to be true either by enumeration, which we have seen to be impossible, or because it is already known that "humanity entails mortality," and this involves an intuition of humanity as an essence.

one whole," he writes, commenting on Newman, "so too we grasp
the full tale of the premises and the conclusion *per modum unius*,
'by a sort of instinctive perception of the legitimate conclusion
in and through the premises, not by a formal juxtaposition of
propositions.' "[1] "There comes a point when the truth shines
out, when the fact or object or meaning is manifested in its unity
through the signs."[2] "There is good reason . . . for thinking that
the mind has the power of recognizing when the complexity has
reached the requisite degree for certainty," though "no rule of
thumb can be given which will tell us once and for all when and
where on all possible occasions this requisite complexity is
present."[3] Yet, as was said above, this power is finite; "nothing
. . . justifies the pretension that we know exhaustively the inner
nature of reality. There are deeps within deeps, there are
secrecies which the sense-bound mind of man cannot penetrate."[4]

Our case will be considerably strengthened if we see in more
detail the light which this view throws on the problem of induction, for that problem is one which logicians have found extremely
baffling. "Why," asked J. S. Mill, "is a single instance, in some
cases, sufficient for a complete induction, while in others myriads
of concurring instances, without a single exception known or
presumed, go such a very little way towards establishing a universal
proposition? Whoever can answer this question knows more of
the philosophy of logic than the wisest of the ancients, and has
solved the problem of induction."[5] "I am convinced," writes
Bertrand Russell, "that induction must have validity of some
kind in some degree, but the problem of showing how or why it
can be valid remains unsolved. Until it is solved, the rational man
will doubt whether his food will nourish him, and whether the
sun will rise to-morrow."[6]

It will be clear that if the ultimate elements of which the world
is composed are isolated and unrelated particulars there is no
justification for the principle of induction at all. If a number of
flashes in the sky, which are sufficiently similar to one another to
be all called "lightning," are each followed by noises which are
sufficiently similar to one another to be all called "thunder,"
while these similarities are purely accidental and in no way manifest any real common characteristic of the flashes or the noises,

[1] *Nature of Belief*, p. 137.   [2] Ibid., p. 187.   [3] Ibid., p. 198.   [4] Ibid., p. 196.
[5] *Logic*, III, iii, 3. Quoted by H. W. B. Joseph in *An Introduction to Logic*, p. 400.
[6] *Outline of Philosophy*, p. 14. Russell hastens to add that he is not a "rational man."

then there is no reason whatever to suppose that another flash
called lightning will be followed by another noise called thunder.
There can be no such thing as induction in a nominalistic universe.
On the other hand, if it is possible for similarities to manifest
common natures, how can we distinguish when these cases arise,
and how can we be quite sure that, in such a case as that of
lightning being followed by thunder, there is a genuine case of
causal connection in view of which we may expect lightning to be
followed by thunder next time, and that the sequence was not a
pure coincidence or due to some other cause? There is a well-
known story of a man who, having got drunk on three successive
nights on whisky-and-water, brandy-and-water and rum-and-
water, decided by applying the method of agreement that it must
have been the water that was bad for him. And even when on
the fourth night, by applying the method of difference and
drinking whisky neat, he decided that his conclusion was wrong
and that the real intoxicant must have been some hypothetical
common constituent of whisky, brandy and rum which we may,
for convenience, designate by the name alcohol, why should we
suppose that, if drinks containing alcohol made a man drunk four
nights running, they should necessarily make him drunk on the
fifth? There is no mood of the syllogism that enables us to argue
as follows:

> "A, B, C, D contain alcohol.
> A, B, C made me drunk.
> Therefore D will make me drunk."

We could indeed draw this conclusion if we knew that *all*
alcoholic drinks were intoxicants. But that would involve our
having discovered that D was an intoxicant, and this is the very
conclusion which we are trying to prove. It is clear that mere
enumeration of instances can never give us a logically coercive
induction.

Nevertheless, the attempt to prove that it can has been made by
more than one logician. J. S. Mill argued that, given the law of
causation, induction could be reduced to deduction. Bertrand
Russell outlines the argument thus: "We know that B must have
a cause; the cause cannot be C or D or E or etc., because we find
by experiment or observation that these may be present without
producing B. On the other hand, we never succeed in finding A
without its being accompanied (or followed) by B. If A and B

are both capable of quantity, we may find further that the more there is of A the more there is of B. By such methods we eliminate all possible causes except A; therefore, since B must have a cause, that cause must be A." But, as Russell remarks, "all this is not really induction at all; true induction only comes in in proving the law of causation. . . . We are left with the problem: Does mere number of instances afford a basis for induction?"[1]

The most thorough investigation of this question that has been made is due to the late Lord Keynes. He "holds that an induction may be rendered more probable by number of instances, not because of their mere number, but because of the probability, if the instances are very numerous, that they will have nothing in common except the characteristics in question. . . . If we can so choose our instances that they have nothing in common except the qualities A and B, then we have better grounds for holding that A is always associated with B. If our instances are very numerous, then, even if we do not *know* that they have no other common quality, it may become quite likely that this is the case."[2] Keynes concludes that, as a consequence, without any appeal to law or causality, it has been shown that the probability that A and B will occur together next time increases with the number of times that they have been observed to do so in the past. But unfortunately it does not follow that this probability approaches certainty as a limit or even that it becomes greater than one-half (i.e. that A and B are more likely to occur together than not).

To achieve this last requirement Keynes has to introduce a postulate called the "principle of limitation of variety." This, as corrected by Nicod, demands that, for each of the objects in the field, there shall be a finite number *n* which is such that there is a finite probability that the number of independent qualities of the object is less than *n*, where "independent qualities" means qualities that do not cohere together in groups of invariable connection. We might express this roughly by saying that it is necessary that some limitation should be placed on the variety in the universe. But it seems very difficult to see any *a priori* reason why this principle should be true, and the slight indications that point that way rest on scientific data which have been derived by

[1] *Outline of Philosophy*, p. 281. (I have taken the outline of Keynes's investigation, which will be found in his *Treatise on Probability*, from this same work.) A more recent discussion, leading to the same conclusion, is given in Weinberg's *Examination of Logical Positivism*, ch. iv. Unfortunately this last book contains a large number of very confusing misprints. [2] Russell, *Outline of Philosophy*, p. 281.

90 HE WHO IS

the use of induction and therefore cannot be validly used to prove
that induction is itself valid.

Since, then, the attempts to set the method of induction upon a
firm basis of deductive logic have come to a dead end, in spite of
the fact that both science and life are impossible without a constant
use of the method, we may not unreasonably fall back upon
Fr. D'Arcy's contention that the validity of the inductive method
depends upon an inherent power of the human mind to recognize
the element of causality in nature when it receives an adequate
stimulus to do so. "Induction," he writes, "is neither by syllogistic inference nor by exhaustive enumeration, but a type of what
I have named interpretation. The multiplication of experiments,
the refinement of data, serve to eliminate the irrelevant and leave
the way open for the mind to detect the essential; once that has
been discovered the rest slide into their place."[1]

It may be well to emphasize again what is the precise point for
our purposes of this discussion of induction. It is simply this: that
the validity of induction is universally accepted by modern
philosophers, since they can neither philosophize nor live without
it. Nevertheless, they find it impossible to justify it rationally on
the basis of the subjectivist and particularist theory of perception
which, in some form or another, most of them hold. On the other
hand, the theory of perception which we have been maintaining
here does provide a rational basis for induction.[2] This fact may
therefore be reasonably urged as providing strong corroboration

[1] *Nature of Belief*, p. 177. Whitehead significantly remarks: "The very baffling task
of applying reason to elicit the general characteristics of the immediate occasion, as
set before us in direct cognition, is a necessary preliminary, if we are to justify induction; unless indeed we are content to base it upon our vague instinct that of course it is
all right. Either there is something about the immediate occasion which affords
knowledge of the past and the future, or we are reduced to utter scepticism as to
memory and induction." (*Science and the Modern World*, p. 61 (58).) Mr. A. J. Ayer,
in expounding his mitigated logical positivism, tries to sidestep the issue by maintaining that the problem set by induction is meaningless. "It appears," he writes,
"that there is no possible way of solving the problem of induction, as it is ordinarily
conceived. And this means that it is a fictitious problem, since all genuine problems
are at least theoretically capable of being solved." (*Language, Truth and Logic*, p. 50.)
But all that this really shows is the inadequacy of logical positivism, which denies the
problem instead of solving it.
[2] It is not, of course, claimed that we have solved in this chapter all the problems
connected with induction; that is not, in any case, our business here. But it is alleged
that only on some such view as we have put forward can the problem even begin to be
fruitfully discussed. We cannot attempt in a footnote to appraise the treatment given
in Mr. W. H. V. Reade's recent book, *The Problem of Inference*, but it is of interest to
note that he refuses to accept the view that inference is merely equivalent to the
recognition of logical implication, and that he insists that our immediate knowledge
in perception is not just of particulars but of universals. Cf. Maritain, *An Introduction
to Logic*, p. 258 f.

for the truth of our theory, though it does not of course prove that no other theory can be devised to meet this need. But we must now return to Fr. D'Arcy.

When he passes on to consider the evidence for the existence of God, Fr. D'Arcy's argument is in substantial agreement with our own, though he does not give a detailed discussion of the classical Five Ways. He denies the validity of the argument from religious experience in the forms in which it is commonly stated. "Its value," he writes, "seems to me not to consist in any appeal to feeling or interior conviction which cannot be brought before the footlights, nor to some imaginary contact with God by intuition. There is no need to return to the occult to escape the atheism of science."[1] (In passing, it must be observed that the "contact with God by intuition" which D'Arcy rejects is the immediate awareness of God as the direct object of knowledge taught by ontologism, not, as we shall see, the intuition of God's existence as the ground of the existence of finite beings.) The truth is rather that, by unity of indirect reference, God is apprehended as the ultimate reality upon whose creative act the world depends. "The certainty rests on the infinite complexity of the evidence which is afforded by indirect evidence [query, reference?] and given to us under the form of unity. . . . In one and the same kind of act it is seen that what we know has no ground or unity without a whole, and that we interpret this whole not abstractly but as a cause or power or spirit. . . . Simple people . . . have a world of discourse and a universe in which they view things, and they have no difficulty in identifying this unity with a God who is not the universe but the ground of it. They interpret, that is, what they see as the work of a spirit in an analogous way to that in which they interpret the bodily actions of their fellows as the signs of a human will." The bearing of this on Garrigou-Lagrange's general proof, which includes the Five Ways as special cases, will be obvious, but D'Arcy's discussion becomes still more relevant to our present concern as he proceeds. After remarking that the refutation which Kant claimed to have provided of the classical arguments "depends upon the limitations which he himself imposes on the extent of human knowledge," he insists that we must not begin with the phenomena of nature as science relates them to us, since these are confessedly nothing but appearances. "The objects which we meet in knowledge when we are not

[1] *Nature of Belief*, p. 259.

working as scientists are always sensible *things*, that is to say, they
are made up of a sensible and an intelligible content," and even
"scientists abstract from things in themselves in order to be able
to learn more about them. . . . Their methods . . . bear out . . .
that we know something, that we are looking through the appearances at reality." And, he continues, "once this is granted the
existence of God must be admitted without more ado." For, in this
act of knowledge, either "we do nothing but know the one, complete, self-sufficient reality—and this we must call God—or, if
we know the dependent, we are bound to assert the existence of
its source and ground," and this latter again is God. Since, therefore, we do not know completeness in every act of knowledge, what
we know is the contingent, and the contingent as "a suppliant for
its existence and its meaning on what is not itself."[1]

Fr. D'Arcy's conclusion, therefore, is that the alleged "Argument from Religious Experience," in so far as it is valid, is simply
what the argument from contingency becomes in a world in which
thought has become more and more subjective, in which men have
focused their attention less and less upon outside things and more
and more upon themselves. "The modern," he says, "has made
a discovery that in his own experience he cannot escape God,"
but "the experience which modern writers on religion uphold is
not a direct awareness of God but the consciousness of their own
state as creatures." As we said on an earlier page, "the arguments for the existence of God start from the recognition of finite
being, and this involves the recognition that we are finite ourselves."[2] And we may agree with Fr. D'Arcy that the argument
from religious experience may well turn out to be "nothing but
the old argument from contingency looked at from inside instead
of from outside."[3]

It would, of course, be unfair to claim from another writer more
agreement with one's own argument than can be certainly sustained. In particular, we have not laid quite as much stress as he
has upon religious experience in relation to the unity of indirect
reference. But on our two main points we have his support:
namely, the inherent power of the human mind to penetrate into
the heart of beings and obtain a true, even though a limited, grasp
of their ontological status, and the consequent possibility of an
immediate recognition that that status demands as its ground the

[1] *Nature of Belief*, pp. 258–62.   [2] See p. 77 *supra*.
[3] *Nature of Belief*, p. 263. Cf. E. I. Watkin, *Theism, Agnosticism and Atheism*, pp. 129–36.

existence of that infinite Being whom, as the Angelic Doctor tells us, all men are agreed in calling God.[1]

ADDITIONAL NOTE *A* TO CHAPTER VII

CERTAINTY AND CERTITUDE

It may appear that insufficient care has been taken to distinguish between objective certainty and subjective certitude, and that the statement that the existence of God can be known with certainty from the consideration of finite beings is in effect annulled by the admission that the human intellect, like every other human faculty, is not infallible. It may be replied that, while the great majority of the beliefs upon which we rely for our daily living are ultimately based merely upon that "probability which is the guide of life," our apprehension of the existence and status of finite beings is of a different order altogether. The more we examine the former beliefs the more clearly they are seen to be inferential, while, as was pointed out on page 80 above, the more carefully we contemplate the beings which surround us the more their dual character as real beings and yet finite ones manifests itself. If it is objected that dreaming or over-indulgence in alcoholic stimulants may result in the presentation of spurious sense-data which *prima facie* seem to have as much objectivity as the objects of our normal experience, it may be replied that such data do not, by the nature of the case, lend themselves to contemplative inspection, nor is the person who experiences them in a condition in which he can achieve it. Furthermore, such

[1] Such a presentation of the rational approach to God as has been given above may go some way towards meeting the criticisms made by Dr. John Baillie in ch. iii of his work, *Our Knowledge of God.* If we draw together Abbot Chapman's insistence on the essentially abstract nature of natural theology (p. 26 *supra*), Fr. Garrigou-Lagrange's "general proof which is necessary for every man" (p. 37 *supra*), and Dr. Baillie's doctrine of a "mediated immediacy" (op. cit., sec. 16), we may conceivably find that the difference is not as great as appears at first sight. We may, however, suggest that Dr. Baillie's upbringing in a devoutly Christian family may have led him to assume an immediacy of God to the mind of man that others would dispute. In any case, it must be remembered that, as St. Thomas himself remarks, "faith is a kind of knowledge" (*S. Theol.*, I, xii, 13 ad 3), but this does not make natural theology illicit. And the distinction between the *ordo essendi* and the *ordo cognoscendi* must never be forgotten (p. 1 *supra*). Cf. the short but penetrating review of Baillie by Fr. Ivo Thomas, O.P., in *Blackfriars*, February 1940, p. 123.

sensory presentations either have as their content imaginary
figures which have had real counterparts in the past experience
of the experient (as, e.g., rats and snakes) or else are constructed
from elements in various objects of past experience (as are, e.g.,
unicorns and dragons); there is thus always an ultimate appeal
to real beings.[1] The appeal is made in the text not merely to crude
awareness of the world which is our environment, but to careful
attention to its nature. We may agree in principle with Dr.
Tennant that the deliverances of "psychic" immediacy need to
be checked by "psychological" reflection and discrimination,[2] but
we must insist that this discrimination must be applied not merely
to the *mechanism* of perception, which (through its expression in
terms of the functioning of the sense-organs, nerves, etc.) itself
involves an assumption of the real existence of finite beings, but
also, and primarily, to the *object* of perception, in order that it
may be plainly understood what is the ontological status of the
objects perceived.

[1] Cf. p. 85, n. 1, *supra*.   [2] See p. 162 *infra*.

CHAPTER VIII

GOD AND THE WORLD: *ANALOGIA ENTIS*

THE foundation of the argument for the existence of God which has been built up in the preceding chapters is the existence of finite beings which demand the existence of an infinite Being as their ground. Indeed, the argument has been little more than an elaboration of the Pauline thesis that "the invisible things of him since the creation of the world are clearly seen, being perceived through the things that are made";[1] to adapt the title of a famous book by Cardinal Bellarmine, we have made an ascent to God by a ladder of created things. We have proceeded from that with which we are immediately acquainted to that which is less familiar; we have started from the evident fact of the existence of the world of which we ourselves are part, and have ended with the God who infinitely transcends it.

Once, however, we have been led to affirm God's existence, our whole perspective changes, and we see that it is not God's existence that requires explanation but the existence of anything else. "This proposition 'God exists'," says St. Thomas Aquinas, "of itself is self-evident," but "because we do not know the essence of God, the proposition is not self-evident to us; but needs to be demonstrated by things that are more known to us, though less known in their nature—namely, by effects."[2] The real miracle is not that God exists but that the world does. God—the self-existent, perfect, changeless Being, the Pure Act in whom all that supremely *is* is comprised—how could he not exist? The self-existent cannot but be; but that he in whom nothing is lacking should confer existence on *us*—that is the wonder which may well stagger our minds.

In the words of a modern theologian, "the relation between God and his creatures is a wholly one-sided relation, in that while the creation depends absolutely upon God, God in no sense depends upon his creation. God would be neither more nor less perfect if the creation dissolved into utter nothingness. The

---

[1] Rom. i, 20.   [2] *S. Theol.*, I, ii, 1c.

absolute perfection of perfect being would still exist." This doctrine, continues Prebendary Hanson, "is dualistic, it is miraculous, it presents great difficulty to the human reason, and still more to human conceit, for though the modern man gets on very well without God and can even make it his boast, he finds the conception of a God who can get on very well without him highly offensive."[1] As Gilson says, "God added nothing to himself by the creation of the world, nor would anything be taken away from him by its annihilation—events which would be of capital importance for the created things concerned, but null for Being who would be in no wise concerned *qua* being."[2]

In view of the widespread tendency even among theologians to-day to be satisfied with a doctrine of God as in one way or another conditioned by or dependent on his creation, it is important to stress the absolute necessity of the conception of the entire independence of God. The very essence of our argument has been that the only hope of explaining the existence of finite beings at all is to postulate the existence of a Being who is *self*-existent. A first cause who was himself in even the very least degree involved in the mutability, contingency or insufficiency of the universe would provide no more in the way of an explanation of the existence of the universe than it could provide itself; such a God would provide a foundation neither for himself nor for anything else. Unless we are prepared to accept the God of classical theism, we may as well be content to do without a God at all. If we admit any dependence of God upon the world, the very basis of the arguments by which we have been led to him is destroyed; a "first cause" who is not self-sufficient explains nothing.

The God that philosophy demands is thus nothing less than the God of *Exodus*, the God whose name is *I am*. The Thomist transformation of the Aristotelian deity into the God of Christian theism is thus not a subtle and illicit importation into philosophy of concepts derived from an alien sphere; it is the provision of the Aristotelian arguments with the only conclusion that can ultimately satisfy them. If anything exists, then self-existent Being must exist; if self-existent being does not exist, then nothing can exist—this is the fact of the matter.

---

[1] "Dogma in Medieval Scholasticism" in *Dogma in History and Thought*, p. 105.
[2] *Spirit of Medieval Philosophy*, p. 96.

This point may be made in many ways. One way of expressing it is in the form of Dr. William Temple's two quasi-mathematical equations:[1]

$$\text{God} - \text{the world} = \text{God},$$
$$\text{The world} - \text{God} = \text{O};$$

another way is in the dictum that the world exists not for God's utility but for his glory, where "glory" must be understood in the theological sense of the "accidental" and not the "essential," glory of God; yet another way is in the words of the Vatican Council that God made the world "not in order to achieve or increase his own happiness but in order to manifest his perfection."[2] As Thomas Jackson wrote, "The world is created, and yet it was not necessary that it should be created. . . . It was likewise free for the Almighty to create or not to create man or angel; but his free purpose to create them after his own image being supposed, it was not merely possible, but altogether necessary, that they should be created good."[3] We must altogether reject the assertion of Hegel that "God without the world is not God,"[4] or of Whitehead, that "God is completed by the individual, fluent satisfactions of finite fact,"[5] or of Tennant that "God without a world, or a Real other, is not God but an abstraction."[6] Since the world can find its explanation only in the creative act of a God who is self-existent Being, God must be a creator in the sense that he can create if he wills to do so; but precisely because he *is* self-existent Being, he need not create unless he does so will. In Gilson's words, "it is quite true that a Creator is an eminently Christian God, but a God whose very essence is to be a creator is not a Christian God at all. The essence of the true Christian God is not to create but to be. 'He who is' can also create if he chooses; but he does not exist because he creates, nay, not even himself; he can create because he supremely is."[7]

The relation that obtains between the self-existent God and the world whose existence is completely dependent upon his will is thus absolutely unique; it has therefore a special name, which is *creation*. Creation is, in the scholastic definition, "the production

[1] *Nature, Man and God*, p. 435. A similar formulation is quoted from Coleridge by A. S. Pringle-Pattison: *The Idea of God*, p. 315.
[2] *Const. dogm. de fide cath.*, I: "*non ad augendam suam beatitudinem nec ad acquirendam, sed ad manifestandam perfectionem suam.*" (Denzinger, *Enchiridion*, 1783.)
[3] *Works*, V, pp. 296–7.   [4] Quoted by James Ward, *Essays in Philosophy*, p. 287.
[5] *Process and Reality*, p. 492.   [6] *Phil. Theol.*, II, p. 168.   [7] *God and Philosophy*, p. 88.

of the whole substance of a thing in the previous absence both of itself and of any other subject."[1] It is literally *making out of nothing*, where "nothing" is not some kind of *Ungrund* or formless prime matter co-eternal with God, as much Greek philosophy taught, but the entire non-existence of anything. We may admit that creation cannot be imagined by us; if it could it would not be creation, for our mental images are invariably made up out of elements in our past experience, and to nothing in our experience does creation, in the strict sense, apply. But what we cannot imagine we may nevertheless conceive, as we saw in discussing the Anselmian definition of God. Creation is the calling into existence of the being itself, not merely the imposition of new qualities upon it; it is therefore the act of one who is Pure Being and of no one else, and this is why there is nothing that we can do which is precisely like it.

Some light is, however, thrown upon the meaning of creation by the secondary and improper use of the word in ordinary speech. When a great painter or musician is described as a "creative artist," or when the noun "creation" is applied to some triumph in the world of feminine fashion, in either case what is implied is the note of novelty. Something has been brought into the world which is different from everything that existed before; the opposite of creative art is art that is purely imitative, and the word "creation" would, one imagines, hardly be applied to utility clothes made by mass-production methods. In all such cases the element of novelty is, of course, strictly relative; neither Michael Angelo nor Mozart nor a Parisian dress-designer can work in complete independence of all that has gone before, and each of them requires some material upon which to exercise his craft. But the fact remains that in the common use of the word "creation" the idea of novelty is uppermost; the word is there used in a sense which bears a distant and very imperfect analogy to its primary and proper sense, in which it signifies the absolute novelty that is involved in the production of being from complete non-existence.

Since, then, "creation" is not the name of a change produced in pre-existent matter but of the act by which finite being is posited in existence, it has nothing to do with the question whether

---

[1] *Creatio est productio totius substantiæ rei ex nihilo sui et subjecti.* Cf. *S. Theol.*, I, lxv, 3c: *Creatio autem est productio alicujus rei secundum suam totam substantiam, nullo presupposito quod sit vel increatum vel ab aliquo creatum.*

the world had a beginning in time or not.[1] We have been led to
affirm the existence of God as the ground of the world's being;
as has been pointed out more than once, the postulation of a first
cause which is first in a merely temporal sense gets us nowhere.
The existence of a world that is changing and contingent necessitates the existence of a God who is by his very essence changeless
and necessary, upon whose creative fiat not merely the world's
beginning but its continued existence depends. Therefore, while
time is the inevitable mode under which finite beings exist,[2] God's
existence is of necessity supra-temporal or, to use the technical
term, eternal. Eternity does not, it must be insisted, merely mean
"going on for ever," nor does immutability mean remaining
the same for an infinitely long time; eternity means existence

[1] Cf. S. Theol., I, xlvi, 2. S.c.G., II, xxxi–xxxviii. De Pot., iii, 14. It has already
been remarked that St. Thomas caused something of a scandal in the thirteenth
century by maintaining that it is impossible to prove by reason alone that the world
had a beginning in time. There is, however, a modern argument, based upon contemporary physical theory, which has been claimed as demonstrating that the world
cannot have been in existence for an infinite time, or at least that at some past epoch
not infinitely distant some extra-mundane intelligence must have intervened to impose
some ordered arrangement upon it. Since it involves the physical quantity known as
entropy, this has been dignified with the name of the "entropological argument." It
rests upon the highly general statement called the Second Law of Thermodynamics.
Briefly the argument is that the interchange of energy between material systems results
in a progressive evening-out of the heterogeneity of the universe, analogous to the
process of shuffling a pack of cards. Now if the universe had existed for an infinite
time, the shuffling would be complete and the universe would be entirely homogeneous.
But it is not entirely homogeneous, therefore it cannot have existed for an infinite
time. Taken in conjunction with the theory of the expanding universe, this suggests
a date about 10,000,000,000 years ago for the "beginning of the world." (See
Eddington, *New Pathways in Science*, ch. iii; cf. *The Nature of the Physical World*, ch. iv.
See also E. T. Whittaker, *The Beginning and End of the World*.) Professor Eddington's
attitude to the argument is very reserved; he writes as follows: "Philosophically the
notion of an abrupt beginning of the present order of Nature is repugnant to me, as
I think it must be to most; and even those who would welcome a proof of the intervention of a Creator will probably consider that a single winding-up at some remote
epoch is not really the kind of relation between God and his world that brings satisfaction to the mind. But I see no escape from our dilemma." He then discusses possible
solutions, and leaves the matter undetermined. (*New Pathways*, p. 59 f.) (Cf. the
discussion of Eddington's attitude on this matter given by Professor L. S. Stebbing in
her refreshingly realistic work, *Philosophy and the Physicists*, ch. xi.)
    It may be added that, for similar reasons to the above, arguments for or against the
existence of God from considerations of the evolution of the universe can hold only a
secondary place in Christian theism. For evolution is concerned with the becoming,
the *fieri*, of the world, whereas we are concerned with a God who is not just a *causa in
fieri*, but a *causa in esse*. Cf. the passage from Garrigou-Lagrange quoted on p. 38 *supra*.
[2] It is unnecessary in this connection to discuss the difference made by the
scholastics between time (*tempus*) in the strict sense, which is the mode of existence
of material beings, and aeviternity (*ævum*), which is the mode of existence of pure
spiritual creatures such as the angels. Note also: "The being of things corruptible,
because it is changeable, is not measured by eternity, but by time; for time measures
not only things actually changed, but also things changeable; hence it not only
measures movement, but it also measures repose, which belongs to whatever is naturally movable, but is not actually in motion." (*S. Theol.*, I, x, 4 ad 3.)

19   *outside time, and immutability means independence of that subjection
to duration which is inherent in temporal existence.*[1]   It is even
more difficult to imagine eternity than to imagine creation, for in
the relation of creation between the Creator and the creature one
term of the relation—the creature—is embedded in the temporal
process, whereas eternity is something altogether in God.   It is,
of course, true that, *as we view him*, God appears to be subject to
change; because the universe that he has created is a changing
universe, God's action upon it when viewed from within it appears
to be a changing action.   Nevertheless, the change that is observed
is not a change in God but in his creation; as St. Thomas says, in
words that have been already quoted, "Newness of movement
is consequent upon the ordinance of the eternal will to the effect
that movement be not always."[2]

We are thus forced to reject the "receptacle theory" of time as
taught by Sir Isaac Newton in his famous scholium in the *Principia*.
"Absolute, true, and mathematical time," he wrote, "of itself, and
from its own nature, flows equably without regard to anything
external. . . .   All things are placed in time as to order of situation."[3]   We agree, in contrast, with St. Augustine, St. Thomas
and, it may be added, the Relativity physicists, that time is
impossible except in connection with the things that exist in it.[4]
The world, we shall say, is created not *in tempore* but *cum tempore*,[5]
while God's existence is independent of time altogether.   It is
impossible in speaking of God to avoid the use of terms that suggest time, if only for the reason that all our verbs, as a matter of
mere grammar, are either past, present or future in tense; but,
even if we cannot imagine supra-temporal or non-temporal
existence, we can conceive it by divesting the words that we use of
their suggestions of temporality.   With these precautions we can
apply to God's mode of existence such terms as *nunc stans* and can

[1] Cf. St. Augustine: "Nor dost thou by time precede time; else shouldest thou not
precede all times.   But thou precedest all things past by the sublimity of an ever present
eternity. . . .   Thy years are one day; and thy day is not daily, but To-day . . . Thy
To-day is eternity."   (*Conf.*, XI, 16, tr. Pusey.)
[2] *S.c.G.*, II, xxxvi.   See p. 62 *supra*.
[3] Quoted by Whitehead, *Process and Reality*, p. 97.
[4] Cf. Eddington, *Nature of the Physical World*, ch. iii.   It may be remarked that there
is nothing in the scholastic view (though there is in the Newtonian view) inconsistent
with the modern theory that, in a carefully defined sense, each being has its own time.
But it is necessary to make a careful distinction between physics and metaphysics.   See
Maritain, on "Our Knowledge of Sensible Nature" in *Degrees of Knowledge*, ch. iv.   It
may also be noticed that St. Augustine tends to look upon time as an impression made
by a changing thing upon the mind of an observer, and St. Thomas as a measure
inherent in the changing thing itself; cf., e.g., *Conf.* XI, 36, with *S. Theol.*, I, x, 4.
[5] The phrase is St. Augustine's: *De Civitate Dei*, XI, vi.

say that to him all things are present *simul et semel*, once for all and simultaneously.[1]

A further consequence of the doctrine of creation is that there is no real distinction between God's creation of the world and his preservation of it. Both are aspects of one extra-temporal act by which the world in the whole of its temporal history receives its existence. If we consider the fact that, but for this act, the world would not enter into existence, we give it the name *creation*; if, on the other hand, we consider the fact that, but for the same act, the world which exists would collapse into non-being, the word that we use is *preservation*. "As the production of a thing into existence depends on the will of God," writes the Angelic Doctor, "so likewise it depends on his will that things should be preserved; for he does not preserve them otherwise than by ever giving them existence; hence if he took away his action from them, all things would be reduced to nothing, as appears from Augustine. Therefore as it was in the Creator's power to produce them before they existed in themselves; so likewise it is in the Creator's power when they exist in themselves to bring them to nothing."[2] In other words, God's concern with the world is not to be thought of as relating merely to the provision of the world with its initial impulse into being, but as an incessant and intimate care for the beings to which he has given all that they have and all that they are. This is a truth which the Bible is never tired of asserting. "I have graven thee upon the palms of my hands." "He hangeth the earth upon nothing." "Are not two sparrows sold for a farthing? and not one of them shall fall on the ground without your Father."[3] We may compare the words in which the thirteenth-century English mystic, Julian of Norwich, describes one of her revelations:

"He showed me a little thing, the quantity of an hazel-nut, in the palm of my hand; and it was as round as a ball. I looked thereupon with eye of my understanding, and thought: *What may this be?* And it was answered generally thus: *It is all that is made.* I marvelled how it might last, for methought it might suddenly have fallen to naught for little[ness]. And I was

[1] Cf. the discussion of the nature of time and eternity and their mutual relation in F. H. Brabant, *Time and Eternity in Christian Thought*, lect. v, vi.
[2] *S. Theol.*, I, ix, 2c. The reference is to Aug. *De Gen. ad lit.*, IV, xii: *Creatoris namque potentia, et omnipotentis atque omnitenentis virtus, causa subsistendi est omni creaturæ quæ virtus ab eis quæ creata sunt regendis, si aliquando cessaret, simul et illorum cessaret species omnisque natura concideret.* Cf. *S. Th.*, I, viii, 1c; *De Pot.*, v, 1; Hooker, *Eccl. Pol.*, V, lv, 3.
[3] Isa, xlix, 16; Job xxvi, 7; Matt. x, 29.

answered in my understanding: *It lasteth, and ever shall* [*last*], *for that God loveth it.* And so All-thing hath the being by the love of God.

"In this Little Thing I saw three properties. The first is that God made it, the second is that God loveth it, the third, that God keepeth it."[1]

And here we have all the answer that should be needed to the familiar accusation that the God of classical Christian philosophy is a distant celestial autocrat who has none of the attributes demanded by religion.

Two great questions remain to be discussed concerning the creation of the universe. The first is: If God is in himself the fullness of being, how can there be anything else that is possible of existence? The second is: Granted that God can create a world, why should he decide to do so?

(1) It was asserted at the beginning of this chapter that the real difficulty for philosophy is not to explain the existence of God but to explain the existence of anything else. Whatever may be their respective natures, it might be urged, surely God *plus* the world is something more than God. Creation has increased the sum-total of existence. Hence God without the world must be something less than the fullness of being.

It must be replied to this objection that the statement, "God *plus* the world is more than God," is not true of a God who is the unique self-existent and infinite Being, in the sense in which we have attributed those terms to him. Of any merely finite God, however great he might be, the objection would hold. The sum of any two finite beings is always greater than either of them taken separately. But if God is literally infinite this simply does not hold. God and the world being of radically different orders of reality cannot be added together.[2]

To add beings together we must add them in respect of their common qualities. Two cows *plus* five cows make seven cows, for they are all cows. Even two cows and five horses can be added

---

[1] *Revelations of Divine Love*, ed. Warrack, ch. v.

[2] I am tempted to bring out this point by a simple illustration from elementary mathematics and to remark that, whatever finite quantity *a* may represent, infinity *plus a* merely equals infinity. In other words, while adding infinity to *a* makes all the difference to *a*, adding *a* to infinity makes no difference whatever to infinity. And I do not think that the non-mathematical reader will be misled by this. But, in view of the extremely elaborate nature of the mathematical theory of the infinite and the many points in connection with it which are still a matter of violent controversy, it would be almost certain to mislead any reader who is a trained mathematician, and to cause him to assume that I am merely transferring to God the notion of the mathematical infinite in its crudest form.

together in a certain way, for, although they are neither all cows
nor all horses they are all graminivorous quadrupeds; and the
answer is seven graminivorous quadrupeds. We might even,
passing to an extreme case, add together the four lions at the base
of Nelson's Column, the Thirty-nine Articles and the four cardinal
virtues, and say that as a result we had forty-seven beings conceivable by the human mind, though the statement would be of
no practical importance owing to the excessively small common
content. But when it is a question of adding finite beings to God,
the sum simply cannot be made. As Gilson says, God and the
world "are, in all rigour, incommensurable, and that is also why
they are compossible."¹ In Thomist terminology God is not in
any genus and any argument that treats him as if he were is
illicit at the start.³

(2) But if we admit that God could create a world if he wanted
to why should he want to? And, if he did decide to do so, why
should it be this particular world rather than any other; why this
particular one out of all the possible worlds? This is, we may
freely assent, the question which above all others is shrouded in
mystery; it must, however, be replied that, if it is true that we
cannot give a direct answer to it, the impossibility of giving a direct
answer is itself a consequence of the position that is being maintained and is not an extraneous objection coming from some
independent source. We must again urge that, if the doctrine of
God which is here maintained is correct, the question does not so
much demand an answer as refuse to admit one. The very basis
of our argument for the existence of God is that no reason can be
assigned why the world should exist; hence we have been led to
postulate a God who by a sheer and unconditioned act of will has
given it existence. In so far as we are able to say why a will acts
as it does, we are limiting its nature as a will. It is possible to
assign motives for the acts which our human wills perform, precisely because their freedom is limited; but even in this case no
complete reason can be assigned, for, if it could, the act concerned
would be not free but necessary. In the case of God, whose will is
supremely perfect and whose freedom is absolute, there is no

¹ *Spirit of Med. Phil.*, E.T., p. 96.   ² See p. 9 *supra*.
³ One way of stating this is to say that, when God has created the world, there are
plura entia but not *plus entis*, more beings but not more being. The problem raises the
very difficult question of the doctrine of analogy; perhaps the best exposition of this is
to be found in Penido's *Le Rôle de l'Analogie dans la Théologie Dogmatique*. For a vigorous
attack on the doctrine of analogy, and indeed upon rational metaphysics as such, the
reader may be referred to Berdyaev's *Freedom and the Spirit*, ch. ii. See Chapter X *infra*.

reason whatever that we can assign. We shall indeed maintain, against the late medieval voluntarists, that God's will must act in accordance with his own moral nature, but that is all that we can say. The only being that God wills necessarily is himself, and if we are forced to say that, in some sense, the act by which God wills the world must be included in the act by which he wills himself, this does not make the willing of the world necessary, for the reason on which such stress has been already laid, that, God and the world being of radically different orders of reality, we cannot class them together.[1] Whether the act by which God wills himself includes the willing of this world or of some other world or of no world at all, in every case no difference is made to that supreme act. For God and the world simply do not add up.[2]

For this same reason the Leibnizian argument that, if God is supremely good, the world which he has made must be the best of all possible worlds is equally irrelevant.[3] For, although different possible worlds may differ widely among themselves, in relation to the infinite Being which is God they all have the same character of complete un-self-sufficiency.[4]   In other words,

[1] This point does not seem to have been given sufficient attention by Professor A. E. Taylor in his remarks in *The Faith of a Moralist*, I, p. 244 f.

[2] Cf. the following passage from Mr. D. M. MacKinnon's very challenging (and by no means slavishly Thomist) paper in *Malvern*, 1941:

"In metaphysics . . . the question of the why of contingent being remains always unanswered. The goal of the metaphysician was not the achievement of a theoretically satisfying system, such as certain forms of monism have claimed to provide. It was the derivation of the contingent from the necessary, but the question of why the necessary should thus have generated the contingent remained always unanswered. And there is a sense in which always it must. For there is no necessity why God should have brought us into being. We are utterly unnecessary to him, we cannot make of our existence (unless we deny its character) a matter of any necessity whatever, yet we cannot deny that through revelation the character of our relation to God is profoundly illuminated by the disclosure in an act, that is necessary to its achievement, of his relation to us." (Op. cit., p. 87.)

[3] "Now as there is an infinite number of possible universes in the ideas of God, and as only one can exist, there must be a sufficient reason for God's choice, determining him to one rather than to another.

"And this reason can only be found in the *fitness*, or in the degrees of perfection, which these worlds contain, each possible world having the right to claim existence in proportion to the perfection which it involves.

"And it is this which causes the existence of the best, which God knows through his wisdom, chooses through his goodness, and produces through his power. . . .

" . . . if we could sufficiently understand the order of the universe, we should find that it surpasses the desires of the most wise, and that it is impossible to make it better than it is." (*Monadology*, 53–5, 90. *Philosophical Works of Leibniz*, Everyman's ed., pp. 12, 20.)

[4] With the reservations made in the note to p. 102 I am tempted to refer to the fact that in mathematics the various finite integers bear very varied relations to one another but that in relation to infinity they each bear the ratio zero. Thus:

$$\frac{0}{\infty} = 0; \quad \frac{1}{\infty} = 0; \quad \frac{2}{\infty} = 0; \text{ etc.}$$

whether God creates the world, or no world, or a different world, the result in relation to his own infinite Being is the same. No world, however perfect, can add anything to him; none of them can increase his beatitude, but any of them can manifest his glory. "All that he has done is well done because it is he who hath done it, said Christian reason. It is he who has done all, since it is well done and since I know why, and besides, he is bound to do the best, says Leibnitzian optimism": this is Maritain's summary of the matter.[1] And again, "Leibniz pretended to justify God by showing that the work which proceeded from the hands of that perfect Workman was itself perfect, whereas in reality it is the radical imperfection of every creature which best attests the glory of the Uncreated."[2]

The truth is, as a matter of fact, as Gilson has pointed out in expounding St. Bonaventure, that, while any world made by God is bound to be good, the very fact of its finitude involves that God could have made a better one. "There is no conceivable world, however perfect, about which the same question could not be raised as has been raised about our own. If God had made a better world, we could always ask why he has not made one still better, and the question would never be meaningless, for no term of the series of possible worlds contains in itself the necessary and sufficient reason for its realization. The only solution possible to such a question does not reside in creatures but in God, and therefore it escapes us. . . . What he has given, he has given by pure grace, in an act of goodness which allows of no dissatisfaction; the rest is his secret."[3] As Fr. Sertillanges puts it, "The best possible world is not possible, for God could always improve on it."[4]

To many present-day Christians the view that the creation of the world is entirely unnecessary to God will, no doubt, seem inconsistent with the Christian revelation of God as a God of love, who has a most intimate concern with all his creatures; it may suggest that God made the world, as it were, in a fit of absent-mindedness and has little or no interest in it. Thus Dr. W. R. Matthews asserts that the "*Deus philosophorum* is not the God and

[1] *Degrees of Knowledge*, E.T., p. 226.
[2] *Religion and Culture*, E.T., p. 40. Cf. Ossuna: *Quo majus est creatura, eo amplius eget Deo*, quoted by Bremond, *Lit. Hist. of Rel. Thought in France*, E.T., I, p. 11.
[3] *Phil. of St. Bonaventure*, E.T., p. 175.
[4] *Foundations of Thomist Philosophy*, E.T., p. 127. He points out, with St. Thomas (*S. Theol.*, I, xxv, 5, et 6 ad 1), that to say that God could have made a better world is not to say that God could have made this world in a better way. Cf. Garrigou-Lagrange, *Dieu*, E.T., II, p. 345 f.

Father of our Lord Jesus Christ. Those who thought out the system," he says, "in spite of their profoundly Christian experience, did not succeed in fusing the Aristotelian metaphysic with the Christian Gospel. We cannot believe in the Deity who emerges from their logic, not because he is too high but because he does not really sustain the Christian values."[1] And again, while admitting that "to maintain that God in and for himself is not self-sufficient is, from the standpoint of traditional Christian theology, a gross heresy," he asserts that, in his opinion, "the doctrine of the self-sufficiency of God should be rejected" and that "the conception of the self-sufficiency of God in and for himself is an abstract idea which cannot be allowed to dominate our theology without disastrous results."[2]

Dr. Matthews is, it must be admitted, careful not to put God and the world on the same level. "When we assert," he writes, "that it is of the nature of God to be creative and infer that every moment of time must be filled with the exercise of his creative power, we do not equate the product of creative activity with the Creator. . . . It certainly is implied in our argument that the being of God as personal is dependent upon the existence of a created order, and that we see no way of holding the personality of a Deity 'prior to creation.' But we must," continues Dr. Matthews, "make two remarks upon this which will remove the real weight of the objection. Our argument most emphatically does not imply the eternity of this physical universe in which we are, nor of any universe; it will be satisfied by the admission that, in any possible time, there must be created being of some kind. And further, we do not suggest, nor can it be inferred from our position, that God depends on creation in the same manner as the creation depends upon him. Created being depends upon God in an absolute sense. It derives its existence wholly from him. God depends on creation only in the sense that, being what he is, it is a necessity of his nature to create."[3]

To deal with Matthews's positive assertions first, it is surprising to find a Christian theologian asserting that "the being of God as personal is dependent upon the existence of a created order."

---

[1] *God in Christian Thought and Experience*, p. 104.
[2] *The Purpose of God*, p. 173. He adds: "I observe that Dr. Temple, in the valuable Gifford Lectures [*sc. Nature, Man and God*] which he delivered in this place, adheres to this venerable theological tradition, with the consequence that his views on purpose and freedom seem to me to be obscure."
[3] *God in Christian Thought and Experience*, p. 206.

Christian theology has always held that, in so far as the being of God as personal can be said to depend upon anything, it is dependent upon those eternal and internal processions by which the unity of the Godhead is differentiated into the Trinity of Father, Son and Holy Ghost.[1] In any case, the real objection to Matthews's view is not that it equates the product of creative activity with the Creator, but that it deprives God of that status of self-sufficiency which alone provides an explanation for the existence of the world and so makes creation possible. And while we may admit the truth of the two remarks which Matthews goes on to make, they do nothing to remove this objection. The assertion that, in any possible time, there must be created being of *some* kind is no less repugnant than would be the assertion that, in any possible time, there must exist this particular physical universe in which we are. Nor does the denial that God depends upon his creation in the same manner as it depends upon him help the matter; such a statement is equally true of the relation between any human artist and his work. There is, however, no doubt that Matthews is voicing a widespread opinion when he says that the *Deus philosophorum* is not the God and Father of our Lord Jesus Christ.

In a certain sense we may readily allow this contention. Traditional theology has not only admitted but has vehemently asserted that the God that philosophy displays to us is *less than* the Christian God; this is why it has maintained the necessity for our natural knowledge of God to be supplemented by revelation. But it has not admitted that the God of philosophy is *inconsistent with* the God of Christianity, as Matthews implies; and this is the real point.

[1] Needless to say, Matthews does believe in the Trinity, but he does not consider that the sphere of life contained therein is sufficient for the exercise of personality. He argues that personality involves the pursuit of ideals, and hence an imperfect sphere in which to pursue them. But, since God is himself perfect, that sphere cannot be within himself. "If therefore we hold that God is personal, we are forced to the conclusion that he finds in the created world, or in the creatures, the sphere, distinct from himself, in which his ideal ends are to be attained." (*God* etc., p. 178.) But this view of personality as fundamentally constituted by striving, while it would be congenial to voluntaristic philosophies such as those of Fichte, Schopenhauer and Hegel, has little to justify it; traditional Christianity asserts that the infinite and perfect life of mutual self-giving of the three divine Persons is far more fully personal than any striving to achieve ideals. And, incidentally, Matthews's view would involve that either God will ultimately achieve his ideals, in which case he will thenceforth cease to be personal, or else he will remain for ever personal at the cost of never achieving his ideals. (The second of these alternatives seems to represent Matthews's own position, op. cit., p. 202.) Later on, it is urged that there are strong reasons for believing that "the thought of God as personal involves us in the conclusion that there are distinctions within the Godhead" (op. cit., p. 193). But, if Matthews's earlier argument is sound, it is difficult to see why. Cf. an article by T. M. Parker in *Sobornost'*, March 1938, p. 14 f.

Is the idea of God's self-sufficiency inconsistent with the idea of his Love? At first sight we might think so, but a little reflection may lead us to a very different view. In the first place, the statement that the world is necessary to God can have two very different meanings. It might mean that by some inherent metaphysical urge God has to create a world whether he wants to or not, or, on the other hand, it might mean that God's sphere of action would be limited and circumscribed without a world, and so he creates it because he wants to. The first meaning is clearly inadmissible; if God had as little voluntary decision in the creation of the world as an automatic machine has in the delivery of a bar of chocolate, we certainly could not describe creation as an act of love. We must assume, therefore, that the statement that the creation of the world is necessary to God means that without it something would be missing from the realm of God's experience; that is to say, that he creates it because without it his activity would be incomplete.

But, it must now be said, if, in creating the world, God was simply fulfilling his own being, then creation, while it might be an act of love, would certainly not be an act of purely unselfish love. Even taking into account the consequences that creation may be foreseen by God to involve—for example, admitting the most crudely patripassian doctrine of the Atonement—the fact would remain that, by creating a world, God was not only doing something for the creatures composing it, but was also doing something for himself.[1] We may take an illustration from human parenthood. In consenting to procreate a child, the parents are certainly not being entirely selfish, nor are they necessarily oblivious of the sufferings which the child may cause them; their motives are, however, inevitably (and rightly) mixed, and among them is the conviction that they will be, on the whole, happier with a child than without one. As the famous controversies between St. Bernard and Abelard and between Bossuet and Fénelon made plain, human love can never be totally disinterested, not even our love for God;[2] but to assume that God's love cannot be entirely disinterested is sheer anthropomorphism. So far from diminishing the love shown by God in creation, the doctrine that

---

[1] Cf. p. 107, n. 1 *supra*.
[2] See, e.g., the discussion in Gilson, *The Mystical Theology of St. Bernard*, App. II, "Abelard," and Baron von Hügel's extremely illuminating exposition and assessment of Fénelon in *The Mystical Element of Religion*, II, p. 160 f. Cf. also *The Pilgrim continues his Way*, pp. 100–1; John Burnaby, *Amor Dei*, ch. ix (on "Pure Love").

creation is unnecessary to God enhances it. It is precisely because creation can give nothing whatever to God which in any way enhances his beatitude, that creation is an act of entire giving on the part of God. God would not be lonely or bored or idle if we did not exist; his life as Trinity is a life of infinite activity, of inexhaustible fullness. In creating the world he gains nothing for himself; that is why creation is an act of supreme love.

The classical doctrine of creation is thus both mysterious and paradoxical, but it is far more profound than the alternative view. Since creation adds nothing to God, there is a very true sense in which God has made us for our own sake and not for his; thus St. Thomas says that "God seeks glory, not for his own sake, but for ours."[1] Nevertheless, just because our whole being derives from him we can attain our beatitude only by seeking him as our last end, and the duty of doing so is the highest law of our being. In other words, although created things can be of no utility to God, it is of their very essence to be for his glory; and God's demand that we shall glorify him is not the selfish claim of a tyrant but an act of the most astounding condescension. "It is infinitely more glorious for us to have been created for the glory of *him who is*," writes Garrigou-Lagrange, "than to have been created for ourselves."[2] That the self-sufficient God deigns to be glorified by his entirely dependent creatures, whose service can add nothing to him, is the supreme privilege and honour that God has conferred upon them. When it is asserted that *either* God demands our service, in which case he must be insufficient without us, *or else* he is sufficient without us, in which case he can have no need of our service, the answer simply is that the very formulation of this dilemma assumes that God is finite. Of any finite being, however great, the dilemma would hold; but it does not hold of God.

"The glory of God," it has been said, "does not consist in receiving something from us which will make him richer! It consists rather in giving us the means of being no longer nothing."[3] "Thus did the Word himself bid the people offer oblations," wrote St. Irenæus, "not that he had need of them but that they might learn to serve God."[4] And what is true of the glory which man, as a rational being, can give to God by his rational service is in its measure no less true of the glory which lifeless or sub-rational living creatures give to God by the mere fact of their existence.

[1] *S. Theol.*, II II, cxxxii, 1 ad 1.   [2] *Dieu*, E.T., p. 106.
[3] P. Charles, S.J., *Prayer for All Times*, E.T., II, p. 60.   [4] *Adv. Hær.*, iv, 18.

If it is true, then, that in one sense God has made us not for his sake but for ours, there is also a sense in which it is equally true that we exist not for our own sakes but for his, for the value of our service to God is set up precisely by this fact—and by this fact alone—that God is ready to accept our freely willed offering of it. We can find an illustration drawn from the realm of human life which, however inadequate it may be, will help to make the point clear. Of all the attributes of God the one which the modern world is most ready to admit is that of fatherhood. Now most fathers receive presents from their small children on their birthdays, and receive them gladly, in spite of the fact that the presents are usually quite useless and in any case have to be paid for by the parent in the last resort. They are none the less readily accepted because of that, and the normal human parent has a joy in receiving such a gift which far exceeds the satisfaction obtained from a much more expensive and useful present given by a business client or even by a grown-up friend.

We must maintain, then, that God created the world by an act of love for which no reason can be assigned except the free operation of his creative will. "*God made the cosmos*," wrote Abbot Chapman in one of his letters, "Why? It was a very odd thing to do!"[1] And we shall never attain to that humility and wonder which are essential to the true practice of Christianity unless we realize that creation, so far from being what might reasonably be expected of God is the most incalculable and, we might even say, superfluous expression of the complete freedom and limitless fecundity of self-existent Being.[2] That creation is eminently congruous with God's nature we may readily admit—*bonum est*

---

[1] *Spiritual Letters of Dom John Chapman*, p. 207.

[2] It will be seen from what has been written above that there is a very close connection between the metaphysical problem of the existence of the universe and the moral and ascetic problem of the duty of man to love and serve God. Mr. John Burnaby has discussed it most interestingly in the Introduction, on "The Embarrassment of the Anti-mystic," to his study of St. Augustine's religious teaching, *Amor Dei*. He first of all shows how Professor Macmurray emphasizes man's duty of serving God to the extent of making God for all practical purposes completely immanent in the world-process, while, on the other hand, Professor Nygren lays such an unbalanced stress upon the transcendence of God as to deny that it is possible for man to love God at all. The Catholic doctrine, as expounded by Augustine, lies between these extremes. It insists as strongly as Nygren on the transcendence of God and as strongly as Macmurray on the duty of man. But it insists that this transcendent God does condescend to be served by his creatures, and that the duty that man has to fulfil finds its end not just within the world-process but above it, in God. The heart of the answer is that man's ability to love God, like his very existence, is a free gift from God himself. (See Burnaby, *passim*; J. Macmurray, *Creative Society* and *The Structure of Religious Experience*; A. Nygren, *Agape and Eros*, E.T., especially Part II.)

diffusivum sui; but that it is in any way necessary to him we must emphatically deny.

The doctrine that the world is unnecessary to God, and the various corollaries that this involves, do not in the least imply that God is uninterested in his creation, though it has often been asserted that this consequence must follow from it. Thus Dr. Matthews writes: "The main object of the Scholastic thinkers was to disengage the conception of love in God from the taint of 'passio,' from the suggestion, that is, that God needs anything or can be affected by anything outside himself"; and he alleges that "this is surely very near to a rejection of the belief that God loves the world or human persons at all."[1] This objection, like the previous ones, rests upon an implicit denial of the absolute infinity of God. There is no need whatever for us to overlook or minimize the truth which the Bible throughout so plainly teaches: that God enters into the most intimate details of the life of all his creatures, that he rejoices in our happiness and sympathizes with our sorrows, that he is glorified by our good acts and grieved by our sins. We will go further and say that the intensity with which our actions as personal beings affect him is infinitely greater than that with which they affect our fellow human beings, for God, as our Creator and Preserver, is present to us more closely than we are present to ourselves.[2] But when that has been said, it must be added that even this is infinitely surpassed by the beatitude which God enjoys in the interior fullness of his own divine life, which it therefore can neither augment nor diminish. Therefore there is no incompatibility between the compassion and the impassibility of God.

Closely connected with this is the much misunderstood doctrine that God loves things in proportion to their goodness.[3] Dr. Matthews objects that "a love nicely proportioned to the merit of the object seems too coldly reasonable to engage our admiration," it "falls short of the best human devotion."[4] We must take into account, however, the fact that God confers upon every being that exists all that it has and is, and that he preserves it in being, however much, in its own freedom, it may violate his will. Behind the act of love by which God loves it in accordance with its good-

---

[1] *God* etc., p. 227.

[2] Solovyev is right when he says that "to assert that God does not 'interest himself' in our material wants is to justify atheism by putting limits to the Godhead." (*God, Man and the Church*, E.T., p. 44.)

[3] Cf. *S. Theol.*, I, xx, 3.   [4] *God* etc., p. 228.

ness, there lies the far greater act of love by which he has called it
into being from non-existence, an act which is in the fullest sense
of the word gratuitous, since before it existed it could have no
claim upon him at all, and while it exists can have no claim upon
him for its preservation. The fact is that not only does God love
whatever goodness we possess but he has himself conferred it upon
us. "Since our will," writes St. Thomas, "is not the cause of the
goodness of things, but is moved by it as by its object, our love,
whereby we will good to anything, is not the cause of its goodness;
but conversely its goodness, whether real or imaginary, calls forth
our love . . . : whereas the love of God infuses and creates goodness."[1] "There is only one reason," writes Mr. Charles Williams,
"why anything should be loved on this earth—because God loves
it."[2]

To sum up the discussion of this chapter, it has been maintained
that nothing less than a strictly infinite God can provide the
explanation of the world's existence, and that, in consequence, the
world must be in the fullest sense, contingent and altogether
unnecessary to God. Various objections have been considered,
which all, in one way or another, complain that, on such a view,
God could not have the intimate interest and concern with his
creatures that is manifested in the Christian Religion. To this we
have replied that, while this would certainly be true if God was a
finite being, it is not true if God is infinite. In other words, the
doctrine of an infinite God not only raises the difficulties, but also
solves them.[3] The doctrine of a finite God, on the other hand,
neither raises nor solves them; but nor does it answer the question
which clamours for a reply: why anything exists at all.

And in the course of this discussion we have touched upon
various aspects of the relation of God to the universe.[4]

---

[1] *S. Theol.*, I, xx, 2c.   [2] *He came down from Heaven*, p. 141.

[3] It may be suggested that the failure to realize this truth is the main defect in
Professor John Laird's very stimulating Gifford Lectures on *Theism and Cosmology*.
Cf. especially lectures iii and iv of that work.

[4] The question as to whether creation adds anything to God is obviously similar to
the question as to whether, in the Incarnation, the humanity of Jesus adds anything
to the Divine Word, and, *mutatis mutandis*, the same answer is to be given. The
Incarnation involves, on the part of the Divine Word a human life that is every whit
as real and concrete as that of any man or woman who has ever lived; nevertheless,
since *qua* human it belongs to the created order, it cannot "add up with" the fullness
of being which the Word enjoys as the eternally begotten Son of the Father. In saying
this, we are not, of course, forgetting that the relation of hypostatic union set up
between the Word and the world by the Incarnation is essentially different from the
relation of "presence of immensity" which God has to the world through the act of
creation.

ADDITIONAL NOTE *B* TO CHAPTER VIII

GOD AND THE WORLD IN THE THEISM OF JAMES WARD

This is a convenient point at which to insert some remarks upon the view of the relation between God and the world expounded in the teaching of the late Professor James Ward, since Ward's reputation stands sufficiently high, through the magnificent refutation of nineteenth-century anti-theistic doctrine which he gave in his first set of Gifford Lectures on *Naturalism and Agnosticism*, for any divergence from his teaching to need some justification. In almost the opening paragraph of the discussion of theism which forms the second part of his later Gifford lectures, *The Realm of Ends, or Pluralism and Theism*, he wrote as follows:

> "There are objections to all attempts to proceed altogether *a priori*. It seems obviously puerile to ask, for example, for a sufficient reason why there is something rather than nothing. This notion of being absolutely thoroughgoing, of building up a metaphysic without presuppositions, one that shall start from nothing and explain all, is, I repeat, futile. Such a metaphysic has its own assumption, and that an absurd one, viz., that nothing is the logical *prius* of something. Well at any rate, it may be said, if we must start from something, let us at least start from what is absolutely necessary, or rather let us not stop till we reach it: let us not rest in what is merely actual, for that can only be contingent. But, paradoxical though it may sound, necessary being is but another aspect of contingent being; for within the limits of our experience only that is called *really* necessary which is inevitably conditioned by its cause, and is thus contingent on this, that is to say, follows from it."[1]

Now, if by "attempts to proceed altogether *a priori*" Ward meant such argumentation in complete independence of all basis in existent being as we find in St. Anselm, or in later days in Descartes and Hegel, we might well agree. It is, no doubt, metaphysically absurd to assume that nothing is the logical *prius* of something. And it would be obviously puerile to ask why there was something rather than nothing if the being about which the question was asked provided the reason for its own existence.

[1] Op. cit., p. 225.

Such a being all men, as St. Thomas would say, would unite in calling God. But Ward condemns equally the argument which refuses to rest in what is "merely actual" (by which presumably he means actual and finite) and so only contingent; and he condemns it on the ground that, in our experience, necessary being is necessary only in the sense that it is necessarily contingent on some anterior cause. But, we must reply, classical theism has never asserted that God is necessary in this sense; on the contrary, he is necessary precisely because he depends on nothing but himself. The truth is, not that necessary being is but another aspect of contingent being, but that contingent being, when it exists, is *necessarily the result—not*, be it observed, *the necessary result*—of a creative act on the part of necessary Being. That is to say, *given the world*, it necessarily follows that a God exists as its Creator, but, *given God*, it does not necessarily follow that a world exists as his creature. It is this distinction that Ward overlooked.

After expressing his agreement with the Kantian objections to the traditional arguments for the existence of God, Ward rightly remarks that there is nothing in our experience comparable with creation in the strict sense of the word. "The idea," he says, "is, in fact, like the idea of God, altogether transcendent." And he immediately adds: "It is impossible therefore that experience should directly give rise to it at all." "But," he continues in the following paragraph, "it has been urged, the universe cannot have existed for ever, since in that case, at any assigned moment, an infinite time would be completed, and that is impossible. The universe must then have had a beginning and so must have had a First Cause." And to this he replies that, "if this argument were valid, it would apply equally to the existence of God. . . . Keeping within experience we can only endlessly regress with no prospect of ever reaching the beginning or of forming any concept of what it was like."[1] Clearly Ward failed altogether to understand the issue. For, in the first place, so far from asserting that the world cannot have existed for ever, the traditional position, at any rate as it is stated by St. Thomas, refuses to admit that there is any reason, apart from the Christian revelation, for supposing that the universe had a temporal beginning at all. And, in the second place, the very essence of that position lies in its denial that God is merely the first term in a causal series. With every bit as much emphasis as Ward it affirms that such a God would provide no

[1] *Realm of Ends*, p. 232.

explanation of the existence of either the world or himself. For this very reason it insists that he is outside and above the order of the universe and is radically different in status from all the beings that compose it.

The result of this approach is that Ward, while he is willing to admit, at least as extremely probable, the existence of a God who makes a cosmological unity out of a universe that is ontologically a plurality, and indeed goes on to say that "the idea of God would . . . be meaningless, unless God were regarded as transcending the Many, so that there can be no talk of God as merely *primus inter pares*," is led to assert that "a God that was not a Creator, a God whose creatures had no independence, would not himself be really a God."[1] He develops this thought as follows:

> "No theist can pretend that the world is coordinate with God: the divine transcendence is essential to the whole theistic position. No theist again assumes that creation involves external limitation. But the point is that if creation is to have any meaning it implies internal limitation. It is from the reality of the world that we start: if this is denied, the divine transcendence becomes meaningless, nay, God, as the ideal of the pure reason, sinks to a mere illusion within an illusion. On the other hand, if the reality of the world be admitted, then this reality stands over against the reality of God. God indeed has not been limited from without but he has limited himself."[2]

The reply to this will now be obvious: it has already been given on pages 102–5. But it may be remarked, in concluding this note, that Ward never seems to have realized that there was any other alternative to his own pluralistic theism than some kind of monistic absolutism. For him Reality was identical with Experience, and the essence of theism was the doctrine that "beyond the universe of the Many there is a single transcendent experient, who comprehends the whole."[3] The doctrine of *analogia entis*[4] was quite absent from his thought. Either, he implies, being is univocal, and then God must be limited by the world which he has made, or it is equivocal, and so in comparison with God the world has no real existence. In following the former course, he was, we may admit, choosing the lesser of two evils, but in it there lies the one really unsatisfactory point in the whole of his system.

[1] *Realm of Ends*, p. 241. [2] Ibid., p. 243. [3] Ibid., p. 228. [4] See p. 126 *infra.*

CHAPTER IX

THE DIVINE ATTRIBUTES

IT is not the purpose of this book to give a complete and systematic exposition of natural theology, and only those points have been dealt with in detail which are directly relevant to its main theme. It seems worth while, however, to devote a chapter to some brief remarks on some points to which so far little or no reference has been made.

It has already been said that, in spite of his assertion that natural theology is competent to demonstrate not *what* God is, but *that* he is, St. Thomas Aquinas deduces from the fact of God's existence a remarkably large number of facts about him.[1] He assumes that, although we cannot obtain by the exercise of reason an essential or quidditative knowledge of God, we can know certain of his attributes, by establishing first of all the fact that in God essence and existence are identical and then deriving the consequences of this identity. This has already been discussed; here we shall merely offer some observations upon the problem of the divine attributes.

The divine attributes have been defined as "those absolutely simple perfections, unmixed with imperfection, which exist necessarily and formally, though in a higher mode, in God."[2] For the sake of clearness it will be well to comment on some of the terms contained in this form of words.

(i) "Absolutely simple perfections, unmixed with imperfection." Perfections are indeed found in created beings, but they are always limited. Creatures are good, but their goodness is finite; they may know, but they are not omniscient. God, on the other hand, is not merely good, he is Goodness itself; he is not merely true, but is the Truth.

(ii) "Which exist necessarily." The attributes of creatures are, at least for the most part, contingent; they can be increased and diminished, they can even be acquired and lost, without the being which is their subject ceasing to be the same being. I can have

[1] p. 69 f. *supra.*
[2] Phillips, *Modern Thomistic Philosophy*, II, p. 307. We shall not discuss the distinction between the *entitative* and *operative* (*metaphysical* and *moral*) attributes of God (op. cit., ad loc.).

116

my hair cut, I can become wiser or more foolish, without ceasing to
be myself. But in God nothing is accidental; he *is* all that he *has*.

(iii) ". . . and formally." Formally, that is as opposed to
virtually. Skegness is healthy, not in the sense that it enjoys
health but that it causes it; it is healthy virtually. Its residents,
presumably, are healthy formally, for they enjoy the health that
Skegness causes. Now God is not only the cause of goodness,
beauty and so on; he is the Supreme Good and Beauty itself.

(iv) ". . . though in a higher mode." Perfections exist in God,
not merely *formaliter*, but *formaliter eminentius*. Goodness in God
must, in some way, mean the same as goodness in his creatures;
otherwise, since our only immediate idea of goodness is derived
from the world of which we are part, the statement that God is
good would be simply meaningless; we might as well say that God
was bad or that he was pink. But, as the Fourth Way of St.
Thomas insisted, goodness in God must be realized in an essentially different and superior mode to that in which it is realized in
us. The word *eminentius* expresses this fact, but it does not tell us
precisely what that mode is, for it must clearly exceed the capacities
of our understanding. All we can really say is that God's goodness is
related to his infinite Being in a similar way to the way in which
our goodness is related to our finite being. This last statement is
an example of what is technically called analogy of proportionality; this is not the place for a full discussion of the extremely
difficult problem of analogy, but, for the sake of accuracy it is
well to register the fact.[1]

The main problem in connection with the divine attributes is
how to reconcile their multiplicity with the simplicity of God.
Mr. G. K. Chesterton has a story about a lady who, after spending
some time on the Thomist exposition of the simplicity of God, was
heard to remark in despair that, if that was his simplicity, she
wondered what his complexity was like! She might have been
comforted to discover that there is no complexity in God, but it
must be admitted that, in view of the multiplicity of the divine
attributes—unity, goodness, truth, eternity, omnipotence, omniscience, immutability and so forth—it certainly looks as if there
were. The difficulty is to steer a middle course between the

[1] The doctrine of analogy is discussed at length in Penido's book, *Le Rôle de l'Analogie
dans la Théologie Dogmatique.* See also Garrigou-Lagrange, *Dieu*, E.T., II, p. 203 f. The
Rev. W. W. S. March has pointed out how Bishop Berkeley was forced to adopt the
doctrine of analogy in order to provide a rational reply to the deists of his day. (See
article, "Analogy, Aquinas and Bishop Berkeley," in *Theology*, June 1942.)

extremes of either, on the one hand, stressing the simplicity of
God in such a way as to deny that the various attributes mean
anything inherently different from one another, thus reducing
them to the level of purely subjective impressions made upon our
minds by the concept of God and having no objective counterparts in God himself, or, on the other hand, insisting on the
distinction between the attributes to the extent of depriving them
of any real common unity and of making them merely accidental
to the divine Being. How, it will be asked, can we assert that the
attributes are distinct from one another and yet all identical with
the divine essence? A simple illustration may take us some way
towards the answer, though, like all such parallels, it will land us
in the gravest error if it is pressed beyond the strict limits within
which it is applicable. A building may present quite different
appearances when it is viewed from different aspects, and yet
these appearances all cohere in the unity of the building. Their
differences do not mean that they are nothing but subjective
hallucinations; they, all of them, each in its particular and partial
way, give a real knowledge of the building itself. Nor are they
disconnected from one another, for they are elaborately and
intricately connected by the laws of solid geometry and perspective; this can be seen from the fact that it is possible for the views
that we should describe as the east and south elevations of Lincoln
Cathedral to cohere in one object, while it is quite impossible for
the east elevation of Lincoln Cathedral to cohere with the south
elevation of the Temperate House in Kew Gardens. In other
words, the attributes of God do represent God, and are not merely
misleading impressions made by God upon our minds; while at
the same time they cohere and coalesce in the complete and
absolute simplicity of the divine essence. A more picturesque
illustration is provided by the story of the blind men who set out
to investigate the nature of an elephant. One of them walked into
its side and concluded that an elephant was a kind of wall; one
ran up against its tusk and asserted that it was a kind of spear;
one caught hold of its trunk, and said that obviously it was a
species of snake; while the fourth, who grasped the tail, said that
the others were all wrong and that obviously an elephant was
nothing but a piece of rope.[1] The various characteristics which
they attributed to the beast were not subjective hallucinations;

---

[1] The earliest version of this story seems to be in the Buddhist *Udana;* see *The Bible of the World*, p. 277.

they were genuine properties of the elephant. But their mistakes arose through their not understanding that such widely different characteristics were all united in the elephant's essence. Where the illustrations break down is, of course, in the fact that the co-existence of the various attributes in God is not due to any kind of structural relatedness similar to the laws of geometry in space, but to the unimaginable fullness and interior fecundity which is of the essence of Absolute Being.[1]

A word on certain of the attributes may not be out of place. It has frequently been alleged that a radical omniscience on the part of God is incompatible with human freedom. If God knows to-day what I shall decide to do to-morrow, how can my choice be free? And if my choice is genuinely free, how can God know now what I am going to do? The controversies around these questions raised by the Molinist doctrine of *scientia media* must surely represent one of the most elaborate and unnecessary discussions in the history of philosophy.[2] And if the questions are posed in these terms it seems impossible to give a satisfactory answer, for the simple reason that the very posing of the questions introduces an error into the discussion. For, if God's existence is outside time, it is strictly meaningless to talk about what God knows *to-day*, since God's "to-day" is eternity. It is *true to-day* that God knows what I shall do to-morrow, but it is not true that God *knows* it *to-day*. And so the question falls to the ground. But if, as a

[1] Some nominalists taught that the distinction between the divine attributes was purely *nominal* (so that, e.g., to them justice and mercy in God were pure synonyms); Duns Scotus, in reaction, taught that it was *formal and actual*. Cajetan, summing up the Thomist tradition, teaches that the attributes are formally in God, but that their distinction is not formal but *virtual*. (See Garrigou-Lagrange, *Le Sens du Mystère et le Clair-obscur intellectuel*, p. 211 f.; cf. *Dieu*, E.T., II, p. 190 f.)

Dr. Edwyn Bevan, we may note, in his *Symbolism and Belief*, having stated correctly the Thomist doctrine that perfections are *formally* in God (p. 314), later on assumes that this involves that the distinction between the attributes is purely *nominal* (p. 320 f.). It is hardly surprising that he feels impelled to reject the doctrine of analogy altogether. But the form of symbolism which he constructs after his resurrection of Dean Mansel does not appear to be a satisfactory substitute (lect. xiv). His final argument for theism clearly leads to nothing more than the idea of God as a regulative principle for human life (lect. xvi), until in the last sentence of his work he suddenly asserts that "what actually causes anyone to believe in God is direct perception of the Divine" (p. 386), a surprising assertion in view of his earlier statement that "even among religious people mystics are only a small minority" (p. 346). Cf. the review-article by Bernard Kelly, T.O.S.D., in *Blackfriars*, December 1938.

[2] Molina taught that God has a special kind of knowledge, *scientia media*, of the way in which each particular free agent will make his free choice in every possible situation, and that this knowledge, whose object is the conditional future or *futuribile*, is specifically different from his *scientia simplicis intelligentiae*, whose object is the pure possible, and from his *scientia visionis*, whose object is the really existent. See Garrigou-Lagrange, *Dieu*, E.T., II, p. 59 f. A quite admirable discussion of divine foreknowledge is given by Thomas Jackson, *Works*, V, p. 83 f.

concession to the limitations of the human imagination, we feel obliged to speak as if God's knowledge was in time, we shall be compelled to say, however reluctantly, that God does to-day know my future free choices, for the alternative is to deny God's omniscience *tout court*. But then we shall have to add quite simply that there is a mystery beyond our power to unravel.

As regards the attribute of omnipotence, it has frequently been remarked in recent years that, in the original Greek and Latin Creeds, the words Παντοκράτωρ and *omnipotens* do not possess the same nuance as the English word *almighty*; that they assert God to be the Ruler of all things or powerful in all matters, rather than to be able to do anything. Such a contention may be admitted as a matter of etymology, for the simple reason that the terms of theology are normally drawn from the vocabulary of human speech and that, of no human being, however exalted, would it be asserted, except perhaps in addresses which were exaggeratedly flattering and insincere, that he was literally able to do anything whatever. It must not, however, be concluded from this that the early Church would have been ready to admit the possibility that God was limited in his power. Nor is such a limitation consistent with the argument that has been here developed. If God is in any absolute sense the Ruler of all things and powerful in all matters, if creatures depend upon God's incessant creative action for all that they have and all that they are, if he is the very source of their existence and nature, then it is absurd to suppose that his power over them is limited by anything outside himself.[1] But this must not be taken as denying that there

[1] For a discussion of the reconciliation of divine omnipotence and omniscience with human freedom, the reader may be referred to Garrigou-Lagrange, *Dieu*, E.T., II, p. 268 f. For some reflections on the historical and sociological bearings of the problem see Maritain, *True Humanism*, ch. i, and *Freedom in the Modern World*. If we maintain that the Thomists are right against the Molinists, it is not because they provide a more complete answer (which is doubtful), but because they refrain from distorting the question in order to make it more easily tractable.

Thomas Jackson, writing against the Calvinists, states the issue admirably:

"There is a fallacy, though the simplest one that ever was set to catch any wise man, wherein many excellent wits of these latter ages, with some of the former, have been pitifully entangled. The snare, wherein it were not possible for any besides themselves to catch them, they thus frame or set: 'Whatsoever God hath decreed must of necessity come to pass: but God hath decreed every thing that is: therefore every thing that is comes to pass of necessity. All things are necessary, at least in respect of God's decree.' The extract or corollary whereof, in brief, is this: 'It is impossible for aught, that is not, to be; for aught that hath been, not to have been; for aught that is, not to be; impossible for aught to be hereafter, that shall not be.' But if it be (as here I suppose) very consonant to infinite wisdom, altogether necessary to infinite goodness, and no way impossible for infinite power, *to decree contingency as well as necessity*; or that some effects should be as truly contingent as others are necessary; a conclusion quite contradictory

are certain limitations imposed upon God's action by his own nature; so that, for instance, he cannot decide that two *plus* two should be equal to five,[1] or that cruelty should be a virtue instead of a vice. For he is, by his very nature, the supreme Truth and the Sovereign Good, and any violation of these attributes would be not a perfection but a deficiency. St. Thomas neatly expresses this in the dictum: "It is better to say that such things cannot be done, than that God cannot do them."[2] It is, indeed, one of the marks—and, we might suggest, one of the strong points—of a philosophy whose ultimate category is that of being, that it refuses

---

to that late inferred will be the only lawful issue of the former maxim, or major proposition matched with a minor of our choosing. Let the major proposition stand as it did before, 'Whatsoever God hath decreed must of necessity come to pass,' with this additional, 'Nothing can come to pass otherwise than God hath decreed it shall or may come to pass': the minor proposition, which (if our choice may stand) shall be consort to the major, is this, '*But God hath decreed contingency as well as necessity*'; or, 'that some effects should be as truly contingent as others are necessary: therefore of necessity there must be contingency, or effects contingent.' The immediate consequence whereof is this: 'There is an absolute necessity that some things which have not been, might have been; that some things which have been, might not have been; that some things which are not, might be; that some things which are, might not be; that some things which shall not be hereafter, might be; that some things which shall be hereafter, might not be.'" (*Works*, V, p. 88.) And again: "Free it was for me to have thought or done somewhat in every minute of the last year, whereby the whole frame of my cogitations or actions for this year following might have been altered; and yet should God have been as true and principal a cause of this alteration, and of every thought and deed thus altered, as he is of those that *de facto* are past, or of that which I now think or do." (Ibid., p. 93; italics in original.)

This might almost be an expansion of the following passage in St. Thomas:
"Since then the divine will is perfectly efficacious, it follows not only that things are done, which God wills to be done, but also that they are done in the way that he wills. Now God wills some things to be done necessarily, some contingently, to the right ordering of things, for the building up of the universe. Therefore to some effects he has attached necessary causes, that cannot fail; but to others defectible and contingent causes, from which arise contingent effects." (*S. Theol.*, I, xix, 8c.)

Two vital points have often been overlooked in discussing the question: (1) that we are concerned with the relation of two voluntary beings—God and man—and not with two lifeless mechanical forces which could be compounded by a psychological counterpart of the parallelogram-law; (2) that because God's creative act is at the ontological root of the being of all his creatures it is possible for him both to conserve their freedom and to maintain his own sovereignty, in the most complete and harmonious balance. But that there is a mystery in all problems in which the will is concerned we need not deny; indeed it is quite essential to assert it. (Cf. p. 103 *supra*.)

[1] Whitehead has asserted that "it is perfectly possible to imagine a universe in which any act of counting by a being in it annihilates some members of the class counted during the time and only during the time of its continuance. . . . [There follows the well-known story of the counting of the members of the Nicene Council.] Such a story cannot be disproved by deductive reasoning from the premises of abstract logic. We can only assert that a universe in which such things are liable to happen on a large scale is unfitted for practical application of the theory of cardinal numbers." (*Encyc. Brit.*, 14th ed., XV, p. 88.) But the mere fact that Whitehead describes such an occurrence as "annihilation" involves an appeal to the accepted laws of arithmetic as true. (Cf. Ayer, *Language, Truth and Logic*, p. 100, and Maritain's remarks on non-Euclidean geometry, *Degrees of Knowledge*, E.T., p. 165 f., especially p. 168, n. 1.)

[2] *S. Theol.*, I, xxv, 3c.

to exalt one attribute or operation of God above another. To the Scotists, who taught that the formal constituent of God was infinity and that will was essentially superior to intellect, it was natural to say that the moral law rested simply on the arbitrary decree of God and that actions are good because God has commanded them; to the Thomists, on the other hand, it was *being* that was fundamental, with the necessary corollary that the moral law is neither an antecedent prescription to which God is bound by some external necessity to conform, nor a set of precepts promulgated by him in an entirely arbitrary and capricious manner, but something inherently rooted in the nature of man as reflecting in himself, in however limited and finite a mode, the character of the sovereign Good from whom his being is derived. The moral law is thus in its essence neither antecedent nor consequent to God; it is simply the expression of his own self-consistency. To say, therefore, that God is bound by it is merely to say, from one particular angle, that God is God.

We may remark, in passing, that the contrast generally drawn between Thomist intellectualism and Scotist voluntarism is not wholly exact. The Scotist tradition is no doubt voluntarist in spirit, and in this sense Scotus may be considered as the ancestor of Kant, Fichte and Schelling. But, with all the stress that it lays upon the intellect, the fundamental concept of Thomism is not intellect but being, not truth but unity. For this very reason it is able to preserve a balance between intellect and will, between the true and the good, which otherwise is all too easily lost.[1] And it is not altogether fantastic to surmise that the belittling of the intellect in comparison with the will, which has been so marked a feature of post-Kantian philosophy, may be closely connected with the rise in our own day of an attitude to life which is in effect an idolatry of arbitrary power.

When we have said, however, that, because he is God, God cannot do anything that is in itself either arbitrary or immoral, we have not denied the possibility of miracle. Here, as in other matters, we must adhere closely to the doctrine of a God who, in relation to the world, is both independent of it and yet is its Creator. The idea of a miracle is essentially the idea of an

---

[1] The extraordinary intricacy of the Thomist presentation of the structure of the human act, as it is, for example, expounded in Gardeil's *La Crédibilité et l'Apologétique*, ch. i, while it will no doubt appear to many as unnecessarily subtle, is the result of a determination to give due weight to both the intellectual and the voluntary elements and to exalt neither at the expense of the other.

occurrence which is a break with the order of nature, and this involves necessarily that there must be an order of nature to be broken with. We cannot defend the possibility of miracles by arguing that nothing at all exists except by the deliberate creative act of God and that miracles are no more surprising than anything else, though it is by no means rare to find the possibility of miracles defended on this ground. Such a view attributes our surprise at what we should call a miracle simply to the fact of its unfamiliarity to us. It makes the essence of a miracle purely psychological. It is sometimes expressed by saying that everything is miraculous, which is another way of saying that nothing is miraculous. It implies a view of the world as being merely the successive concretion by God of momentary configurations of created being, which instantaneously collapse into non-existence and have no more organic or causal connection with one another than have the pictures that appear in rapid succession on a cinema screen.[1] And once we allow ourselves to become sceptical that the external world consists of persisting beings, possessing determinate natures and exerting action on one another, it will not be long before we find ourselves denying that there is an external world at all; as Gilson has shown, there is a straight line of development from Descartes through Malebranche to Berkeley and Hume.[2] The very basis of the position from which we have argued to the existence of God is the fact, which we have alleged is evident to us as soon as we grasp the nature of the world of our experience as it really is, that, on the one hand, the world consists of really existing beings and that, on the other hand, these beings are not *self*-existent. Looking back at this fact in the light of the doctrine of creation, we can now see that it implies that God creates finite being not by giving momentary existence to a succession of entirely disconnected particulars, but by maintaining in being a universe which persists in time and in which there is genuine continuity and causality. Thus God is not the only cause, though he is the only ultimate one; and he maintains the order which is discernible in the universe not by annihilating the causal relationship of beings towards one another, but by preserving it.

[1] It may be objected that the pictures on the screen produce an illusion of continuity and that therefore, for all we know, the continuity of the world in which we live may be just as illusory. We cannot argue the point in detail here, but the heart of the reply would lie in the fact that the very possibility of the illusion in the cinema depends upon the existence of beings whose existence is not discontinuous, such as the screen, the celluloid film and, above all, the audience.

[2] See *The Unity of Philosophical Experience*, ch. vii, viii.

Were this not so, then the whole idea of an order of nature and, indeed, of the existence of beings with definite characteristics would be a complete illusion; and, among other consequences, science would be reduced to the level of pure description, giving us no valid insight into reality.[1] The fact that potatoes nourish me to-day would give me no reason to suppose that they may not poison me to-morrow; and I should have no more objective ground for surprise if the cat which I can see walking across the garden were to assume successively the forms of a purple cow, a chest of drawers and the President of the Royal Society than I shall have if it continues to exhibit its familiar feline appearance.

There is, then, a course of nature, and God has created a world in which finite beings, while subject to generation, development and corruption, have, in a certain relative sphere, determinate characteristics and behave according to definite laws. They manifest a combination of permanence and change: of permanence because they are, in the strict sense, beings; of change because they are only finite and relative ones. Each of them has a determinate ontological status; yet, because of its finitude, its future depends not only upon its own particular nature but upon the influence of other finite beings and in the last resort upon God himself.[2] Its determinacy, being strictly relative, includes a certain indeterminacy; for only in God are existence and essence identified.

The question of the possibility of miracles, then, is simply the question whether, in addition to the act by which God preserves in existence the world of finite beings and the operation of their

---

[1] It is a little startling to see how many scientists are prepared to save the autonomy of science at the expense of denying that it gives any genuine knowledge about an external world. It may be left to the despised Thomist philosophers to save from the scientists the claim of science to be what its name implies. Cf., e.g., Eddington's *Philosophy of Physical Science* with Maritain's *Degrees of Knowledge*, ch. iv; also E. I. Watkin, *Theism, Agnosticism and Atheism*, pp. 85–8. The scientists of the last century tended to claim for science far too high a status of insight into objective reality; their present-day successors often go to the other extreme.

The importance for theology of recognizing the reality of secondary causes is well expounded by Thomas Jackson: "By this concession of some true power and property of working unto natural agents, more is ascribed to the Creator of all things than can be ascribed by the contrary opinion, which utterly denies all power or property of working to the creatures; for he that denies any effects to be truly wrought by them cannot ascribe their abilities or operative force (which in his opinion is none) unto their Creator." (*Works*, V, p. 279.) In other words, since we attribute causality, in the supreme and primary sense, to God by a way of analogy based on the (secondary and limited) causality which we see in the finite realm, any denial of secondary causality will deprive us of our ground for attributing causality to God.

[2] This fact is presumably what lies at the root of Whitehead's philosophy of organism with its "principle of relativity" (*Process and Reality*, p. 30), though as will be seen later on we do not give it the same interpretation as he does.

secondary but real causality, it is also possible and proper for him to intervene in the sphere of their operation by a direct initiative of his power. That this is possible will be sufficiently evident; that it is fitting may be less immediately so. But, if we remind ourselves that operations are always directed to ends, it is difficult to deny that, at any rate on certain occasions, God's purposes may be more fully achieved by such an intervention than without it. To be able to predict precisely when a miracle would be fitting is more than a finite mind has a right to claim; that would need a knowledge of the relation of particular events to the ultimate fulfilment of the divine purpose for the world which no one but God —and, perhaps, human minds under the direct illumination of God—possesses. We shall not expect miracles to happen with very great frequency, since we can reasonably assume that the order of nature which God has established is sufficient for the normal operations of the world. But when a miracle is alleged to have occurred, we need not deny its possibility; and, so far as philosophy is concerned, the matter is then one for investigation by ordinary rational and scientific methods.[1]

---

[1] A very careful analysis and discussion, from the scholastic standpoint, of the relation between the natural and the supernatural, the various senses in which the word "supernatural" is used, and the relation between the supernatural and the miraculous will be found in Verrièle's book, *Le Surnaturel en nous et le Péché originel*, ch. i. In view of the extreme looseness with which such terms as "supernatural" and "miracle" are often used, the discussion there given is most valuable.

Dr. Tennant, in his *Miracle and its Philosophical Presuppositions*, gives a very convincing vindication of the existence of an order of nature (though he overstresses its independence through his doctrine of God as finite) and of creatures as dependent upon God's sustaining activity for their perduring existence (lect. ii; cf. *Phil. Theol.*, II, pp. 212, 215 f.). But he looks upon miracles as due to an action by God similar to that by which man makes use of natural forces rather than as a direct intervention by the Creator as sovereign over the natural order.

CHAPTER X

TRANSCENDENCE AND IMMANENCE

THE God of traditional Christian theism is both transcendent and immanent. He is transcendent because, as we have maintained in a previous chapter, "a first cause who was himself in even the very least degree involved in the mutability, contingency or insufficiency of the universe would provide no more in the way of an explanation of the existence of the universe than it could provide itself; such a God would provide a foundation neither for himself nor for anything else."[1] He is immanent because unless every finite being was sustained at its ontological root by his incessant creative action—unless, to use the scholastic terms, he was in it by "essence, presence and power"[2]—it would collapse into non-existence through sheer insufficiency; it would, in Julian of Norwich's phrase, "fall to naught for littleness." And both the terms "transcendent" and "immanent" are relative to the created world; God is transcendent *to it* and immanent *in it*. Furthermore, they are intimately related to each other, for they both arise out of the fact that the world is God's creation. As Fr. Przywara puts it, God, "as the pure 'Is,' is on the one side so inward to the creation that the transient 'is' of the creation is only *from* him and *in* him—and yet on the other side, differentiated from the creation, above it as the pure 'Is,' for whom no relationship to anything which is 'becoming' is in any way possible."[3] The precise relation of these two elements of transcendence and immanence, and their consequences for religion, have been worked out with great profundity of thought and profusion of detail in the work from which these words are quoted, and the doctrine of *analogia entis* (that is, the doctrine that creation is a similitude of God's being, deriving both essence and existence from his creative act, while being in no way necessary to him) is there made the foundation of a general theory of religion which is of quite exceptional significance. In the present chapter we shall attempt a more modest task, and

---

[1] p. 96 *supra.*   [2] Cf. *S. Theol.*, I, viii, 3.
[3] *Polarity*, E.T., p. 33. An exposition of this difficult but most illuminating book, by its translator, Dr. A. C. Bouquet, appeared in *Theology*, December 1934. A short discussion of Przywara's teaching will be found in W. M. Horton's *Contemporary Continental Theology*, p. 65 f.

simply give some discussion of the distortions that result when either of the two characteristics is stressed to the partial or complete exclusion of the other, concluding with some remarks on the relevance of the balanced Catholic doctrine to two important branches of theology.

The doctrine of transcendence in its extreme form results in the view that God has no real concern with the universe. He must presumably have created it, or it would not be here, but it would be ridiculous to suppose that he can have any present dealings with it. Historically this view was embodied in the Deism of the eighteenth century, to which it was particularly congenial. For, since it believed nature to be God's handiwork and therefore to manifest his character in the same way in which a sculptor or an author is made known to us in his works, it provided the basis for a sincere, if restrained and chilly, religious reverence, while at the same time involving no untidy interference with the orderly course of natural law as expounded by Newton and his successors. As Whitehead says, "God made his appearance in religion under the frigid title of the First Cause, and was appropriately worshipped in whitewashed churches."[1] Whatever God might have done in the past when the world first came into being, his present relation to it is simply that of an artist to his work; in Addison's famous hymn it is as "their grand Original" that "the spacious firmament on high and all the blue ethereal sky" manifest the Deity, as rejoicing in "reason's ear," they roll "in solemn silence . . . round the dark terrestrial ball"; and the attitude to God which the contemplation of nature is expected to produce in us is presumably not unlike the attitude to Sir Christopher Wren that is induced by walking round St. Paul's Cathedral.

The great instance of a religion of divine transcendence is of course to be found in Mohammedanism. "The fundamental conception of Allāh among orthodox Muslim theologians is negative. He is unique, as well as a unit, and he has no relation with any creature that partakes of resemblance."[2] No practical religion can, of course, deny all connection between the world and God, and in Mohammedanism this doctrine of transcendence is combined with an extreme voluntarism which makes God not only transcendent but arbitrary and ruthless. The very name by which the religion of the Prophet of Medina is known bespeaks man's complete helplessness before this implacable deity; *Islam* is

[1] *Adventures of Ideas*, p. 157.   [2] L. Bevan Jones, *The People of the Mosque*, p. 100.

submission, submission to the will of God. And by that *enantio-dromia*, which is so marked a feature of human activity, Moham-medanism becomes the most militant religion in history, for once the believer has made his submission he becomes himself devoted to the divine will and so sees himself as an instrument of the divine ruthlessness.

A religion of unbalanced transcendence allows no place for intimate communion between man and God. In eighteenth-century Deism, worship becomes the orderly admiration by man of the divine perfection; there is more than a suggestion of the notion that worship is not so much something that man does for the glory of God as something that he does for his own good; it becomes what has been aptly called "the art of spiritual cosmetics." It therefore easily passes into a Voltairean cynicism. And, para-doxically, just because it locates God at such a distance from the world in which we live, it can easily deny that he has any effective control over it, and then we are not far from the concept of a God who is helpless before his own creatures. The practical out-come of eighteenth-century thought has been described by Professor Tawney in these words: "God had been thrust into the frigid altitudes of infinite space. There was a limited monarchy in heaven, as well as on earth. Providence was the spectator of the curious machine which it had constructed and set in motion, but the operation of which it was neither able nor willing to control."[1] All that could be conceded—and, in a society where belief in the Incarnation had not become entirely extinct, there was some demand for this concession—was that, on very rare occasions, the Creator might perhaps make some transitory intervention in the affairs of his world, in the way in which an absentee landlord will sometimes visit his property to see whether it is in order or to cope with some crisis. But, to quote Professor Tawney again, concerning the divine Providence, "like the occasional intervention of the Crown in the proceedings of Parliament, its wisdom was revealed in the infrequency of its interference."[2]

Side by side with this transcendence we can discern an apparent immanentist tendency, but it is an immanentism of God not as efficient but as formal cause. It is strongly manifested in Pope's *Essay on Man*, which must surely be one of the most complacent theological discussions ever written.

[1] Tawney, *The Acquisitive Society*, p. 13.   [2] Ibid.

> "All are but parts of one stupendous whole,
> Whose body Nature is, and God the soul;
> That, changed through all, and yet in all the same;
> Great in the earth, as in th' ethereal frame;
> Warms in the sun, refreshes in the breeze,
> Glows in the stars, and blossoms in the trees,
> Lives through all life, extends through all extent,
> Spreads undivided, operates unspent;
> Breathes in our soul, informs our mortal part,
> As full, as perfect, in a hair as heart:
> As full, as perfect, in vile Man that mourns,
> As the rapt seraph that adores and burns:
> To him no high, no low, no great, no small;
> He fills, he bounds, connects, and equals all."[1]

Have we, we might wonder, passed over into a religion of complete immanence? Not really, for there is no suggestion that man should enter into communion with this God who is the soul of the world. The proper study of mankind is man, and virtue alone is happiness below. Man's ultimate duty, it appears, is neither to a transcendent nor to an immanent God, though there is enough talk about God and about virtue; it is rather to man himself. For this is the conclusion of the discussion:

> "That REASON, PASSION, answer one great aim;
> That true SELF-LOVE and SOCIAL are the same;
> That VIRTUE only makes our Bliss below,
> And all our Knowledge is, OURSELVES TO KNOW."[2]

We might add that, to an eighteenth-century philosopher, no very intimate union was implied by describing God as the soul of nature; Descartes had seen to that. For the classical Christian doctrine of man as a psycho-somatic unity had given way to the Cartesian view that the relation between body and soul was purely external and accidental; man was, in Maritain's phrase, "an angel driving a machine,"[3] and mind and matter were so essentially disparate that even the word "driving" is almost an exaggeration. The God of deism, in short, oscillates between a genuine transcendence and a spurious immanence; but he is far from being the God of Christian theism.

The transcendentalism of Islam is of a very different order. In the first place, Mohammedanism is a historical religion. It is based upon a revelation alleged to have been made through an

---

[1] *Essay on Man*, Epistle I, ix.   [2] Ibid., IV, vii.   [3] *Religion and Culture*, p. 24.

Arab born in Mecca about the year 570 and to be contained in
the book which he left behind him. For it there is one God, and
Mohammed is his prophet. The extreme voluntarism of the
transcendental revelationism of orthodox Islam reduced religion
almost entirely to the unreasoning performance of certain specified
duties; God has demanded their fulfilment and that is all that
there is to say about it. But very early in the history of Islam
another trend becomes evident in reaction from this, and finally
establishes itself as the tradition of Sufism. It has both a philosophical and a mystical side, and on the latter it represents the
attempt to satisfy a desire for union with God for which the pure
Koranic doctrine makes little or no provision. Perhaps its most
interesting manifestation is in the Persian mystic, al-Hallâj, who
has been made the subject of a remarkable and sympathetic study
by Fr. Maréchal.[1] Hallâj was executed in A.D. 922 at Baghdad as
a heretic, on the charge of having denied the Koranic doctrine of
the divine transcendence and of claiming to have achieved an
actual identification of himself with God. The conclusion of
Fr. Maréchal's investigation is that Hallâj had, in all probability,
attained to a genuine mystical union with God of a very high
order. In support of this he points out that Hallâj had a profound
veneration for Jesus of Nazareth and that much of the doctrinal
content of the Koran itself derives from the Judæo-Christian
tradition. He sees, therefore, no insurmountable objection to the
possibility of the achievement of the height of mystical experience
by such a thoroughly sincere seeker after God as was Hallâj, and
he believes that the evidence shows its actual realization. But the
task of reconciling Koranic Doctrine with Sufism has been a
perpetual embarrassment to Muslim theologians, and it seems to
be generally agreed that even the great attempt at a synthesis on
the part of al-Ghâzali in the eleventh century was not successful.[2]

A very different type of revelationist transcendentalism is
represented by such typical figures of the modern continental

[1] *Studies in the Psychology of the Mystics*, E.T., p. 241 f., "The Problem of Mystical
Grace in Islam." Cf. also the essay on "Islamic Mysticism" in Mr. Christopher
Dawson's *Enquiries into Religion and Culture*. For a short summary of the history and
characteristics of Sufism, see L. Bevan Jones, *The People of the Mosque*, III, v, vi, or
R. A. Nicholson in *E.R.E.*, XII, p. 10 f., *s.v.* "Sûfîs." Maréchal's study is based upon
the researches of M. Louis Massignon.
[2] See Maréchal, op. cit., p. 273; Bevan Jones, op. cit., p. 146 f. For a study of the
early development and interrelations of early Christian and Muslim mysticism, see
Margaret Smith's *Studies in Early Mysticism in the Near and Middle East*. This writer has
also published a detailed study of Hallâj's predecessor, Mohâsibî, under the title *An
Early Mystic of Baghdad*.

Protestant dogmatic revival as Nygren, Barth and Brunner. In spite of their not inconsiderable differences—Nygren is a Lutheran and the other two Calvinists, and Barth and Brunner have themselves parted company—they agree in denying that man can enter into any real union with God and hence they assert that mysticism is impossible.[1] Man can have faith in God—justification by faith is for these writers the very essence of religion—man can even obey God, though his obedience is bound to be vitiated by sin, but to love God or to be united with him is altogether beyond man's power. It is interesting to see how this thesis is worked out by Nygren in his great study, *Agape and Eros.* God loves man in spite of man's worthlessness, indeed the divine *agape* is precisely love for that which is worthless; but for man to love God is hardly proper, in spite of the scriptural texts. Faith. not love, is man's proper attitude to God, though apparently nobody between St. Paul and Luther knew this.[2] In the course of his historical study Nygren most scrupulously and charitably defends the great Catholic saints from practically all the charges that Protestantism has ever brought against them; there is only one fault of which he cannot acquit them, that of trying to love God. For to him the assertion that man can love God and achieve real union with him is clearly the supreme heresy; it is a contradiction of man's creaturely character and a sin against humility. In Barth this same trait takes the form of denying that man can have any knowledge of God that counts for anything except by divine revelation; no effort from man's side can do anything to pierce the barrier that creaturehood and sin together have set up between man and God. And the whole of Barth's Gifford Lectures consist of a vehement and sustained denial that the science about which he is lecturing—namely, natural theology—has a right to exist.[3] Brunner, it must be

---

[1] I use " mysticism " here in the strict sense of a quasi-experimental knowledge of God. Cf. Maritain's definition of mystical experience as " a possession-giving experience of the absolute." (*Redeeming the Time*, p. 225.) A discussion of the various meanings, proper and improper, which the word has borne and of how it may best be defined will be found in Dom C. Butler's *Western Mysticism*, p. 1 f. Cf. Maréchal, op. cit., pp. 286-7. It is typical of William James that he defines mysticism entirely in terms of its psychological characteristics without any reference to its object. (*Varieties of Religious Experience*, ch. xvi.)

[2] Thus Nygren refers to "the tendency . . . towards a weakening of the idea of Agape in the Johannine conception." (Op. cit., I, p. 117; cf. II, p. 24 f.)

[3] *The Knowledge of God and the Service of God*, especially ch. i. It is interesting to note how many of the continental Protestant theologians are forced on theological grounds to condemn their own subject-matter. Nygren writes about mysticism, Barth about natural theology, Troeltsch about the social teaching of the Christian Churches, but each of them has to maintain that what he is writing about is an aberration.

admitted, is less violent than Barth about human corruption, but he is none the less opposed to mysticism. For, according to him, mysticism means either that man can jump over the gulf separating him from God or that he can find God as immanent in his soul. And, in either case, the transcendence of God is denied.[1]

What can be said in reply to this we shall see later on. It will be well now to see what happens when an exaggerated stress is laid upon immanence.

The logical outcome of a purely immanentist theology is pantheism, the doctrine that God and the world are simply identical. But in practice such a view is very difficult to maintain, if only for the reason that the multiplicity of the world and the evil with which it is infected seem clearly to contradict it. Pantheism, therefore, tends to take certain modified forms; it may, with some doctrine of *maya*, teach that the world of appearance is merely illusion, it may hold on to belief in the reality and deity of the world but take refuge in the notion that deity is impersonal—both tendencies seem to be present in philosophic Hinduism;[2] it may, as in Taoism, reduce God to the position of a mere principle of order, to which human life ought to conform;[3] or it may combine, in an unnatural union, all three tendencies. But there is one caution which it is most important to bear in mind.

Europeans have become so accustomed to interpret the notion of God in the context of their own tradition that it is almost impossible for them to divest it of the fully developed characteristic of personality which it has acquired in the theology of Christendom. They tend, therefore, in discussing such a matter as the movement of Hindu religious thought, to assume unconsciously that the deity of whom immanence is asserted is the Christian God. "If the God in whom we believe were merely immanent," they ask themselves, "what would follow?" To which the obvious reply is that the God in whom we believe could not be merely immanent, for he is transcendent as well. Before we can even begin to discuss the great Asiatic religions we must divest our minds,

---

[1] *The Mediator*, p. 292 and p. 293, n. 1.

[2] Cf. the discussion of Buddhism and Brahmanism in Coomaraswamy's *Buddha and the Gospel of Buddhism*, III, iv.

[3] Cf., e.g., the *Tao-te-King* of Lao-Tse, printed in full in *The Bible and the World*, p. 471 f. Any suggestion of a personal deity is still more remote in Confucius; cf. the *Analects*.

so far as is possible, of concepts which are incompatible with them.

We can illustrate this point by reference to the much discussed question as to whether Brahmanism and Buddhism are really inconsistent. To the European mind it seems at first sight perfectly obvious that they are, and that, from the standpoint of Brahmanism, Buddhism ought to appear as a pernicious heresy. For Brahmanism places before man as his ultimate beatitude the identification of himself with the ground of the world—the soul becomes the One, the *Atman* is the *Brahma*—while Buddhism sets before him the ideal of complete extinction of personality. But we must be careful. For what is this ground of the world, and what is the world of which it is the ground? In Christian thought it would be a personal God, and the world would be his creation; moreover, men would be individual, substantial, personal beings. For Brahmanism, on the other hand, the ground of the world is certainly not personal, and the world itself is of doubtful status; it is we are told, *maya*, appearance, but what does that mean? Appearance of something that really exists, or mere illusion? And what of men? They, too, are impermanent, and their personality is only superficial and accidental. Is there really any ontological difference between absorption into the impersonal ground of an illusory world and complete extinction? Admittedly there is a difference between the technique of Brahmanism—at least in some of its forms—and that of Buddhism, for the former is an attempt to identify oneself with the ground of the world, while the latter is an attempt to escape from the world altogether. Yet even here the difference is perhaps not so marked as might appear. For the Brahmanist, identification involves an entire break with the world as we experience it in order to attain union with its ground. The things that surround us are mere appearance or illusion, and so must be altogether rejected, whether this is done by the way of intellectual *gnosis* (*jñana*), disinterested activity (*karma*), or devotion (*bhakti*). A Christian mystic may reject the things of this world in order to attain union with a transcendent God. But if God is purely immanent, what sort of union can be attained by such renunciation? Is not the world renounced in fact identical with the deity sought after? And if so, how can we find him by this renunciation? It might well appear that the negativism of Buddhism is the logical outcome of Brahmanism rather than the contradiction of it. For if all existence is illusion, is it not better to try to escape from it altogether rather than to seek to be identified with its ground?[1]

For a Christian there are few phenomena in the history of religion more puzzling than the contrast between Gautama Buddha and his teaching. It is quite impossible to read the description of his life and doctrine in the Buddhist scriptures without being overawed by the sheer moral beauty of his character and the utter genuineness of his desire to lead his fellow-men into the way of salvation. But what is this salvation that he offers them? Extinction. And what is his ultimate philosophy? Sheer atheism. And the final issue of it all is a kind of despairing scepticism. For, Buddhism teaches, man will not achieve beatitude merely by desiring it, even if beatitude is extinction. He will only achieve it by being indifferent as to whether he achieves it or not.[2] And in that case, what can it matter whether he does achieve it? Blessed is he that expecteth nothing, for he shall not be disappointed; this is the end of the matter. *Parinirvana* may or may not be extinction; *nirvana* is mere indifference.[3]

In practice, pantheism is bound to be mitigated in some way, for the distinction and conflict between the various beings in the universe make it impossible to identify either each of them separately, or the totality of them all, with God without making some qualification. This point is brought out well in a parable by the nineteenth-century Hindu teacher, Sri Ramakrishna:

[1] In his essay on " The Natural Mystical Experience and the Void " in *Redeeming the Time*, Maritain suggests that the Buddhist *nirvana* is fundamentally the same as the Brahman *mukti*, though inadequately interpreted owing to the phenomenalistic philosophy of Buddhism (p. 248). He works out in detail the view that this " void " is a metaphysical experience of the substantial *esse* of the soul by a negative (or, rather, annihilating) connaturality. Its object is the Absolute, as *Atman* or self. It thus bears upon the soul itself and, through the soul, upon God as the source of the soul's being, but, on account of its entire negativity, cannot distinguish between them. Hence the inclusion within *Atman* of both the human and the Supreme Self. The Indian mystic is thus seeking the Absolute within his soul by a stripping-off of the soul's operations which leaves him equally unable either to distinguish God and the soul from each other or to confuse them with each other, since the experience is purely negative.

[2] Cf. *Buddha and the Gospel of Buddhism*, II, iv. "Nibbāna."

[3] The distinction is sometimes drawn between *Parinirvana*, the "Complete or Final Dying-out" at death, and *Nirvana*, the "Dying-out" which can be achieved in this life: op. cit., p. 122. It is difficult for a Westerner to discover whether Buddhism can validly be considered a gospel of ontological suicide; in a letter to the writer, Dr. A. Coomaraswamy asserts that no such view can be substantiated from the Buddhist texts. In any case, general statements about anything as many-sided as Buddhism are bound to be over-simplified. For a full discussion of the various views as to the exact nature of *Nirvana* see Mrs. Rhys Davids, *Buddhism*, ch. vii.

Whitehead remarks that "Buddhism is the most colossal example in history of applied metaphysics. . . . Christianity . . . has always been a religion seeking a metaphysic, in contrast to Buddhism which is a metaphysic generating a religion." (*Religion in the Making*, p. 39.)

"The master said, 'Everything that exists is God.' The pupil
understood it literally, but not in the right spirit. While he was
passing through the street he met an elephant. The driver
shouted aloud from his high place, 'Move away! Move away!'
The pupil argued in his mind, 'Why should I move away? I am
God, so is the elephant God; what fear has God of himself?'
Thinking thus, he did not move. At last the elephant took him
up in his trunk and dashed him aside. He was hurt severely,
and going back to his master, he related the whole adventure.
The master said: 'All right. You are God, the elephant is God
also, but God in the shape of the elephant-driver was warning
you from above. Why did you not pay heed to his warnings?'"[1]

As examples of modern attempts to construct a Christian
theology on an immanentist basis we may mention the works of
Professor Nicholas Berdyaev and Fr. Alexis van der Mensbrugghe,
both members of the Eastern Orthodox Church and both strongly
influenced by the "sophiology," or teaching concerning the
Divine Wisdom, which looks back to the fourteenth-century mystic
of Mount Athos, St. Gregory Palamas,[2] and which became
prominent in Russian theology in the last century through the
thought and writings of Vladimir Solovyev.

Berdyaev launches a violent attack upon what he describes as
"naturalist metaphysics and theology," in which term he includes
practically the whole of the historic theology of Christendom. For
him the truth about religion is to be found by exploring the content of the religious consciousness: "an abstract metaphysic cannot exist, but a philosophy or a phenomenology of the spiritual life
is possible."[3] He thus condemns rational theology no less
vigorously than does Karl Barth, though from a diametrically
opposite position; and it is well known that Berdyaev and Barth
consider each other to represent the extreme of theological error.
To Barth rational theology is anathema because it is an attempt by
sinful man to comprehend a God who is incomprehensible; grace
and nature have nothing in common. To Berdyaev, on the other
hand, rational theology is anathema because it turns into an
object of discussion a God who is already comprehended in the
depths of the human spirit; grace and nature are really identical.
Berdyaev accuses the Thomist tradition of a vicious dualism and

---

[1] "The Sayings of Sri Ramakrishna" in *The Bible of the World*, p. 163.
[2] See the article on "The Ascetic and Theological Teaching of Gregory Palamas,"
by Fr. Basil Krivoshein, in *Eastern Churches Quarterly*, January–October 1938. See
p. 140, n. 1, *infra*.   [3] *Freedom and the Spirit*, E.T., p. 6.

also of a vicious monism. "Religious metaphysics and theology," he says, maintain "an opposition between the Creator and creation and between grace and nature. But in making this opposition . . . creation is naturalized and objectified, with the result that the Creator himself is subjected to the same process."[1] We must not, he urges, rationalize religion. "Spirit is not a substance, an objective reality, in the same sense as other substances. Spirit is life, experience, destiny. A purely rational metaphysic of spirit is impossible. Life is only disclosed in experience."[2] Hence to prove the existence of God is impossible, for "the reality of the spiritual world and of the divine do not correspond in any way to the reality of our sense-perceptions and our thoughts. . . . It is impossible to ask the question whether there is a reality which corresponds to the experience of the great saints, to that of the mystics, to that of men who live on a higher spiritual plane, for that is a question arising only within the sphere of psychology, naturalism, and a naïve, and non-spiritual, realism."[3]

The result of this denial of the validity of rational theology is that discussion becomes impossible, for there is no common ground from which Berdyaev and his critics can even begin to argue. There are pages in which Berdyaev appears to be stating what is practically a Thomist thesis, but they are followed by denunciations of Thomism; there are pages that read like pantheism, but pantheism is violently repudiated. This is hardly to be wondered at, since, if Berdyaev's fundamental contention is correct, his own formulations fall under the same condemnation as those of his opponents; for he, no less than they, is attempting to express in the categories of human speech what, on his own theory, is ineffable. We come to the heart of the matter when he states his ultimate postulate that freedom is prior to being,[4] for this means that it is prior to God. Adopting the distinction made by Eckhart between God (*Gott*) and Divinity (*Gottheit*) in a way from which, one imagines, Eckhart would have fled in horror, and identifying Divinity with Boehme's *Ungrund*, he asserts that "both philosophy and theology should start neither with God nor with man (for there is no bridge between these two principles), but rather with the God-Man. The basic and original phenomenon of religious

---

[1] *Freedom and the Spirit*, p. 6. Cf. the vigorous attack on "objectification" in *Solitude and Society*, II, ii.
[2] *Freedom and the Spirit*, p. 9.   [3] Ibid., pp. 10, 11.
[4] Ibid., p. 119. Cf. *Solitude and Society*, p. 24.

life is the meeting and mutual interaction between God and man, the movement of God towards man and of man towards God."[1] But we must beware of giving such statements as this the meaning which a rational theology would attribute to them, since, as we have seen, the very idea of a rational theology is denied. The real problem that Berdyaev raises, though he fails to face it, is what the relation of theology to reality can possibly be once this denial has been made. Berdyaev would not admit that he is merely describing the psychological phenomena of the religious consciousness, yet it is impossible on his own principles to see what else he can be doing. Denying the doctrine of analogy, he insists that his mode of thought is symbolic.[2] Yet, since he maintains that his is "a symbolic mode of thought which brings us face to face with ultimate realities,"[3] it is not easy to see how this denial of analogy can be justified.

The conclusion would seem to be that Berdyaev is attempting the impossible. There are few modern writers whose work is more provocative and stimulating, and there is probably none who is able so profoundly to read the signs of the times. With his desire to find a place in his discussion of religion for the whole content of the religious consciousness, and to avoid that type of abstraction which substitutes bloodless categories for the full experience of life, we cannot but sympathize. But we cannot admit that he has succeeded. Indeed he himself seems to be prepared to confess as much. "I recognize," he writes, "that there is something essential which I cannot put into words. . . . I put my problems in the form of affirmations. But my thought as it moves within my own being is that of a man who, without being a sceptic, is putting problems to himself."[4] The only question is whether the very way in which he is putting them may not deprive him of the possibility of getting an answer.

Berdyaev's immanentism seems to derive at least as much from German idealism as from Eastern Orthodoxy; this could hardly be said of Fr. Alexis van der Mensbrugghe, who claims that his views are firmly based upon Platonism, patristic theology, Byzantine iconography and the thought of Russian Orthodoxy.[5] He

---

[1] *Freedom and the Spirit*, p. 189. Cf. p. 194. Cf. also the remarks on the "theandric idea" in *Solitude and Society*, p. 40 f.
[2] *Freedom and the Spirit*, ch. ii, "Symbol, Myth and Dogma."   [3] Ibid., p. 83.
[4] Ibid., Introduction, p. xviii.
[5] *From Dyad to Triad*, p. 2. See also a review by the present writer and a reply by the author in *Sobornost'*, December 1935 and March 1936.

maintains what he describes as a doctrine of analogy, though it is very different from the *analogia entis* of the scholastics, and this doctrine becomes a universal principle, which is applicable to morphology, mythology, logic, ontology, axiology, and theology alike. There are two modes, he asserts, in which the One differentiates itself: a "horizontal" threefold differentiation of Modality, and a "vertical" twofold differentiation of Quality. In its theological application, the former corresponds to the coexistence of the three Persons of the Godhead, while the latter distinguishes God's Existence from his Essence or Wisdom (*Sophia*). In this *Sophia* there is included the created universe, both in its ideal essence and in its concrete reality. For the ideal essence and the concrete reality of the world are not admitted to be distinct from each other. "There is no first 'conceptual realization' in God, and after that, apart from that, later on, another 'realization in reality.' God does not think first and create afterwards. His Act, as that of a pure Spirit, is absolutely simple; if he thinks a form that form is created *ipso facto*; his thinking is creative. We, on the contrary think first and make afterwards, because we are only secondary agents (*causæ secundæ*). We can only work on a given material already existing. . . . But that is exactly where we are only transformers, not creators in the adequate sense of the word."[1]

Several comments seem to be called for on this passage. The temporal presentation—"later on" and so on—is, we may suppose, merely for verbal convenience. But the denial of any distinction whatever between God's knowledge of things as possible and his creation of them as actual presumably involves the consequence that everything that is possible is actual as well, or, to put this in another way, that this world is the only possible one. And the comparison with human work, while the assertion that is made must be admitted, is quite irrelevant, for no one (except possibly David of Dinant, whose "ravings" were so sternly rebuked by the Angelic Doctor[2]) has claimed to find within the God of Christian theism the matter out of which the world is constructed.

But the crux of the matter is reached in the question of the nature of evil. "Dualism (or Pluralism)," writes Fr. van der Mensbrugghe, "is wrong in seeing Creation as a movement *ad extra*, the raising of a second subject of Being. . . . Sophian or Dual Orthodoxy [his own theory] is right in seeing Creation at once as a movement *ad intra sed ad infra*. Its definition of Creation is

---

[1] *Sobornost'*, March 1936, p. 20.   [2] *S.c.G.*, I, xvii.

Internal Inferiorization of Being."[1] The obvious objection to this doctrine is that, if it is true, evil, as indeed everything in the created world, becomes something happening in the interior of God.

To this criticism Mensbrugghe replies as follows:

> "The theory does indeed deny *absolute* evil; but the relative evil consisting in splitting the lines of action of Wisdom along the double axis of the Better and the More is amply safeguarded, and is, I think, sufficient to explain the evil in this world. . . . Peccability could only be predicated of Sophia as far as it has nothing to do with rebellion or even with sluggishness in answering God's Will, so far as no meaning of moral guilt be attached to it. . . . There is thus as much difference between Sophia's Sin and Moral Sin as between Original Sin in the babe and Actual Sin in the grown-up. . . . Sophia is sinless in her service of God (except for that Φθορά which makes her oscillate between Better Service or More Service), although physical and moral evil arise in and through the relation of the created forms between themselves."[2]

It is difficult to be satisfied with this reply, for the mutual relations of the created forms are, on this theory, themselves included in Sophia. If creation is, as is alleged, internal inferiorization of Being, so that "the Container needs the Contained, the Absolute needs the Relative in order to become God,"[3] then moral evil must itself be within God, for there is nowhere else for it to be. The idea that there is anything which is in any sense outside God is rejected quite definitely: "once and for as long as an actual 'outside' of God is granted, any further dependence or unity of Origin cannot prevent Dualism *in actu*."[4]

It is easy to see what is the danger that Mensbrugghe fears from the admission that anything is exterior to God; it is the setting up of a dualism in which God and his creatures appear as ranged on the same level in some sort of medium anterior to both; indeed, he explicitly says so, when he quotes a phrase from Pringle-Pattison about the "impropriety in placing God and men in the same numerical series, and in speaking as if we and God together, in a species of joint ownership, constituted the sum-total of existence."[5] (Berdyaev, it will be remembered, made just this objection to all

[1] *From Dyad to Triad*, p. 61.   [2] *Sobornost'*, March 1936, pp. 20, 21.
[3] *From Dyad to Triad*, p. 62.   [4] *Sobornost'*, March 1936, p. 21.
[5] Ibid. The quotation is from *The Idea of God*, p. 389.

systems of rational theology.) But this is precisely what the doctrine of creation as we have interpreted it in line with the Thomist
tradition refuses to do. A God who is merely a *primus inter pares*
provides, as has been repeatedly urged, no ground for either his
own existence or that of anything else; but it is not true that the
only alternative view is that creation is internal to God. According
to the doctrine of *analogia entis*, God as self-existent Being is altogether distinct from the world, while the world is entirely insufficient and dependent, although, at the same time and indeed for
this very reason, it is most intimately interpenetrated by the
creative act through which he is present to it at the heart of
its being. And we shall argue, in concluding this chapter, that
only a doctrine in which transcendence and immanence are combined in this way is capable of providing a satisfactory basis for
religion.[1]

[1] It should be pointed out that Mensbrugghe is by no means the only modern
Russian theologian who has discussed the problem of creation in the light of the
conception of the Divine Sophia. There is a line of development going back through
Fr. Paul Florensky to Vladimir Solovyev. And a sophiology in many respects different
from that of Mensbrugghe has been worked out by the distinguished Dean of the
Russian Theological Academy in Paris, the Archpriest Sergius Bulgakov; his only
work on the subject in English, apart from a few articles in *Theology* (July and August
1931, January 1934), is *The Wisdom of God*. For him, the divine *ousia* and *sophia* are
identical; *sophia* is the self-revelation of the Godhead and belongs to all three Persons
of the Trinity. *Sophianity* (which is identical with *theandrism*, the ultimate unity of
Godhead and manhood which is manifested in the fact that man is made in the
image of God) is a general metaphysical and theological principle, which provides a
particular understanding not only of the doctrine of God, but also of cosmology,
anthropology, Christology, pneumatology, Mariology and ecclesiology. Bulgakov
insists very strongly upon the distinction between God and the world, and upon the
fact that the world is not necessary to God; "The world as such maintains its existence
and its identity, distinct from that of God. . . . There is no such ontological necessity
for the world as could constrain God himself to create it for the sake of his own
development or fulfilment; such an idea would indeed be pure pantheism" (op. cit.,
p. 110). Distinction is made between the uncreated *sophia*, which is the *locus* of the
divine prototypes of all possible creatures, and the creaturely *sophia* found in the actual
world. "Here we have at once Sophia in both its aspects, divine and creaturely.
Sophia unites God with the world as the one common principle, the divine ground of
creaturely existence. Remaining one, it exists in two modes, eternal and temporal,
divine and creaturely" (op. cit., p. 112).
Bulgakov's supporters claim that his treatment solves the problem of the relation
between God and the world, whereas the treatments of both the Barthians and the
Thomists are unsatisfactory. Berdyaev, as we have seen, claims also to steer a course
between these two positions; he dissents from sophiology, though from a quite opposite
reason from that of most of Bulgakov's critics, namely that he considers Bulgakov to be
too conservative! It must be added that Bulgakov's thought is extremely difficult for
a Western mind to follow; also, it has given rise to a painful domestic controversy in
the Russian Church, which led to a condemnation by the Moscow Patriarchate in
1935 (see *Orient und Occident*, March 1936). The opinion may be ventured that, whatever its inadequacies in the realm of trinitarian theology and Christology (and on this
see the review by J. P. Arendzen in *Eastern Churches Quarterly*, January 1938), in the
cosmological sphere Bulgakov's sophiology would appear to approximate to the
scholastic doctrine of analogy, though the obscurity of the language makes a **precise**

For a religion of pure transcendence places God too far away from us for him to be relevant to our life; if there is no line of communication between him and us, he ceases to be our concern. And if the attempt is made to correct this deficiency by super-imposing an extreme revelationism, as in Barthianism, so that, although there is no way up from us to God, God has blasted a way down to us, God's accessibility has been saved at the cost of making him unintelligible. If the way between earth and heaven is an entirely one-way street, God may indeed utter his word, but we can never understand it, for it comes to us simply as a bolt from the blue and there is nothing in our experience with which we can relate it. On the other hand, a religion of pure immanence places God too close to us to be of any real use. It immerses him in the very predicament in which we ourselves are entangled; it makes him neither our judge nor our saviour—and it is noteworthy that neither Brahmanism nor Buddhism offers us a saviour; at best they tell us how we may hope to save ourselves. Dr. Demant has shown with devastating clearness what this involves in the sphere of human history, but it is equally true in the sphere of personal piety.

"God conceived as the immanent spirit in the march of his-tory," writes Dr. Demant, "makes religion an appendage of events and secular movements. Such a religion can neither interpret human history nor help man to make it. It registers religiously what transpires under a natural and secular ægis. But, the abstract transcendentalism of theological Protestantism leads to the same attitude. For the actual work of living in the world the dogma that all is equally under the divine 'No' is as useless as the dogma that all is equally under the divine 'Yea.' In either case man has to find his criteria of judgment and action

---

assessment practically impossible. It may be noted that he rejects Solovyev's doctrine of *sophia* as "undoubtedly syncretistic" (p. 23).

Owing to the inaccessibility of the material it is very difficult for Western theologians to investigate sophiology in detail, though a thorough examination in the light of traditional Western theology would be of great interest and value. A long discussion of the cosmology of Solovyev, whom he convicts of "univocity," was given by Dom Theodore Wesseling in *Eastern Churches Quarterly*, January–October 1937, and this was followed by a series of articles by Fr. Basil Krivoshein on St. Gregory Palamas, January–October 1938. The words of so rigid a "westerner" as Maritain may be worth quoting here: "I would add that Greek and Russian piety, which differs apparently from Catholic piety not so much in divergences of dogma as in certain characteristics of spirituality, is much less hostile, in my opinion, to the philosophy of St. Thomas than might at first be supposed. It approaches the problems from another angle and the scholastic presentation as a rule irritates and offends it. These are merely questions of modality." (*St. Thomas Aquinas*, E.T., p. 70.)

from some source extraneous to his central religious conviction. Luther had to posit that, outside the realm of grace and faith which affected only man's inner orientation, worldly affairs were by God entrusted to the princes; Calvinism, with its valiant effort to make the world Christian, succeeded only in making Christianity worldly. Much modern Christianity is avowedly confined to encouraging a 'change of heart' and a change of nothing else. The historic scene is left to 'the experts' who have inherited the function of Luther's princes."[1]

Again, Dr. Demant remarks that the Christian mind has

"split, in its innermost outlook, into cosmic interpretations which bring God within the world process and purely redemptive theologies which take man as religious out of it, leaving his actual existence at the mercy of its floods."[2]

In contrast with these one-sided distortions,

"the dogma which sees existence in terms of Being and Becoming, Eternity and Time, Creator and Creation, gives us the right to make choices in the actual world without identifying our choice with the absolute good."[3]

We can follow out this same point in the realm of Christian piety. Here, as before, the doctrine of a God who is both immanent and transcendent produces a tension which has seemed to many to be paradoxical and even inconsistent. God is, on the one hand, to be approached by me only if I leave all created things beneath me in a cloud of forgetting, while I strive to pierce the cloud of unknowing which separates me from the ineffable superessential Deity;[4] on the other hand, the one and only place in which I can find him is in the "apex" or "depth" or "fine point" of my soul.[5] Furthermore, these two apparently entirely opposite movements do not seem to those who describe them to involve any contradiction; certainly St. Francis of Sales was not conscious of any antithesis between his own doctrine and that of the great Spanish Carmelites.

---

[1] *The Religious Prospect*, pp. 180-1.   [2] Ibid., p. 214.   [3] Ibid., p. 154.
[4] Cf. *The Cloud of Unknowing, passim.*
[5] Cf. Blosius: "Therefore should he 'introvert' himself—that is, should turn himself into his own soul, and dwell there in his own heart—for there will he be able to find God." (*Book of Spiritual Instruction*, ch. iii, 3.) And St. Francis of Sales: "Le second moyen de se mettre en cette sacrée présence, c'est de penser que non seulement Dieu est au lieu où vous êtes, mais qu'il est très particulièrement en votre cœur et au fond de votre esprit, lequel il vivifie et anime de sa divine présence, étant là comme le cœur de votre cœur et l'esprit de votre esprit." (*Intro. à la Vie dévote*, II, ii.)

The fact is that the two movements, although their descriptions are so different, are, as regards their object, the same, for that object is the one transcendent and immanent God. For this reason, even from the psychological point of view, their difference is much less than might be expected. For the transcendent God who is sought in the cloud of unknowing is present already in the depth of the soul; while the immanent God who dwells in the centre of our being is infinite, perfect and self-existent.

There is, however, a sense in which the transcendence of God is primary, for God is the giver of existence to the beings in which he is immanent. The primary act is not from man to God, but from God to man; the Barthians are right about this. As Przywara says, "for the Catholic foundation of religion, which is the *analogia entis*, all other bases for religion count as immanental. *The God of Catholicism alone is the truly transcendent deity....* Even for the highest mystical union, God remains the One who dwells in Light unapproachable; even in the most intense form of mystical illumination, as it occurs in St. John of the Cross, the experience is of this inaccessibility, of the 'Night' as well as of the *unio mystica*." As a result, " 'Catholic immanentism' is the immediate consequence of the rigid super-creatureliness of the Universal Creator, while ordinary immanentism simply confines him to being *within* his creation."[1]

It is this, and not Mr. Aldous Huxley's theory that God is really impersonal, that explains the phenomenon of the Dark Night in Christian mysticism. The closer the mystic approaches to a vision of the pure Deity, the more the object of his contemplation exceeds the capacity of his vision. Hence we find in the writings of St. John of the Cross the most terrible descriptions of spiritual desolation side by side with the insistence that it is precisely in this desolation that the soul is both being assimilated to God and being given a clearer knowledge of him.

---

[1] *Polarity*, E.T., pp. 38, 41, 42. It is important to remark that, when the Catholic doctrine of the relation between God and the world is neglected, the distinction between immanence and transcendence very largely vanishes too. Mr. E. I. Watkin points out that "ultra-transcendental pantheism, when it regards the finite as but a manifestation of an underlying Godhead, *ipso facto* regards the finite as a mode of that Godhead, and becomes thus identical with ultra-immanentist pantheism. Catholic mysticism," he continues, "bars both passages to this common error. It bars the immanentist approach by insisting on the absolute distinction of finite beings from God, in virtue of their essential finitude. It bars the transcendentalist approach, and therefore the mystical modernism that is taking that way, by its doctrine of special relationships, including, as it does, its doctrine of personal identity between a created being and God, in the Incarnate Word." (*Philosophy of Mysticism*, p. 72.)

> "O guiding night,
> O night more lovely than the dawn;
> O night that hast united
> The lover with his beloved
> And changed her into her love."[1]

Thus, writes Przywara, Catholic piety is

"a never-ending (relatively infinite) unveiling of the absolute
infinite God in and above the never-ending (relatively infinite)
self-evolution of life in him. It is bounded by two extremes, the
one immanentism, which is an actual self-evolution of God in man,
for which God is only another name for creaturely evolution; the
other, transcendentism, which is the lifeless static adoration before
a wholly remote eternal Deity, for whom human life with its self-
mutation has in general no inward religious meaning except at
the most the negative one of pure abandonment.... The
repose in movement of Catholic transcendentality is the decisive
formula. Two attitudes interpenetrate here to form a twofold
unity: (i) Experience of the infinity of God *in* the endless rhythm
of life, and (ii) Adoration of the same infinity *above* the endless
rhythm of life."[2]

This, then, provides the theological basis of Catholic mysticism.
The psychology of it has received perhaps its profoundest treatment in Fr. Gardeil's work, *La Structure de l'Ame et l'Expérience
Mystique*.[3] As we shall see, it involves just the combination which we
have expounded of divine transcendence and divine immanence.

Gardeil begins by considering the essential structure of the
human soul. It is a mind, a *mens*, a special kind of created spirit
and as spirit it bears in itself the image of the Supreme Spirit,
God its Creator. As spirit it has a natural desire for God, but as
finite spirit it can tend to him only according to the idea which it
can form of him, and it is totally incapable of raising itself to this
infinite object of its desire. Nevertheless, what it cannot do for

---

[1] *Amada en el Amado transformada.* The poem is quoted in full in *Spanish Mysticism*, by
E. Allison Peers, p. 227.

[2] *Polarity*, E.T., pp. 61–2. Przywara specifies three fundamental modes in which
the human ego orients itself in relation to the ultimate object of its experience:
immanence (*Zuständlichkeit*), which looks for God in the depths of the soul; transcendence (*Gegenständlichkeit*), concerned with the "wholly Other"; and, cutting across
these, transcendentality (*Tatständlichkeit*), which postulates no existing object, but is a
pure striving. Transcendentality tries to hold immanence and transcendence in
tension, but such tension is unstable and explosive. Only in Catholicism is it firmly
achieved, for there the unifying principle is God himself, who is both transcendent
and immanent.

[3] There is an interesting discussion of some disputed points of Gardeil's exposition
in Chambat's *Présence et Union*, p. 9 f.

itself God can do for it, for, leaving on one side sin, which is a
distortion of the soul and not an element in its true nature, there
is nothing in the soul that is *repugnant* to the vision of God. The
soul is merely helpless.

Now the soul is, as we have just seen, a created analogue of God,
and, by his presence of immensity, God is more present to it than
it is to itself. Hence we may expect that the best analogue that we
can find to the soul's knowledge of God is its knowledge of itself.
This self-knowledge has one very remarkable characteristic;
namely that, although the soul is, ontologically considered, more
immediately related to itself than to any of the beings which it
apprehends (since it *is itself*, entitatively, while it merely *knows
them*), it knows other beings before it knows itself. Indeed, it comes
to know itself only as a result of those acts in which it turns
towards external beings.[1] (It may be noted that, absurd as it
might seem, children learn to recognize external objects before they
learn their own self-identity.) Therefore, by analogy, and *a fortiori*,
we may expect that the God who is more interior to the soul than
it is to itself will also be known only as a result of the soul's acts.

But as a result of what acts? The act of self-reflection indeed
may give us some kind of knowledge of God, if the soul which is its
object is a created analogue of him. But such a knowledge will be
only a knowledge of him in his effects, not a knowledge of him in
his own proper being. It will be of the same kind as the soul's
knowledge of God through his effects in the external world, though
of a vastly higher degree. Is there, we therefore ask, any kind of
human act through which we may come to know God himself in
the same sort of way as the way in which, in self-reflection, we
come to know our own selves? We know already that God is *near*
enough for this, for he is present by immensity at the very heart
of our being, in the most intimate way conceivable. But is there
any way by which we can be made to see him there, any way by
which our faculty of knowledge can be brought to exceed the
limitations of its finitude and be raised to the apprehension of this
infinite Being?

It is asserted that there is, and its name is grace. Just as,
through the operation of his natural acts of knowledge directed

[1] Professor John Laird expounds this point very usefully in his *Mind and Deity*,
p. 8o f., though he also allows for a direct reflexive self-awareness. Cf. S. Alexander,
Space, Time and Deity, I, p. 16 f. Heim makes a similar point against the idealists in
God Transcendent, p. 129. St. Thomas writes: "The intellect knows itself not by its
essence but by its acts." (*S. Theol.*, I, lxxxvii, 1c.)

towards the external world, man can come to know not only the
external world but himself, so, by sanctifying grace, he can come
to know God. And this means that, in addition to his presence of
immensity, God must be made present in a new and higher mode
in the soul, for only God can know God adequately, and so man
can only know God in a way which is analogous to God's knowledge of himself if he is elevated into God's own act of self-knowledge. Just as by nature the soul knows itself as the principle of its
natural acts, so by grace it knows God as the principle of its supernatural acts. Even so, this indwelling of God in the soul by grace,
which is offered to anyone who is prepared to live by the theological
virtues, is not enough to give us a knowledge of God that is in all
respects parallel to the knowledge of ourselves which we have
through our natural acts.

> "When, by psychological knowledge, the soul reflects upon the
> act which it has just performed, it seizes this act in its entirety—
> in its term, namely the concept, in its movement or intention of
> knowledge, in its efficient principle, namely the soul itself in so
> far as it is activated by its act—for all this is in itself actually
> intelligible. On the other hand, in the intentional life of living
> faith, all that can be actually apprehended are the object of this
> life, constituted by the truths of the Faith (which are themselves
> representatives of the divine reality), and the activity of living
> faith itself." [1]

For anything more than this the *ad hoc* initiative of God himself is
necessary, and in this the soul, whatever it may have previously
done in the way of preparation, is entirely passive. The soul can
neither demand nor expect this; it is a pure gift from God, and it
raises the soul to the highest point of union attainable in this life,
that of the Spiritual Marriage or the Prayer of Union. The pre-
dominant part in this is played by the virtue of charity and the
gift of wisdom.

> "The Holy Spirit . . . communicates to the soul that loves
> God his knowledge of divine things, that is, in particular, what is
> deepest, most formal, *most God* (if we may venture to use the
> phrase), for the Holy Spirit comprehends God in his depths and
> in an infinite mode. . . . The human spirit, having placed itself
> by its use of the gift of wisdom under the rule of the Spirit who

[1] *La Structure de l'Ame*, II, p. 185. In this discussion I have tried to reproduce the
substance of Gardeil's thought, without either making unnecessary use of technical
terms or referring to the many important side-issues which he raises. Cf. W. Bardon,
E.C.Q., July–Oct. 1941, p. 285 f.

uncovers before it the depths of God, allows itself to be joined to this interior God without any concept, *tanquam ignoto et inaccessibili*, and in this attitude of absolute renunciation of seeing or of making for itself ideas of God, it lets itself be carried towards God by the Holy Spirit. . . . No doubt the soul will then contemplate nothing, but if it truly shares in the divine wisdom, it will do better than contemplate; in so far as it has become one spirit with God, it will feel, touch, and experience immediately the substantial presence of God within itself."[1]

Such an experience can come rarely, and then only transiently, in this life; and, as has been said, it is a pure gift from God. Nothing remains beyond it but the Beatific Vision, of which it is itself a kind of foretaste.

It will be readily seen how, in this description of the life of the soul in grace, the divine immanence and the divine transcendence are balanced, and how unjustified is the complaint of the Barthians that Catholic mysticism, and indeed Catholic religion as a whole, is just an attempt of man, in defiance of the divine transcendence and his own creatureliness, to climb up to God. It does indeed find place for both immanence and transcendence. God is immanent in the depth of the soul and it is there that he is to be found. But he is immanent there, not as contained in it, but rather as containing it; not in the sense that he is limited and restricted by man, but in the sense that man, at the very root of his being, is altogether dependent upon God. God, then, is immanent, but the unveiling of this immanent God is not the work of man. All that man can do without grace is to know God as the author of certain effects, and he can only know this because God *is* the author of them; not because man can, as it were, put God under his scrutiny. Anything beyond this is the work of sanctifying grace, of the elevation of man by God to a participation in God's own life; and the very essence of grace is that it is gratuitous, a free gift of God which man has neither the right to demand nor the power to appropriate by his own efforts. Finally, in mystical experience —and it is, it will be remembered, against this that the Barthians raise their strongest protests—the human soul is devoid of all activity whatever, even of the least active co-operation; it loves God, as St. John of the Cross says, "not through itself, but through himself; which is a wondrous brightness, since it loves through the Holy Spirit, even as the Father and the Son love one another."[2]

[1] *La Structure de l'Ame*, II, pp. 258–60.
[2] *Living Flame of Love*, 2nd redaction, III, 82. *Works*, III, p. 206.

"The substance of this soul, although it is not the substance of God, for into this it cannot be substantially changed, is nevertheless united in him and absorbed in him, and is thus God by participation in God."[1] And the unanimous teaching of all Catholic mystical theologians is that, whatever man may do in the way of preparing himself for mystical union with God, and however large or small may be the proportion of souls that God calls to it (questions which have received much discussion in recent years[2]), the actual elevation to mystical prayer is a pure and unconditioned gift of God for which man has nothing more than an entirely passive or obediential capacity.

Non-Catholic mystical doctrine nearly always falls into one of two extremes. It may, on the one hand, envisage the mystical union as the elevation of the soul by its own powers to the level of a deity who is conceived as purely transcendent, the "flight of the alone to the alone" of the neo-Platonists, and in this case there is a virtual denial of the creatureliness of man. It may, on the contrary, set forward a technique for the identification of the human personality with a God who is located purely in the depths of the human soul, in which case there is a virtual denial of the divine transcendence, as in the teaching of Brahmanism and of such Western mystics as Jacob Boehme and, presumably, Angelus Silesius. Against both these types of mystical theory the opposition of Barth, Nygren, Brunner and Niebuhr is justified. Their criticisms do not, however, touch the general theory of Catholic mystical theology, with its two fundamental doctrines that God is both transcendent and immanent and that mystical union is achieved not by any human effort, but by the pure and unconditioned act of God himself, who elevates the soul into a participation of his own divine life.[3] It is most regrettable that so many, both of the supporters and of the opponents of mysticism, in recent years have taken as representatives of Christian mysticism such very untypical figures as Eckhart or even Angelus Silesius, rather than St. John of the Cross or St. Teresa of Ávila. Thus, on the one side, Dr. Inge describes Eckhart as "the greatest of all speculative mystics,"[4] and Berdyaev singles out Eckhart and Angelus

---

[1] *Living Flame of Love*, 2nd redaction, II, 34. *Works*, III, p. 158.

[2] Cf., e.g., the works of Poulain, Saudreau, Farges, etc., and the balanced discussion by Garrigou-Lagrange in *Perfection Chrétienne et Contemplation*.

[3] It is important to notice that mystical experience does not arise, as Dr. Edwyn Bevan among others supposes (see *Symbolism and Belief*, lect. xv), merely from a peculiar type of temperament on the part of the mystic, though this may dispose towards its reception, but from the initiative of God.   [4] *Christian Mysticism*, p. 148.

Silesius for special approval.[1] On the other side, Brunner claims to show that mysticism and Christianity are incompatible by arguing for a substantial identity in the teaching of Eckhart and of the tenth-century Indian Sankara,[2] while Niebuhr similarly uses Eckhart in order to show that mysticism necessarily contradicts human creatureliness.[3] None of these arguments, in fact, penetrates to the heart of the question, for reasons which have been made clear. Finally, it may be remarked that Catholic mystical doctrine in no way neglects the centrality of Christ, in its emphasis on union with God, though it has often been alleged to do so. While, from the psychological aspect, there is, as we have seen, a radical distinction between the obscure and mediate knowledge of God which the Christian non-mystic possesses and the quasi-experimental knowledge which is conferred upon the mystic by God himself, the ontological foundation of the two is the same, namely union with the divine humanity of Christ by sanctifying grace.[4] By incorporation into the manhood of Christ, who is the eternal Son of the Father, the soul is given by adoption a real participation in the Sonship of Christ and so enters into the life of the Trinity. This is simply the other side of the indwelling of God in the soul to which the Johannine Gospel testifies—"If any man love me, my Father will love him and we will come unto him and make our abode with him." It is what St. Paul describes in the text, "Your life is hid with Christ in God." There is thus a fundamental continuity between the state of the ordinary Christian and that of the mystic, or even of the saint in heaven who rejoices in the Beatific Vision, for, as St. Thomas says, "Grace is nothing else than a beginning of glory in us."[5] Because of our finitude, however, this capacity for a quasi-experimental knowledge of God cannot be realized by our own efforts, but only by the deliberate act of God himself. When, where and upon whom he will think fit to bestow this gift is known to him alone.[6]

[1] *Freedom and the Spirit*, p. 194.   [2] *The Mediator*, E.T., p. 110, n. 2.
[3] *The Nature and Destiny of Man*, I, p. 61 f. (cf. pp. 134, 145); II, p. 94 f.
[4] It must be noted that, while there is a real continuity (and indeed, according to many mystical theologians, an identity of essence) between mystical union and the Beatific Vision, mystical union, like all earthly knowledge of God, is knowledge by faith, not by sight. Cf. the teaching of St. John of the Cross and Mother Cecilia as discussed by E. I. Watkin in *The Philosophy of Mysticism*, p. 214 f.; cf. p. 357 f. Only in heaven is the veil entirely taken away; identity of essence is not incompatible with diversity of mode.
[5] *S. Theol.*, II, II, xxiv, 3 ad 2. Cf. Garrigou-Lagrange: "*La vie mystique est la vie chrétienne devenue en quelque sorte consciente d'elle-même.*" (*Perfection Chrétienne et Contemplation*, I, p. 149.)
[6] A further discussion of some questions of mystical theology and philosophy will be found in my book *Christ, the Christian and the Church*, p. 61 f. and ch. xii.

CHAPTER XI

THE COSMOLOGY OF WHITEHEAD

THE outlook which has been adopted in this book has been,
in the broad sense of the word, cosmological; that is to say,
in considering the problem of the existence of God, we have taken
as our starting-point the *cosmos*, the world or universe of which we
ourselves are part. Recent years have seen two quite outstandingly
portentous cosmological investigations, in the work of Dr. A. N.
Whitehead and in that of Dr. F. R. Tennant. It will therefore be
well to add to our discussion a comparison of the position at which
we have arrived with those of these two distinguished thinkers, so
that points of agreement may be registered and an attempt made
to account for any differences that may appear.

The definitive statement of Dr. Whitehead's philosophy is to be
found in his Gifford Lectures delivered at Edinburgh in 1927–8
and published in 1929 under the title *Process and Reality: An Essay
in Cosmology*. Its groundwork was laid as far back as 1919, in two
books entitled *An Enquiry concerning the Principles of Natural Knowledge* and *The Concept of Nature*, while it was immediately preceded
by three other works which appeared between 1926 and 1928,
namely, *Science and the Modern World*, *Religion in the Making* and
Symbolism, its Meaning and Effect. No substantial development is
apparent in the later works, *Adventures of Ideas*, which was published in 1933, and *Modes of Thought*, published in 1938.[1]

It is interesting to reflect that the cosmology of Whitehead and
the work of the logical positivists both derive from the monumental work, *Principia Mathematica*, which appeared in three large
volumes from 1910 to 1913 as the joint product of Dr. Whitehead
and Bertrand Russell, although the final conclusions at which
Whitehead has arrived are of the kind which every good logical
positivist is in honour bound to reject as "metaphysical" and
hence meaningless.

Like all other cosmologists, Whitehead is confronted with the
problem of a universe in which multiplicity is interlocked with

[1] In the present chapter these books will be referred to in the footnotes by their
initials. Attention may also be called to Miss D. M. Emmet's valuable book, *Whitehead's Philosophy of Organism* and to the two articles by Mr. S. E. Hooper in *Philosophy*,
July 1941 and January 1942.

unity, and persistence with fluidity, but in contrast to many he makes the most determined efforts to see that none of these data are neglected for the sake of the others. It is thus very difficult to know whether to describe him as a pluralist or as a monist, as a Parmenidean or as an Heraclitean. There is hardly a philosopher of note from whom he does not borrow, or whom he does not correct, but his main affinities are with the group of seventeenth- and eighteenth-century philosophers who stretch from Descartes to Kant. He designates his system by the name "The Philosophy of Organism."

The fundamental notion of Whitehead's philosophy is that of *creativity*, which he chooses in preference to the scholastic notion of *being*, presumably for its dynamic implications (though it may be observed, in passing, that, for the *philosophia perennis*, being is anything but lifeless, since the supreme Being is God, who is Life, Power and Love). Creativity is the "principle of *novelty*." It is "that ultimate principle by which the many, which are the universe disjunctively, become the one actual occasion, which is the universe conjunctively." For "it lies in the nature of things that the many enter into complex unity."[1] We are reminded here (though not by Whitehead) of the scholastic doctrine of potentiality and act.

The units out of which the universe is made up are "actual entities" or "actual occasions"; these are, as it were, atoms of creativity. But, though atoms, they are not isolated; in each of them all the others are mirrored, either in positive prehensions as being relevant to the prehending entity or in negative prehensions as being discarded.[2] However, the actual concrescence of an entity is not a purely passive reception by it of influences from other entities; it is itself self-creative, and what it ultimately becomes on emerging into concrete existence depends upon its own subjective aim. And out of this perpetual self-creation and interdependence of actual entities the history of the physical world is built up.

[1] *P.R.*, p. 28.
[2] Elsewhere Whitehead writes: "The organic starting-point is from the analysis of process as the realization of events disposed in an interlocked community. The event is the unit of things real." (*S.M.W.*, p. 212 (178). Cf. *M.T.*, p. 205 f.) Again, "it belongs to the nature of a 'being' that it is a potential for every 'becoming'" (the "principle of relativity" (*P.R.*, p. 30). It must be noticed that for Whitehead "relativity" does not mean "non-absoluteness" so much as "universal relatedness.") His meaning of the word has a different nuance to that which it bears in the famous "Theory of Relativity."

It must be observed that, according to Whitehead, actual entities are atomic in their temporality as well as in their spatiality. Their creation is a perpetual perishing; they do not persist in time, for with time they die. The notion of a substance persisting through time is definitely rejected. For Russell, as we have seen,[1] physical objects are simply logical constructs from sequences of particulars, isolated sense-data strung together somehow or other. Whitehead's view is somewhat similar, but, through his doctrine of interrelation of actual entities, he is able to maintain that when a nexus of actual entities has what he calls "social order" each entity absorbs into itself, by a kind of "inheritance," the defining characteristics of its predecessors, so that, while the individual perishes, its character persists.[2] (This is, of course, as true, in Whitehead's view, of lifeless as of living objects, but it is not difficult to see here his predilection for the Buddhist rather than the Christian doctrine of immortality asserting itself.) Such a nexus he calls an "enduring object,"[3] but he does not seem to succeed in his attempt, which he develops in *Adventures of Ideas*,[4] to get "persons" out of "occasions" by the notion of "transference of energy."

We cannot, however, he asserts, account for an ordered universe simply by means of actual entities. An aggregate of actual entities, each of which was pure creativity, would be formless chaos. "The understanding of actuality requires a reference to ideality."[5] There must therefore be a realm of "forms" or "eternal objects," which actual entities prehend as well as prehending one another. So out of actual entities and eternal objects Whitehead proceeds to build up the world, and four-fifths of *Process and Reality* is devoted to the description of the way in which, from these two fundamental types of entity, in which creativity manifests itself, the universe of our experience emerges. It is not necessary for our present purposes to go into this in detail.

Once the category of eternal objects has been introduced, the question of their nature inevitably arises. They cannot have any concrete existence of themselves, or they would be actual entities: "the metaphysical status of an eternal object is that of a possibility for an actuality."[6] And Whitehead is far too much of an empiricist

---

[1] p. 83 *supra*.
[2] For this reason Whitehead is able to make a more satisfactory attempt than Russell at constructing a theory of induction. (*P.R.*, p. 288 f.; cf. *M.T.*, p. 133 f.)
[3] *P.R.*, p. 46 f.   [4] *A.I.*, ch. xi.   [5] *S.M.W.*, p. 221 (185).
[6] Ibid., p. 222 (186).

to attribute reality to pure abstractions. His eighteenth Category of Explanation, the "Ontological Principle," insists that "actual entities are the only *reasons*";[1] "all real togetherness is togetherness in the formal constitution of an actuality."[2] Where, then, are the eternal objects? In the actual entities, we might reply; and so in a sense they are, for the actual entities prehend them and they are ingredient into the actual entities. But if that is all that is to be said, we are back where we started, with the actual entities, and we agreed that actual entities by themselves would produce mere chaos, not a cosmos. What is the way out?

It is at this point that Whitehead introduces a unique actual entity whose function it is to be the non-temporal locus of all the eternal objects; and to it he gives the name God. Actual entities prehend the eternal objects through the valuation of those objects by God. "The differentiated relevance of eternal objects to each instance of the creative process requires their conceptual realization in the primordial nature of God. He does not create eternal objects; for his nature requires them in the same degree that they require him."[3] "Apart from God, there could be no relevant novelty. Whatever arises in actual entities from God's decision, arises first conceptually, and is transmuted into the physical world."[4]

Thus the cosmological scheme, in its fundamental elements, is complete. In *Religion in the Making*, Whitehead sums it up as follows:

"The temporal world and its formative elements constitute for us the all-inclusive universe.

"These formative elements are:

"1. The creativity [embodied in actual entities] whereby the actual world has its character of temporal passage to novelty.

"2. The realm of ideal entities, or forms, which are in themselves not actual, but are such that they are exemplified in everything that is actual, according to some proportion of relevance.

"3. The actual but non-temporal entity whereby the indetermination of mere creativity is transmuted into a determinate freedom. This non-temporal actual entity is what men call God —the supreme God of rationalized religion."[5]

---

[1] *P.R.*, p. 33. [2] Ibid., p. 44. [3] Ibid., p. 363; cf. p. 353. [4] Ibid., p. 229.
[5] *R.M.*, p. 90.

Again he writes:

> "God is that non-temporal actuality which has to be taken account of in every creative phase. . . .
> "God is the one systematic, complete fact, which is the antecedent ground conditioning every creative act. . . .
> "He transcends the temporal world, because he is an actual fact in the nature of things. He is not there as derivative from the world; he is the actual fact from which the other formative elements cannot be torn apart."[1]

Are we then to hail Whitehead as a Christian theist because he thus introduces a being (or, as he would say, an actual entity) to which he gives the name God? We may well hesitate to do so when we see what he has to say about God. Let us turn again to *Process and Reality*. There we read:

> "It is as true to say that God is permanent and the World fluent, as that the World is permanent and God is fluent.
> "It is as true to say that God is one and the World many, as that the World is one and God many.
> "It is as true to say that, in comparison with the World, God is actual eminently, as that, in comparison with God, the World is actual eminently.
> "It is as true to say that the World is immanent in God, as that God is immanent in the World.
> "It is as true to say that God transcends the World, as that the World transcends God.
> "It is as true to say that God creates the World, as that the World creates God.
> "God and the World are the contrasted opposites in terms of which Creativity achieves its supreme task of transforming disjoined multiplicity, with its diversities in opposition, into concrescent unity, with its diversities in contrast. . . . For God the conceptual is prior to the physical, for the World the physical poles are prior to the conceptual poles. . . .
> "God and the World stand over against each other, expressing the final metaphysical truth that appetitive vision and physical enjoyment have equal claim to priority in creation."[2]

Again we are told that "God is the primordial creature,"[3] and that "God's existence is not generically different from that of other actual entities, except that he is primordial in a sense to be

---

[1] *R.M.*, pp. 94, 154, 156.   [2] *P.R.*, pp. 492, 493.   [3] Ibid., p. 42.

gradually explained."[1] We have certainly travelled far from the Thomist doctrine of God as self-existent Being.

For Whitehead's God is essentially an evolutionary deity. Although he is in a certain sense superior to the world, he is very much dependent upon it, and the historic process is a kind of mutual adventure in which God and the world are taking part. "The World's nature is a primordial datum for God; and God's nature is a primordial datum for the World. Creation achieves the reconciliation of permanence and flux when it has reached its final term which is everlastingness—the Apotheosis of the World. . . . Neither God, nor the World, reaches static completion. Both are in the grip of the ultimate metaphysical ground, the creative advance into novelty. Either of them, God and the World, is the instrument of novelty for the other."[2]

There seems to be an inconsistency here. God was described as a non-temporal actual entity, presumably because temporal actual entities are inevitably perishing; yet here we are told that he himself develops as time goes on. Nor can the reply be made that, while God is himself unchanging, from the standpoint of a being within the changing world he appears to undergo change. This might be asserted of a transcendent God, but the Philosophy of Organism knows nothing of a transcendent God. "Any proof," writes Whitehead, "which commences with the consideration of the character of the actual world cannot rise above the actuality of this world. *It can only discover all the factors disclosed in the world as experienced.* In other words, it may discover an immanent God, but not a God wholly transcendent."[3] The Thomist notion of a demonstration *quia est*, as contrasted with a demonstration *quid est*, is thus rejected. In his "primordial nature" which he possesses apart from the world, God is not even conscious. "Viewed as primordial, he is the unlimited conceptual realization of the absolute wealth of potentiality. . . . As primordial, so far is he from 'eminent reality' that in this abstraction he is 'deficiently actual.' . . . Thus, when we make a distinction of reason, and consider God in the abstraction of a primordial actuality, we must ascribe to him neither fullness of feeling, nor consciousness."[4] "The consequent nature of God is conscious; and it is the realization of the actual world in the unity of his nature, and through the transformation of his wisdom."[5] "The completion of God's

[1] *P.R.*, p. 103.   [2] Ibid., p. 493.   [3] *R.M.*, p. 71 (italics not in original).
[4] *P.R.*, p. 486.   [5] Ibid., p. 488.

nature into a fulness of physical feeling is derived from the
objectification of the world in God."[1] (We are reminded of
Dr. Matthews's assertion that without a world God could not be
personal.)

It is important not to be misled by Whitehead's description of
God as "the principle of concretion."[2] This does not mean that
he is the Creator; for every actual entity, as a manifestation of
Creativity, creates itself. As Miss D. M. Emmet says, "Whitehead
would not agree with St. Thomas that creation proceeds by
emanation from the primordial cause, God, but would only claim
that God provides the final causation for the self-creation of actual
entities, and also the initial limitation upon mere creativity in
virtue of which there can be any order, or process of creative
advance whatsoever."[3] In one place after another, Whitehead
makes it plain that, in his view, God merely provides the world
with the vision which it is to follow in its creation of itself. "The
power by which God sustains the world is the power of himself as
the ideal. He adds himself to the actual ground from which every
creative act takes its rise. The world lives by its incarnation of
God in itself. . . . He is not the world, but the valuation of the
world. In abstraction from the course of events, this valuation is
a necessary metaphysical function. Apart from it, there could be
no definite determination of limitation required for attainment.
But in the actual world, he confronts what is actual in it with what
is possible for it. Thus he solves all indeterminations."[4] "The
metaphysical doctrine, here expounded, finds the foundations of
the world in the æsthetic experience, rather than—as with Kant—
in the cognitive and conceptive experience. All order is therefore
æsthetic order, and the moral order is merely certain aspects of
æsthetic order. The actual world is the outcome of the æsthetic
order, and the æsthetic order is derived from the immanence of
God."[5] "God is the measure of the æsthetic consistency of the
world. There is some consistency in creative action, because it is
conditioned by his immanence."[6] It is true that in the earlier
book *Science and the Modern World* there are passages that suggest
leanings to a more orthodox view,[7] but these are not returned to

[1] *P.R.*, p. 488.   [2] *S.M.W.*, p. 243 (203); *P.R.*, p. 345.
[3] *Whitehead's Philosophy of Organism*, p. 121.   [4] *R.M.*, pp. 156, 159.
[5] Ibid., p. 104.   [6] Ibid., p. 99.
[7] *S.M.W.*, pp. 249–51 (207–8). But even here the "habit of paying to [God]
metaphysical compliments" is condemned.

in *Process and Reality*. There we are told that "each temporal
entity, in one sense, originates from its mental pole, analogously
to God himself. It derives from God its basic conceptual aim,
relevant to its actual world, yet with indeterminations awaiting
its own decisions."[1] "He is the unconditioned actuality of conceptual feeling at the base of things; so that, by reason of this
primordial actuality, there is an order in the relevance of eternal
objects to the process of creation."[2] In his primordial nature
"he is the lure for feeling, the eternal urge of desire,"[3] while
in his consequent nature, as himself determined by the world,
he is "the great companion—the fellow-sufferer who understands."[4]

It will be clear from this that Whitehead's doctrine of God is a
doctrine of immanence; this is not altered by such remarks as "It
is as true to say that God transcends the World, as that the World
transcends God," or "He transcends the temporal world, because
he is an actual fact in the nature of things."[5] God is not needed by
Whitehead as the self-existent infinite Being upon whose love and
power the world depends for all that it is and has; he is needed
merely as the locus of the eternal objects without which actual
occasions would not be able to effect their own self-creation. God
provides for them a final cause of an æsthetic kind; it is noteworthy that in one place Whitehead quotes with general approval
the famous passage from Aristotle about God moving the world
as the object of its desire.[6] God also appears as some kind of
formal cause, since the eternal objects of which he is the locus are
ingredient into the actual occasions which prehend them. But he is
certainly not, in Whitehead's thought, what Christian theism
asserts that he is, namely the creative efficient cause of the total
being of everything other than himself. It is therefore hardly surprising that Whitehead's final attitude to God is not one of adoration so much as of sympathy. T. E. Hulme has remarked that it is
at the end of their discussions that philosophers usually give
themselves away. "If you ask," he writes, "what corresponds to the
pantry which betrayed the man in armour, I should answer that
it was the *last* chapters of the philosophers in which they express
their conception of the world as it really is, and so incidentally
expose the things with which they are satisfied. How magnificently

---

[1] *P.R.*, p. 317.   [2] Ibid., p. 486.   [3] Ibid., p. 487.
[4] Ibid., p. 497.   [5] *R.M.*, p. 156.   [6] *P.R.*, p. 487.

they may have been clad before, they come out naked here."[1] It is in his final description of God as "the great companion—the fellow-sufferer who understands" that Whitehead reveals the essential immanentism of his thought.[2]

But it is important not merely to point out the inadequacy of Whitehead's system from the point of view of Christian theology, but also to show precisely why this inadequacy has arisen. Unless we can do this we shall merely have done something towards discrediting Christian theology. It appears, as a matter of fact, that, for all its profundity, Whitehead's cosmology suffers from two grave defects.

In the first place, it assumes without argument that Creativity, in the sense of self-creativeness, can be taken to be the fundamental characteristic of finite beings, and that, in consequence, whatever may be needed in the way of a God to provide what is lacking in them as an æsthetic final cause or formal cause, they have no need of any efficient cause outside themselves. "The concrescence of each individual actual entity is internally determined and is externally free."[3] But this simply means that Whitehead has concentrated his thought so thoroughly upon the *way in which things behave* as never really to inquire *why they are*. He has never properly understood what finite being *is* and so has never apprehended its radical contingency.[4] This may be in part due to the highly individualistic and questionable nature of his metaphysical doctrine, but it can hardly be entirely the result of it. For even if the account of finite beings which is given in *Process*

---

[1] *Speculations*, p. 20. On the previous page Hulme writes: "A man might be clothed in armour so complicated and elaborate, that to an inhabitant of another planet who had never seen armour before, he might seem like some entirely impersonal and omnipotent mechanical force. But if he saw the armour running after a lady or eating tarts in the pantry, he would realize at once, that it was not a god-like or mechanical force, but an ordinary human being extraordinarily armed. In the pantry, the essence of the phenomena is not *arms, but the man*."

[2] We may add that, while, for the reasons suggested below, Whitehead's God falls short of the demands of a thoroughgoing theism, he nevertheless yields more to those demands than Whitehead's philosophical doctrine would seem to allow. Professor L. S. Stebbing, in a very critical review of *Process and Reality*, asserts that "Professor Whitehead's indefensible use of language becomes nothing short of scandalous when he speaks of 'God'." (*Mind*, October 1930, p. 475.) And in view of Whitehead's own description of God's existence as "the ultimate irrationality" (*S.M.W.*, p. 249 (208)), it is a little surprising to find him criticizing the positivists because they "work [themselves] into a state of complete contentment with an ultimate irrationality." (*M.T.*, p. 202.)   [3] *P.R.*, p. 37.

[4] It is noticeable, for example, that in *The Concept of Nature*, ch. i and ii, in spite of a most salutary insistence that natural philosophy is concerned with data that are external to the mind, Whitehead goes on to discuss the structure of these data without any investigation of their ontological status.

and Reality be accepted, we still want to know why they are there at all. To say that they are units of Creativity explains nothing, unless we are also told why they are the particular units that they are, manifesting the particular kinds of Creativity that they do. The one thing that they are clearly not is self-explanatory, but this is the one fact that Whitehead never allows himself to think about. He postulates God as the ground of rationality,[1] but never as the ground of being, and as a result his whole system is left bombinating in a vacuum.

The second defect is, it seems, not unconnected with the first, and may indeed partly explain it. Whitehead apparently has no conception of the doctrine of *analogia entis*. The result is that, having found it necessary to introduce a being which he calls "God" in order to compensate for a certain evident lack of self-explanation in the world, he then assumes that God must be dependent upon the world correlatively to its dependence upon him. His God is thus both evolutionary and finite: "It is as true to say that God creates the World, as that the world creates God"; "a process must be inherent in God's nature, whereby his infinity is acquiring realization."[2] As we have already seen, without the doctrine of analogy it is impossible to provide an explanation of the existence of finite being, for a God who is limited by the world no more provides a reason for his existence than the world does for its own. This has already been expounded at some length in chapters vi and viii; there is no need to repeat the contents of those chapters here. All that need be remarked is that, since it is impossible to answer the question "Why does the world exist?" without the doctrine of analogy, the fact that Whitehead has no such doctrine may be one reason why he refrains from discussing that question. Be that as it may, he certainly fails to discuss it; and, as it is the ultimate problem of cosmology, this must be taken as showing a radical deficiency in his system.

For it is a deficiency rather than a positive error. All that Whitehead has to say about God's relation to the world as its formal and its æsthetic final cause may be accepted in substance as a restatement of the Christian doctrines that the ideas of all created beings are to be found in a more eminent mode in God and that every being tends to God as its last end. And if Whitehead

[1] *S.M.W.*, p. 249 (208).
[2] *A.I.*, p. 357. Cf. the discussion of "Deity" as "that factor in the universe whereby there is importance, value, and ideal beyond the actual." (*M.T.*, p. 140.)

had taken the great tradition of Christian scholasticism as seriously as he has taken the ancient Greeks and the post-Cartesians he might have gone far towards providing the modern philosophical world with the synthesis which it so urgently needs. Professor A. E. Taylor has given it as his opinion that "Dr. Whitehead's work would be even better than it is if it were influenced a little more by St. Thomas and a little less by Spinoza."[1] By taking as his fundamental category a concept of "Creativity" which is essentially *becoming*, rather than a concept of *being* which, in its analogical fecundity, bridges the gulf between the finite and the infinite, he has condemned his cosmology to imprisonment within the realm of finite existence and has thrown away the only key which could release it. Professor Taylor accuses Whitehead of "unconscious tampering with his own sound principle that all possibility is founded on actuality," and remarks that "the attempt to get back somehow behind the concreteness of God to an *élan vital* of which the concreteness is to be a product really amounts to a surrender of the principle itself."[2] But, in spite of its wrongheadedness, the Philosophy of Organism of Dr. Whitehead remains as one of the most impressive and massive cosmological constructions that have been produced, and the Christian theologian may learn much from it, not merely through the valuable positive insights which it manifests but perhaps even more through its ultimate inadequacy.

[1] "Some Thoughts on Process and Reality," in *Theology*, August 1930, p. 79.
[2] Art. cit., p. 78.

CHAPTER XII

THE COSMIC TELEOLOGY OF TENNANT

WE now proceed to consider the approach which is made by Dr. F. R. Tennant and which he elaborates with extreme thoroughness in his great two-volume work, *Philosophical Theology*; his smaller and more recent work, *The Nature of Belief*, does not show any substantial modification of his position. He is one of the most radically empirical and genetic of modern philosophers in method, and he states his view of the whole duty of the philosophical theologian in the most uncompromising way. "The classical proofs of the being of God," he writes, "sought to demonstrate that there is a Real counterpart to a preconceived idea of God. . . . The empirically minded theologian adopts a different procedure. He asks how the world, inclusive of man, is to be explained. . . . He will thus entertain, at the outset, no such presuppositions as that the Supreme Being, to which the world may point as its principle of explanation, is infinite, perfect, immutable, supra-personal, unqualifiedly omnipotent or omniscient. The attributes to be ascribed to God will be such as empirical facts and their sufficient explanation indicate or require."[1] Tennant is the irreconcilable antagonist of all attempts to deduce the existence of God from purely logical premises or from the bare concept of abstract being; St. Anselm and Hegel are equally rejected. But it may be doubted whether he has taken sufficiently seriously the classical tradition of scholasticism with its doctrine of *analogia entis*; certainly he neglects to give any systematic discussion of the presentation of theism by St. Thomas, and the seven references to the Angelic Doctor which occur in his work are all related to merely incidental points. But the relevance of these remarks will become clearer later on in this chapter.

In his first volume, which occupies nearly two-thirds of the whole work, Tennant makes an extremely thorough examination of the basic philosophical principles upon which any consistently empirical theology must rest, and much gratitude is due to him for performing this task; his epistemological doctrine is also expounded, more shortly and with less elaboration, in his later book,

[1] *Phil. Theol.*, II, p. 78.

161

Philosophy of the Sciences. We must, he insists, start from our own experience, for we have nothing else to start from; the *ordo cognoscendi* must precede the *ordo essendi*. And he makes a most valuable distinction between that which is "psychically" immediate to us in our crude acts of perception and that which is recognized as "psychologically" immediate after subsequent reflection upon those acts.[1] Much error, he points out, has arisen from the neglect of this distinction ("the psychologist's fallacy"), and throughout his work the distinction between the psychical and the psychological, denoted by (ψ) and (*ps*) respectively, is never allowed to be forgotten. He plainly affirms that our knowledge of the world is derived from the impressions of particulars received by our senses. "There is no psychological or scientific basis," he writes, "for the opinion that universals exist save *in rebus*, or for identifying the valid with the Real. . . . Universals are obtained by subjects from the particulars in which they are implicit; we know of none that, in the last resort, are not so obtained. In the order of knowing, they presuppose thought; not thought, them. Consequently, universals are not known by acquaintance, or with (*ps*) immediacy; the (ψ) immediacy, with which they eventually come to be explicitly apprehended, is an outcome of process and practice."[2] Proceeding from this starting-point, he builds up, by a very penetrating psychological discussion, a most impressive case for the existence of the human soul as a persistent knowing and willing entity; both Russell's doctrine of the soul as merely a logical construct out of particulars and Whitehead's theory of *nexūs* with "social order" receive implicit refutation here.[3] "The soul," he writes, "cannot be phenomenal. It is that to which phenomena appear, and is known otherwise than is the phenomenal. It is rather the one known being that must be called ontal or noumenal, if we are to avoid indefinite regress; or the one ontal thing that is assuredly known."[4] He does not, it is true, assert, as Gardeil does, that the soul, in reflection upon its acts, has an immediate, though obscure, experimental perception of its own essence;[5] "the apprehension of it is mediated discursively," he says, and "by construction rather than by pure inference."[6] But of the fact

---

[1] *Phil. Theol.*, I, p. 46.
[2] Ibid., I, p. 64. It is important to note that, when words like "real" and "object" are spelt with a small initial in Tennant's discussion, they refer to the content of immediate experience of percipient subjects; when spelt with a capital they refer to the "common world" of many percipients, whether derived from that content by logical construction or assumed to exist in its own right behind the phenomena.
[3] Ibid., I, ch. v. See pp. 83, 152 *supra*.   [4] Ibid., I, p. 97.
[5] Gardeil, *Structure de l'Ame*, II, p. 112 f.   [6] *Phil. Theol.*, I, p. 78.

he has no doubt, and, while he asserts that "Kant was right in teaching that internal experience is only possible through external experience," he agrees with Descartes and Locke that "we have clearer and more certain knowledge of our own existence than we have of the existence of things."[1]

A discussion of Ethical Value is succeeded by a chapter on Thought and Reason, in which the categories of substance and cause are vindicated. "Substance, as unknowable substratum, can well be spared; . . . but the concept of *a* substance remains indispensable. It assigns the *ground* of the conjunction of particulars, which resort to logical concepts, such as class or series, simply ignores. It is the determinedness, as to order, of our sensa, not they themselves or their mere occurrence (which might conceivably be fortuitous but is not), that suggests and calls for an interpretative concept. Thus the concept is not fashioned by the mind itself without objective call."[2] Again, "the concept of constancy of sequence may not logically imply that of necessary connexion or determination; but the fact of constancy of sequence, and of the non-emergence of effect unless the cause be forthcoming, bespeaks or suggests a sufficient ground. As reasonable men, we cannot dispense with the causal category as thus expressing determination of one event by another, whatever we may do as rational logicians."[3] And the accusation of "anthropomorphism" is faced cheerfully. "When we adopt the anthropic category of cause, we may be contenting ourselves with analogy where we cannot have logical cogency: with the 'regulative' where no 'constitutive' function is forthcoming. But if one then speaks 'as a man,' one at least knows what one is doing and what one is talking of."[4]

There follows a discussion of the theory of knowledge, which is, in many respects, of quite extraordinary value. All attempts to make the act of perception terminate with the *sensum*, whether that be conceived as a state of the perceiving soul, as a mere isolated particular, or as a "permanent possibility of sensation," are rejected, and the Kantian doctrine of an unknowable thing *per se* is found to be grossly inadequate. "While we . . . have *acquaintance* only with the sensible or phenomenal, we are having *rapport* with, and phenomenal knowledge of or about, the noumenal.

[1] *Phil. Theol.*, I, p. 78. This last statement is not, of course, altogether in agreement with the position maintained in the present work; see p. 145 *supra*. But what we are concerned with here is simply Tennant's defence of the existence of the soul.
[2] Ibid., I, p. 179.   [3] Ibid., I, p. 181.   [4] Ibid., I, p. 181.

We do not, in this latter sense of 'knowledge,' know the phenomenal only; rather, we know the noumenal through the phenomenal. . . . The thing *per se*, we conclude, must be credited with far more of responsibility and character than Kant, influenced by rationalistic and idealistic propensities, meted out to it."[1] It will be seen how close Tennant is here to the scholastic doctrine of the *species* as being the medium rather than the terminus, the *quo* rather than the *quod*, of perception; nor must we be misled by the fact that he called his theory of knowledge by the name of phenomenalism. For by this he does not mean that phenomena are all that we know, but that phenomena *are phenomena*, that is to say, appearances of noumena which they reveal. "We have," he says, "already substituted for the dictum that we only know phenomena, the more correct statement that we know the noumenal through the phenomenal. The phenomenal is, so to say, the utterance of the ontal *to us*; if the noumenal shines forth, or appears to us, as the phenomenal, it cannot be totally unknowable. And why should the appearing be assumed to be a veiling, rather than a revealing, a distortion or caricature, rather than representation? Philosophers have been wont to assume that phenomena only serve the purpose of deception. But their pessimism is groundless."[2]

Tennant next passes on to consider induction and probability, and it is here that we find the first serious divergence from the position that has been taken up in the present work. Agreeing substantially with Keynes's treatment of induction and probability, he remarks that probability, in order to be amenable to logical and mathematical handling, must be defined as a relation between sets of propositions; no proposition is probable or improbable in itself, but only in relation to certain other propositions. This raises various difficulties, in particular that of relating this purely objective relation between propositions to the fact that the probability with which we are concerned in actual life involves our purely subjective knowledge or ignorance of them. And the crux of the matter appears when we ask what is the basis of the probability which we are forced to ascribe to the ultimate body of knowledge relative to which the probability of all our other beliefs is to be assessed, since, *ex hypothesi*, there can be no "more ultimate" body of knowledge to which it can be referred. "If probability is rational, the rationality is in turn problematic.

---

[1] *Phil. Theol.*, I, pp. 247, 248.   [2] Ibid., I, p. 252.

Probability becomes a logical relation to probabilities."[1] Tennant then concludes that purely logical probability is not the probability with which we are concerned in life, and that, if the process of induction, which is essential to human action, is to be justified, it must be on the ultimate basis of a probability which is, to use his term, *alogical*.[2]

It will be remembered that in chapter vii above, we maintained, in substantial agreement with Fr. M. C. D'Arcy, that, while induction cannot be justified as a purely logical derivation of propositions from one another, it can be justified if we assume that, by its very nature, the human mind has the capacity (which, like every other human faculty, may of course sometimes function erroneously), when confronted with an adequate body of empirical fact, of apprehending, however partially and obscurely, the nature of finite beings, and hence of understanding to a greater or less degree the laws of their behaviour. Tennant does not, however, take this course,[3] presumably for the reason that, while, as we have seen, he thinks that Kant did not go far enough in attributing to us knowledge of things *per se*, he never fully accepts the doctrine that, through the phenomenal, we perceive the noumenal; he treats the "so-called phenomenal World of common sense and

[1] *Phil. Theol.*, I, p. 283. Cf. Tennant's small book, *Miracle*, p. 19 f.
[2] We may note that, while Professor C. D. Broad is on the whole ready to agree with Tennant's doctrine of alogical probability (see review of *Phil. Theol.*, Vol. I, in *Mind*, January 1929, p. 99), Professor J. Laird considers it to be "really incoherent" and to involve a vicious infinite regress. (See review of *Phil. of the Sciences*, in *Mind*, January 1933, p. 111.)
[3] Thus he writes elsewhere: "I would submit that the proposition which we are able to assert without possibility of refutation is not that there must be some certain knowledge [*sc.* of actuality, and not merely of logical implications] which even the sceptic presupposes, but that we possess presumptive knowledge, the ultimate presuppositions of which may in turn be found to be presumptive" (*Phil. of the Sciences*, p. 38), and he goes on to elaborate an epistemological doctrine on the basis of this notion of "presumptive knowledge" (op. cit., lect. ii). But, we must reply, if human knowledge is, of its very essence and not only accidentally, presumptive, there is no justification for the investigations by which we attempt to discriminate between genuine knowledge and error; indeed, the notion of human knowledge as being essentially and universally presumptive would seem to be meaningless. The fact surely is, not that we *have presumptive knowledge*, but that we *presume that we have knowledge*. If "presumptive knowledge" be a convenient term to indicate this, we may accept it, but if all our knowledge of actuality is presumptive, we have no possibility of discriminating between presumptive knowledge which is true and presumptive knowledge which is false. And we may add that, while our (ψ) certitude of truths arrived at by induction is different from (ps) certainty, our (ps) reflection upon it reveals, not that it rests merely upon alogical probability (though this factor need not be altogether excluded), but upon an intuition of the nature of finite essences. Tennant's genetic approach to knowledge, which he expounds so impressively, would seem to supply a very useful tool for discovering when the intellect is in error, but does not, it would seem, succeed in replacing "knowledge" by "presumptive knowledge" as the faculty of the intellect.

conceptual science" as something inevitably made by us "out of" our various private perceptual worlds and the realm of things *per se*, and not as, in the scholastic sense of the word, an *abstraction* from the latter realm, by which (apart from the possibility of error due to sheer human fallibility) it is genuinely manifested to us, however partially, in its actual nature;[1] he speaks of "manipulation of our knowledge-data"[2] rather than of "abstraction," and when he does speak of "abstraction" it is rather in the sense of "construction."[3] At this point Tennant imports into his system the idea of "faith" as essential to epistemology. He declares that his faith is essentially of the same kind as the faith of religion, and suggests that to the catalogue in the eleventh chapter of the Epistle to the Hebrews we might add "By faith, or by hope, Newton founded physics on his few and simple laws of motion; by faith the atomists of ancient Greece conceived the reign of law throughout the material world; and so on indefinitely."[4]

Without inquiring how far this conception of faith is identical with that of Christian theology, or indeed with that of the New Testament, we may observe that at this point there occurs the one considerable break in the rationality of Tennant's system. "Faith," he tells us, "is venture dictated by human interest: it is not mere prudence or probability, for these cannot be, till faith has substantiated somewhat of the hoped for; it is not confined to the realms of moral value and religious ideas, but infects all existential and theoretical knowledge. . . . Science postulates what is requisite to make the world amenable to the kind of thought that conceives of the structure of the universe, and its orderedness according to quantitative law; theology, and sciences of valuation, postulate what is requisite to make the world amenable to the kind of thought that conceives of the why and wherefore, the meaning or purpose of the universe, and its orderedness according to teleological principles. Both are necessarily interpretative, anthropic, interested, selective."[5] And in an eloquent passage he argues that, on the basis of this doctrine of faith, theology and science have the same epistemological status.[6]

We might doubt whether theology should be grateful for being placed upon the same epistemological level as science at the cost of accepting such a doctrine of "faith" as this. It must also be noticed that, in spite of the vigour with which he expounds it, it is

[1] *Phil. Theol.*, I, p. 255.   [2] *Phil. of the Sciences*, p. 83.   [3] Ibid., p. 133 f.
[4] *Phil. Theol.*, I, p. 298.   [5] Ibid., I, p. 299.   [6] Ibid., I, p. 303.

by no means easy to determine precisely what the nature of "faith," as Tennant understands it, is. His explicit repudiation of "rational" theology, by which he means any theological system resting on a purely logical and *a priori* basis,[1] and, it must be added, his criticisms of the ordinary arguments from religious experience as involving a confusion between (ψ) and (ψs) immediacy,[2] seem to be well-founded; but whether an empirical approach to theology necessarily requires the insertion of "faith" at the point where he makes it seems highly questionable, and some of its results will be seen as we consider how he proceeds from it to formulate an argument for the existence of God.

This task is undertaken in the second volume, which opens with a discussion of the conformity of the world to law and of the sense in which the world may be said to be "rational," and then discusses the empirical approach to theism. Argument of a primarily "cosmological" type, such as St. Thomas's first three "Ways," based upon the fact that the world exists although it does not provide the explanation of its own existence, are rejected, though by implication rather than by explicit repudiation. There is, indeed, in an appendix to the first volume an incidental denial of the argument *e contingentia mundi*,[3] which seems to show a misunderstanding of the sense which contingency bears in it, but on the whole it appears that Tennant's avoidance of arguments based upon the mere existence of finite being is related to the fact, mentioned above, of his timidity in accepting wholeheartedly the real existence of extramental objects as substantial beings. "The soul or active subject," he writes, "is the one kind of thing *per se* that we have as yet [*sc.* at the beginning of Volume II] been enabled to assert to be knowable. And, previously to inquiry, the ontal that lies behind or beyond physical bodies and phenomenal events may be supposed to consist of soul-like monads, or to be of essentially different nature."[4] Even "other selves . . . are neither directly apprehended nor provable otherwise than by cumulative pragmatic verification."[5] The consequence of this is that Tennant's inquiry about the world, instead of being directed to the question why it exists, is concerned with the way in which it behaves; and he is able to argue that the design which he claims to see in it implies at least the probable existence of a designer

[1] See, e.g., *Phil. Theol.*, II, p. 79.   [2] See p. 19 *supra.*
[3] *Phil. Theol.*, I, Appendix: Note L, p. 410.   [4] Ibid., II, p. 26.
[5] Ibid., II, p. 78.

without having to decide whether its ontological nature demands
the existence of a self-existent Being as its creative cause.

The chapter on "The Empirical Approach to Theism," which
forms the heart of Tennant's second volume, bears the sub-title
"Cosmic Teleology." The keyword of the argument is "purpose,"
and five fields of fact are examined in which purpose has been
claimed as evident. (1) There is first the epistemological adaptiveness of things to thought, in scholastic language the *convenientia
entium ad intellectum*. In view of the interpretative function which
he ascribes to the mind, Tennant feels justified in concluding only
that "things, or their ontal counterparts, have so much affinity
with us as to be assimilable and to be understood," but that this
"does not of itself testify that the adaptedness is teleological."[1]
(2) Then there is the adaptiveness that is seen in living organisms,
concerning which Tennant remarks that the overthrow of the
Paleyan type of argument by the Theory of Evolution does not
deprive the adaptedness of teleological significance. "The discovery of organic evolution has caused the teleologist to shift his
ground from special design in the products to directivity in the
process, and plan in the primary collocations. It has also served
to suggest that the organic realm supplies no better basis for
teleological argument of the narrower type than does inorganic
Nature."[2] (3) He next considers, therefore, the adaptation of the
inorganic environment to organic life. Against the contention that
different inorganic conditions from those that actually hold might
have been equally compatible with life, albeit life of a different
kind, he urges that "the necessary environment, whatever its
nature, must be complex and dependent upon a multiplicity of
coincident conditions, such as are not reasonably attributable to
blind forces or to pure mechanism,"[3] and that the fact that the
inorganic world is such that life with its purposiveness can emerge
from it is an indication of purpose in the inorganic world itself.
(4) The treatment then proceeds to deal with the æsthetic quality
of Nature, and particular stress is laid on the fact that it is just
where Nature is most "mechanical" and least touched by man
with his attendant abominations of factories, motor-cars and the
like that she is most beautiful. That is, Nature speaks to man of a
purpose beyond herself, and, while coercive force is not claimed
for it, this argument is pressed as providing sound confirmation of
the purposiveness that has been already discerned. "Theistically

[1] *Phil. Theol.*, II, p. 83.   [2] Ibid., II, p. 85.   [3] Ibid., II, p. 87.

regarded, Nature's beauty is of a piece with the world's intelligibility and with its being a theatre for moral life; and thus far the
case for theism is strengthened by æsthetic considerations."[1]
(5) Finally, Tennant considers the moral status of man. He will
not admit that a sound argument for the existence of God can be
built up on moral considerations alone. For him, they "supply
the coping-stone of a cumulative teleological argument. . . .
Isolated from other facts, and used only for the sake of their
alleged *a priori* preconditions, they can supply no rational proof
of the existence of God . . .: the valid and the existent have been
confounded."[2] Kant and Rashdall receive short shrift, the latter
being accused of ambiguity in his use of the word "existence" or,
at least, of having illicitly assumed that "to exist" involves "to be
in some mind" and of having argued from this that, since "the
ideal is not fully apprehended as to its content by any individual
[or] realized in any human life . . . there must therefore be a
Divine Mind in which its 'existence' is to be located."[3] ·For
Tennant the significant fact is that " 'man is the child of Nature.' "[4]
"Her capacity to produce man must be reckoned among her
potencies, explain it how we may. And man is no monstrous birth
out of due time, no freak or sport [; he] is like, and has genetic
continuity with, Nature's humbler and earlier-born children."[5]
"Nature and moral man are not at strife, but are organically
one [, and] the whole process of Nature is capable of being
regarded as instrumental to the developement of intelligent and
moral creatures."[6]

Even from so sketchy and imperfect an outline as the above it
should be clear how weighty are the arguments marshalled by
Tennant in support of his contention that "the only idea of a
world-ground that yields an explanation of these facts in their
totality [*sc.* "the multitude of interwoven adaptations by which
the world is constituted a theatre of life, intelligence and morality"] would seem to be that of an efficient, intelligent, ethical
Being."[7] But, as he is careful to point out, "when we call this
Being 'God' we are borrowing a name, but not any idea, from
religion."[8] Not even any "premature assumption of monotheism
is intended. What is claimed to have as yet been reasonably
established is that cosmic purposing is embodied in the world.

---

[1] *Phil. Theol.*, II, p. 93.   [2] Ibid., II, p. 100.   [3] Ibid., II, p. 97.
[4] Ibid., II, p. 100.   [5] Ibid., II, p. 101.   [6] Ibid., II, p. 103.
[7] Ibid., II, p. 121.   [8] Ibid., II, p. 121.

But oneness of purpose does not imply numerical oneness of purposer,"[1] and the question of the unity of God is left over for later consideration.

We must further notice that the argument is not alleged to be coercive; all through it Tennant is dogged by his doctrine of "faith," which, it will be remembered, he asserts to be implicated in all human theorizing. At the end of his investigation he tells us that "not only theism, but any metaphysical theory or world-view whatsoever, can at best claim to be a reasonable belief ulti-mately grounded on the alogical probability which is the guide of life and of science, and verifiable only in the sense that it renders the known explicable. No *a priori*, rational, logically coercive, or deductive proof is possible."[2] His ultimate claim is merely that "if philosophy can show that theistic belief, such as some take to be the essence of Christianity, is reasonable in the sense that it is continuous with the faith of science and is on a par, in respect of its intellectual status, with the probabilities which are involved in all explanation and in all other knowledge concerning Actuality, it will have provided an answer to a question which will never fail to be of vital interest to human beings."[3] He sums up his judgment on his argument in these words:

"Our world is . . . a cosmos, at least in the humblest sense of the word, and the original determinateness of its terms or *posita* is such as to make it intelligible. This, of course, constitutes a teleological proof of theism no more than does the existence of the world afford a causal or cosmological proof. The mystery of mysteries is that something exists; and if the one underived or uncaused existent be God, the creator of all things else, God is 'the last irrationality,' and creation is the next to the last inexpli-cability. To replace absolute pluralism by theism is to reduce an indefinite number of separate inexplicabilities to these two alone; and so far economy, and therefore explicability of a kind, is secured. It is of no important kind, however: for there is no more wonder about a self-subsistent plurality than about a self-subsistent individual. But when the intelligibility of a cosmos, rather than the mere existence of a world of any sort, is the fact to be considered, teleological theism evinces more conspicuously its advantage, in other respects than that of economy, over absolute pluralism. For over and above the forthcomingness, conceived as self-subsistence, of the many existents, is their adaptiveness, inherent in their primary determinateness and their

[1] *Phil. Theol.*, II, p. 121.   [2] Ibid., II, p. 249.   [3] Ibid., II, p. 250.

relations, to the requirements of intelligibility. This further particularizes their determinateness and so bespeaks more of coincidence in the 'fortuitous.' "[1]

The last sentence but one in this passage might, if it stood in isolation, be taken as a restatement of the Thomist Fifth Way, as asserting that the very existence of finite being involves a final as well as an efficient cause.[2] But the rest of the passage makes it plain that it is the intelligibility of the cosmos *as a whole*, or at least of large sections of it, which is being considered, as is, of course, shown by the previous statement of the whole argument. The really surprising feature is the way in which Tennant assumes that to postulate God and creation, rather than a plurality of finite beings, as the ultimate categories of explanation of the fact that something exists, is to effect merely a numerical economy of concepts;[3] this is presumably possible only in view of his doctrine, on which we shall comment shortly, that God is himself a finite being. Tennant is here in line with his master, James Ward, as is seen in their agreement that creation is necessary to God.[4] To describe God as "the last irrationality" is inevitable in such a case; it is parallel to Whitehead's assertion that "God is the ultimate limitation, and his existence is the ultimate irrationality."[5] But the assertion of traditional theism, that God, in contrast to all other beings, is self-existent and infinite provides not merely a numerical economy but an explanation. Any other God could only be a last irrationality, but the Christian God is the one entire Rationality through which alone all else becomes rational. This has already been expounded[6] and it need not be repeated here.

Tennant's discussion of cosmic teleology is followed by two chapters dealing with the Idea of God: Creation, Eternity, Infinitude and Perfection, the Absolute, Divine Personality, and Self-

---

[1] *Phil. Theol.*, II, p. 104.   [2] See p. 54 *supra*.
[3] Cf. the following passage in *Philosophy of the Sciences*:
"We must recognize at the outset that an alogical factor enters into the foundations of all our knowledge. The *posita*, of which I have already spoken, are prior to logic and determinative of all possibility. No reason, let alone a logical or an *a priori* reason, can be assigned for their being what they are, or indeed for their being at all. Their particular determinateness is inexplicable" (p. 87).
It is, of course, precisely because no logical or *a priori* reason can be assigned for the existence and nature of the *posita* that traditional theism affirms them to be the creatures of a self-existent Being. It does not admit that because there is an element in the world which is alogical in the sense of not being explicable by mere implication between propositions, it is therefore alogical in the sense of being metaphysically inexplicable.   [4] See p. 113 *supra*.
[5] *Science and the Modern World*, p. 249 (208).   [6] See ch. vi *supra*.

limitation. His demolition of all such absolutisms as make the
world merely an appearance or an experience of God would
seem to be unanswerable, as is his recognition that the only
alternative is some doctrine of creation. And he is rightly anxious
to ensure that if terms are used of God they shall have a determinate meaning and shall not be merely vague honorific epithets
savouring, in the phrase which he quotes from Hume, more of
panegyric than of philosophy. But his disregard of the doctrine
of analogy, with the consequence that all terms derived from our
experience of finite beings must be applied to God in precisely
their original sense if they are to have any significance in that
application at all, makes his discussion of the divine attributes,
however illuminating in itself, to some extent irrelevant to the
issue.[1] It will be sufficient here to see what he has to say about
the attributes of infinity and perfection.

Tennant distinguishes three main uses of the word "infinite" in
Christian theology. It can mean either "devoid of all defining
limitations," with the implication of indefiniteness or indeterminacy; it can mean "the limitless in number, time, or space:
that which cannot be reached by successive acts of addition or
division"; or it can have a third meaning, that of "completeness
or perfectness,"[2] and Tennant accuses St. Thomas, in common
with other Christian theologians, of confusion in his use of the
term. When St. Thomas says that the being of God is called
"infinite" because it is pure, self-subsistent or not received, he is
using the term simply to imply non-limitation by other self-
subsistents; and to pass on from this notion of infinitude as self-
subsistence to the connotation of "an *omnitudo* of all qualities
however mutually incompatible" would be, as Tennant clearly
sees, not only a change in meaning, but a change from sense to
nonsense. There is, however, a sense in which God is an *omnitudo*,
which follows immediately from his self-subsistence and which does
not involve any contradiction, and this sense is precisely what is
implied in the traditional theistic doctrine. It has been observed
earlier that *ipsum esse subsistens* and *quo majus nihil cogitari potest* are
mutually equivalent;[3] if God is the one self-subsistent, then he is

---

[1] It is interesting to note how deeply, through the neglect of the traditional doctrine
of analogy, the notion of creation as necessary to God, has implanted itself in modern
philosophical theology, even when this would claim to be "orthodox." We have found
it in Ward, Tennant, and Matthews; it occurs in Pringle-Pattison too (*The Idea of God*,
lect. xvi).

[2] *Phil. Theol.*, II, p. 140.   [3] See ch. ii *supra*.

necessarily the *omnitudo*, not of all qualities however incompatible, but of all perfections. St. Thomas is quite explicit that the infinitude of God does not involve the possession of incompatible qualities. "Whatever implies contradiction," he says, "does not come within the scope of divine omnipotence, because it cannot have the nature of possibility. Hence it is better to say that such things cannot be done, than that God cannot do them."[1] Thus God's infinitude leads immediately to his perfection; but it does not seem fair to accuse St. Thomas, as Tennant does, of "merging" the two terms.[2] Their close connection is inevitable, but that is simply because God's infinitude and his perfection are in themselves both identical with his essence and differ only in that they are different aspects of it. Nor is it the case that St. Thomas confuses the use of "infinite" as meaning self-subsistent with its use as meaning indefinite or indeterminate, because this latter notion is quite foreign to his thought about God. To the Angelic Doctor, Pure Being is not vague or indeterminate, but supremely active and rich;[3] to him, as Tennant realizes, Pure Being is the most perfect of all things, because it actuates all things, and when we remember that, to the Catholic theologian, this Pure Being is none other than the eternal and ever-living Trinity, we see at once how false is the notion that in Catholic theology the infinitude of God carries with it the least suggestion of indeterminacy or indefiniteness. There is no need to deny that words like "infinity" and "perfection" have often been applied to God with vague and overlapping meanings, but, however we precisely define them, there are two mutually implicatory facts for which they stand, namely, that God is unconditioned by anything outside himself and that he is *maxime ens*, the plenitude of all that supremely *is*.

In his treatment of creation, Tennant finds himself in a similar position to that of Whitehead, though he does not force it to the same extreme or express it in so sharply antithetical a form.

> "The human imagination," he writes, "most forcibly represents to itself the dependence of the world on the will of God by supposing God and time to precede creation. But, as early Christian thinkers found, there is no reason to convert this representation into a theistic tenet. One of them regarded creation as an

[1] *S. Theol.*, I, xxv, 3c.   [2] *Phil. Theol.*, II, p. 141.   [3] *S.c.G.*, I, xliii.

endless regress, world preceding world; another taught that
creation was not in time, but the world and time were
created together. . . . A further refinement is made when God
is conceived as *essentially* the world-ground or creator; not another
cause in the series, or a being who might or might not have
created. God *quâ* God is creator, and the creator *quâ* creator is
God: or 'God without the world is not God.' "[1]

And this last is Tennant's own view.

"Thus conceived," he continues, "the theistic idea of creation
is free from the old puzzles concerning temporal relations. If God
be a world-ground, there never could have been no world. The
'possibilities,' prior to any Actuality, between which the Deity
has been thought to have chosen, are but hypostatized abstractions. . . . If we are to speak in terms of time, the theistic
doctrine may be summed up in the statement that the world is
coeval with God and is contingent on his determinate nature
inclusive of will."[2]

There are various suggestions scattered through his work which
make one hesitate to ascribe to Tennant the obvious force of his
statements in the pages from which the above extracts are taken.
Like Ward, he is clear that the world derives its existence from
God: "The world . . . is God's utterance. Its nature depends on
his nature and will, not his nature on that of a self-subsistent
universe."[3]   Such a statement is far more satisfactory than
Whitehead's dictum that "it is as true to say that God creates the
World, as that the World creates God."[4] Yet Tennant tells us
that "God without a world, or a Real other, is not God but an
abstraction,"[5] in much the same way as the primordial nature of
Whitehead's God is not "eminently real" but "deficiently
actual."[6] And it seems clearly fallacious to argue that "if God
be a world-ground, there never could have been no world," for
it is perfectly possible to suppose that God is, by his very nature,
a world-ground in the sense of being able to create a world, but is
only incidentally a world-ground in the sense of having actually
done so. From the contemplation of a picture we can say that
there must have been an artist who was able to paint it; but we
cannot say that he could not help painting it, or that "there

---

[1] *Phil. Theol.*, II, p. 128. Tennant repeats this last assertion in three other places,
viz., pp. 156, 168 and 183.
[2] Ibid., II, p. 129.   [3] Ibid., II, p. 209.   [4] *Process and Reality*, p. 492.
[5] *Phil. Theol.*, II, p. 168.   [6] *Process and Reality*, p. 486.

never could have been no picture." Tennant is, in fact, making a needless capitulation to Broad's belief that the theistic position implies that the existence of the world follows from the existence of God, though, unlike Broad, he sees the necessity as metaphysical rather than logical.[1] The fact is that, having rejected, as traditional theism also rejects, the idea that creation necessarily implies a temporal beginning, Tennant concludes that the world is thereby shown to be necessary to God. All that has been said in chapter viii above is relevant here, and we may sum it up in Gilson's words that "it is quite true that a Creator is an eminently Christian God, but a God whose very essence is to be a creator is not a Christian God at all. The essence of the true Christian God is not to create but to be."[2] Like Whitehead, Tennant assumes that, because we can say that the world *must* have been created by God, we can infer that God *must* have created the world, ignoring the fact that the antecedent conditions presupposed by these two statements are by no means the same. We agree that, *if the world exists*, the world must have been created by God, but we cannot conclude that, *if God exists*, God must create the world. Indeed, the true conclusion is precisely the opposite. Because it is the very insufficiency of the world that implies the existence of a Creator, it follows that this Creator must be himself self-sufficient and therefore under no obligation to create. The world demands as its ground a God who need not have made it. We may sum this up by saying that we have indeed to make our first approach to God by examining the finite world, but that this very examination, while it shows us that God has *necessarily* the power to create and has *as a matter of fact* made use of this power, shows us also that his use of it is not necessary but is an act of free and unconstrained will. This point has been sufficiently elaborated already and needs no more mention here.

Because of his implicit denial of *analogia entis* and because of the explicit denial of divine infinity which results from it, Tennant is forced to envisage God as related to the world in essentially the same way as finite beings are related to one another. He cannot say, with the scholastic tradition, that, whether God creates this world, a different world, or no world at all, his own infinite perfection is unaffected, or that God and the world do not "add up." In consequence he finds himself, in order to save the divine wisdom and goodness, under the necessity of maintaining that, taking into

[1] See p. 57 f. *supra.*   [2] *God and Philosophy*, p. 88, quoted on p. 97 *supra.*

account the conditions under which God has to work, this is the best of all possible worlds;[1] this gives a rather unrealistic flavour to his discussion of the problem of evil. Again, since terms have to be applied univocally to God and to creatures, he has to set limits to God's power and knowledge; God has limited his own activity in creating a world in which there are beings exerting causality, and his conservation of the world is exercised rather in preventing these spontaneously acting independent beings from disrupting the cosmos than in preserving them in existence by a continuous act of creative power. God's relation to us thus becomes far less intimate than traditional theology has taught. "Theism," writes Tennant, "does attribute to God's creatures delegated spontaneity such as conceivably might develop into erratic tendencies. And it is only with the qualification which this attribution involves that the theist can use such expressions as that in God 'we live and move and have our being': to take these words more literally would be to identify the world-ground with the world instead of to insist on the inseparableness and distinctness of God and his world."[2] There thus appears an interesting paradox. Because, through his doctrine that creation is necessary, he has lessened the ontological distinction between God and the World, Tennant has perforce to exaggerate their practical independence in order to avoid confusing them altogether; while traditional theology, secure in its fundamental postulate of God's transcendence as self-existent being, can without fear of any concession to pantheism or determinism, teach that, without any violation of human freedom, God is the primary cause of every human act.

It is unnecessary to follow up these points in further detail; their bearing is obvious. But one further point must be briefly examined. This is the question as to whether God is a unity or a plurality. Tennant is not very much impressed by the argument that "if we are to regard goodness and love as essential attributes of God . . . this implies that within or besides himself there must eternally have been an other to be known and loved with all the fulness of his capacity to know and to love,"[3] apparently because of his view that God always had a world to occupy himself with. "God without a world, or a Real other, is not God, but an

---

[1] This is altogether different from the Thomist doctrine that, while God might have made a better world, he could not have made the present world in a better way. Cf. S. Theol., I, xxv, 5, et 6 ad 1; Garrigou-Lagrange, Dieu, E.T., II, p. 345.

[2] Phil. Theol., II, p. 212.   [3] Ibid., II, p. 169.

abstraction."[1] But, as we have seen, he does not claim that his
argument necessarily leads to monotheism. "Oneness of purpose
does not imply numerical oneness of purposer." And while he
rejects the doctrine of the Trinity in its orthodox form on the
ground that it postulates for the three Persons a status inter-
mediate between the substantival and the adjectival,[2] he sees no
objection to the idea of "God" as a self-subsistent society of divine
beings with equality of nature, identity of essence and harmony of
will.[3] And his subsequent inquiries do not, so far as one can see,
throw any further light on the question: "the issue," we are told,
"does not lie within the sphere of fact-controlled thought."[4] The
plain fact is that he is not able, and apparently does not wish, to
rule out the possibility of polytheism, though it is a highly refined
polytheism which he prefers to describe as "the pluralistic conception of deity."[5] That he is prepared to face this is a great
tribute to his courage and honesty; there are few philosophers
who would be willing to risk the charge of polytheism, with the
uncomplimentary associations which it carries, even if they hoped
to be able to show that those associations were inapplicable to
their particular case.

We may bring this discussion of Dr. Tennant's Cosmic Teleology to an end by remarking that, if, as we have seen, it affirms the
existence of a God who is less than the God of traditional theism in
that, while the universe is dependent upon him for its existence,
nevertheless he is bound to create it and once he has created it is
limited by it, this is only what we might have expected from the
method of investigation adopted. For, if we restrict ourselves to
asking questions about the way in which the beings which compose
the world behave—and this is what Tennant's investigation of
cosmic purposing amounts to—we are most unlikely to arrive at
the notion of a genuinely transcendent cause. As Whitehead,
who is far more consistent than Tennant in following this procedure, says, "Any proof which commences with the *character* of
the actual world cannot rise above the actuality of this world. . . .

[1] The argument is that, while "a self or subject does not depend, *quâ* an existent or
as to its being, upon any object to which it stands in the relation of presentation or
attention," yet "relation or *rapport* is essential for any existent's assuming the rôle of,
and being, a subject." (*Phil. Theol.*, II, p. 167.) This is, of course, precisely the argument which, in conjunction with the notion of *internal* relations, a trinitarian will use
in support of the doctrine of the Trinity. See p. 186 *infra*.
[2] Ibid., II, Appendix: Note D, p. 267 f.   [3] Ibid., II, p. 170 f.
[4] Ibid., II, p. 172.   [5] Ibid., II, p. 170.

It may discover an immanent God, but not a God wholly transcendent."[1] And the transcendence which in places Tennant
verbally ascribes to God is far from being transcendence in the
traditional and thoroughgoing sense. It is only when, dis-
regarding the prohibitions of a philosophical method which
mistakenly bases itself upon the procedures proper to the natural
sciences, we ask the metaphysical question, "Why do finite beings
exist at all?" that we can arrive at the recognition of the true
transcendence of the Deity. And this is a valid question, which
needs asking. Time after time Tennant comes near to asking it,
but he always fails to do so. In addition, the unfortunate introduction of "faith" at the end of his first volume renders the whole
of the subsequent argument professedly tentative and speculative.
As a result he arrives at the merely probable existence of a God
who is less than the God of religion : a God who, whatever else he
may be, is certainly not adorable. If Tennant's contentions were
at all points irrefutable, we should have to accept them and make
the best of a bad job. But reasons have been advanced for supposing that this is not so. The plain fact is that, in his magnificent
refutation of all attempts to build up theology on purely *a priori*
arguments, Tennant never seems to envisage any other alternative
than a God who is essentially implicated in the world-process, and
therefore never takes seriously the traditional doctrine of a God
who is discovered as the creator of the world and yet is at the same
time altogether self-sufficient.[2] But when we have said this, we
are far from denying the importance that attaches to the systematic
working out in such careful detail of the implications of a radically
empirical approach to the problem of the design in the universe.

---

[1] *Religion in the Making*, p. 71. (Italics not in original: I suspect that Whitehead
mentally stressed "actual" rather than "character" and so missed the real point of
his own remark!) This inherent limitation of any approach which is primarily teleological rather than cosmological appears in Dr. W. R. Matthews's development of the
teleological argument in his *Purpose of God*. His final conclusion is that "the doctrine
of the self-sufficiency of God should be rejected" (p. 173).

[2] In an interesting article in the *Harvard Theological Review*, July 1942, Dr. Graham
Frisbee examines Tennant's attempt "to show that the charge that the empiricist is
unable to 'prove' the existence of more than a finite God is damaging on neither its
philosophical nor its religious side," and concludes that "whatever else he has or has
not done, he has not shown that."

ADDITIONAL NOTE *C* TO CHAPTER XII

THE MORAL ARGUMENT AND THE PROBLEM OF EVIL

This book would hardly be complete without some reference to an approach to theism which has become increasingly prominent during the last century, namely that which adopts as its starting-point the fact and the content of the moral consciousness of man. Historically this development is, of course, to be traced to the influence of Kant, who, having, as he thought, demolished all forms of speculative argumentation for the existence of God as involving, in one way or another, the fallacy of the ontological argument, took refuge in the moral sense of man as affirming the existence of a Supreme Moral Being as a necessity for the practical reason.[1] Anything like a full discussion of the moral approach would fall outside our present scope, for, except in so far as it enters as one element into the "Argument from Perfection" which is the Thomist Fourth Way, it is almost entirely absent from traditional theology. Furthermore, an adequate discussion of it would require a book of its own, and not merely a few pages in a book whose primary concern is with something else. What is, however, both relevant and necessary to our present task is to give some consideration to the relation between the moral approach and that of traditional theology; that, and that only, will be attempted here.

It has been argued at some length in the preceding chapters that the fundamental question for theology is, "Why do any finite beings exist at all?" and not merely, "Why has the realm of finite beings the particular characteristics which we observe in it?", though, as we have recognized, it is in practice impossible to ask the one question without at least thinking about the other. In addition we have tried to show that the common modern notions of a finite God or of a God to whom the creation of the world is necessary arise precisely from concentrating on the second question rather than the first; that is one of the main points of our discussion of the works of Whitehead and Tennant, as well as of the writings of several other philosophers who have been referred to in less detail. It may, however, be added, in qualification of this

[1] E. I. Watkin, however, argues with some force that the moral argument is in essence contained in St. Augustine's argument from the abstract absolute of Truth (*Theism, Agnosticism and Atheism*, pp. 119–21).

statement, that if there *is* any question about the nature, rather than about the existence, of finite beings which might offer some hope of arriving at the existence of a God who is, in the fullest sense, independent of his creation, it will presumably be some question about the nature of the human mind; for, among all the beings of which we have experience in this world of ours, the human mind is, so far as we know, the only one which has the capacity of transcending the limits of the finite order and of directing its operation to affairs which are not altogether bound up with finite being.[1] It was asserted above, in our discussion of mysticism, that, while the natural object of the finite human intellect is finite being, its only adequate and completely satisfying object is the infinite Being which is God. In a similar, but not quite identical, way we can assert that, while the immediate object of the human will, in its fallen state, is finite good, its only adequate and completely satisfying object is the supreme Good which is God.[2] We cannot, however, argue with any safety from this fact of unsatisfiedness alone to the existence of a perfect Good in which man's moral needs are to be satisfied. If we already have reasons to believe in the existence of God, we can see why man is unsatisfied with finite good and can also see that God is the one Good in which man can find full satisfaction. But until we have those reasons such an inference is at best extremely precarious. This reservation is very similar to the objection which Tennant brings against Kant when he asserts that "if the *summum bonum* has its possibility of realization guaranteed by the concept itself, Kant in principle employs the ontological argument in ethics after demolishing it in theology," since Kant "merely argues that God, a regulative idea for the theoretical reason, is a postulate for the practical reason: *if* the moral order of the world (as Kant conceived it) is to stand, and what ought to be is to be, God must

[1] The possibility of the existence of pure spirits or of rational psychosomatic beings other than man need not be taken into account here, as in any case the content of their moral experience is not accessible to our examination.

[2] "Similar, but not quite identical," because, whereas the intellect bears immediately upon finite being because of its own *finitude*, the will of fallen man bears immediately upon finite goods not because of its finitude but because of its *fallenness*. The essential difference is that intellect is a faculty of possession, while will is a faculty of tendency; we can know only what is present to our mind, whereas we can desire what is absent. Even the intellect of the saint cannot have God-in-his-essence as its object until it has been altogether "deified" by God himself in the Beatific Vision (or in some transient foretaste of it), while even imperfect Christians, if they are in a state of grace, can have God-in-his-essence as the object of their will. (This does not, of course, mean that the *degree* in which the will loves its object is necessarily perfect.) With this explanation the statement in the text may stand.

exist."[1] And it is of importance to notice that most philosophers who have elaborated the moral argument in recent years have refused to take man's moral sense in isolation as the basis of their treatment. Thus Dr. W. R. Sorley wrote that "the argument . . . may be looked upon as a special and striking extension of the cosmological argument,"[2] while Tennant affirms that moral considerations "supply the coping-stone of a cumulative teleological argument."[3] Again, Dr. William Temple, in his massive work *Nature, Man and God*, while he adopts the moral value or the Good as his fundamental category, builds up his case for theism not upon the mere occurrence of man's intuition of the Good, but upon the fact that the world is of such a character as to give rise to minds in which, among other properties, this intuition is found. And, while Professor A. E. Taylor, in the first volume of his *Faith of a Moralist*, seems to go further than any of the writers just mentioned towards finding a foundation for theistic belief in the moral consciousness of man alone, it is significant that when, in his essay on "The Vindication of Religion," he sets out to give a complete presentation of the case for theism, the moral argument forms only one strand in a threefold cord, of which the other two strands are formed by the cosmological and teleological arguments and by the argument from religious experience respectively.[4] Nor must we forget the vigorous defence of the cosmological approach in his long article on "Theism" in the *Encyclopædia of Religion and Ethics*. It should also be noticed that, in developing the moral argument, he is careful to insist that what he is dealing with is not the bare concept of morality, but the moral life as a concrete constituent of human experience.

It appears from such instances as the above that, while the moral approach is to be accepted as the great constructive addition which modern philosophy has made to the edifice of traditional theology, it depends for its full force upon the prior, or at least the simultaneous, acceptance of a more metaphysical investigation. We must add that the consequences of a religious kind which the moral argument will involve will depend very largely upon the form that this metaphysical investigation has taken. If the moral argument is taken in conjunction with a cosmological doctrine

[1] *Phil. Theol.*, II, pp. 97, 96.
[2] *Moral Values and the Idea of God*, p. 348.   [3] *Phil. Theol.*, II, p. 100.
[4] This is the second essay in *Essays Catholic and Critical*. It is only right to add that Taylor does not claim demonstrative certainty for his arguments, and that he introduces "faith" in much the same way as Tennant does (op. cit., p. 32).

that asserts as the ground of the cosmos a "God" who is finite or to whom the cosmos is necessary for the full expression of his activity, the response which the moral consciousness demands being directed towards the object thus postulated, religion will tend to lay its main emphasis upon fellowship and co-operation with the Deity; this trend is strongly marked in Whitehead's system and less strongly in Tennant's and Ward's. If God is conceived as purely immanent, man's effort will be directed inwards in a quietistic self-stultification, as in the religions of India. But if God is conceived as strictly infinite and the world as adding nothing to his inherent perfection, the dominant note will be one of adoration and self-abandonment, and of supplication for a union with God which only God can confer; this is the position of historical Christianity.

A few words must be added about the problem of evil, if only because it provides the objection which the modern man or woman nearly always falls back upon as his or her conclusive reason for rejecting the theistic position, however convincingly this may seem to have been stated. It is commonly alleged that academic theologians are remarkably insensitive to its gravity; with the implication that this is due to the seclusion of their lives from the hard realities of the contemporary world. To some extent this accusation may be admitted;[1] the system of McTaggart was woefully deficient in any real understanding of the problem, Tennant deals with it better, though still unsatisfactorily,[2] and Taylor better still.[3] But one of the most profound discussions of it in recent years is due to one who is not a professional philosopher or theologian at all, namely, Mr. C. S. Lewis, in his short book, *The Problem of Pain*. His discussion is not merely philosophical, but theological; it is based upon a rigidly orthodox, but by no means cut-and-dried Christian position. It is indeed doubtful whether one can get very far towards a solution by purely philosophical considerations; the theist will, in the last resort, go on repeating, "I have proved that God exists and is both good and almighty, therefore the problem of evil must be somehow soluble, although I can't solve it," while the objector will as often reply, "But the problem is obviously insoluble, therefore there must be some flaw in your arguments about God, although I can't see where it is."

---

[1] On the other hand, it is right to remark that very few ordinary men and women have so gloomy an outlook upon life as the radically pessimistic philosopher.
[2] *Phil. Theol.*, II, ch. vii.   [3] *Faith of a Moralist*, I, ch. v.

Only one or two remarks which seem relevant will be offered here.

In the first place, the problem is one which religion creates for itself, not one which it finds awaiting a solution. If there is no God, then there is no problem of reconciling the existence of pain and sin with his love and power; and, while the atheist may with reason urge against theism that it has set itself a problem which it cannot solve, he has no business to feel evil as constituting a problem for him, except in the purely intellectual sense of causing him to wonder where it came from. In actual fact, however, very many atheists appear to labour under a gigantic sense of resentment for the existence of evil, although, on their own hypothesis, there is no one for them to be resentful against; this note is, for example, very marked in Bertrand Russell's famous essay on "A Free Man's Worship."[1] This is very mysterious, and almost leads one to suspect that the atheists have been indulging in a little surreptitious theism on the quiet.

Secondly, evil, at any rate in the form of pain (which is the form in which it troubles most people), is only a problem because people rebel against it. No one, so far as is known, has ever lost his faith as a result of the muscular and dermatic pain involved in rowing for Cambridge in the Boat Race, though, if the mere existence of pain as such is incompatible with theism, it should provide the material for as strong an argument against religion as is furnished by all the suffering involved in a world-war. The fact is that suffering is rebelled against only if no end can be seen which appears to be proportionate to it. In the case mentioned, the suffering is believed to be amply compensated for by the hope of arriving at Mortlake Brewery before the Oxford Boat. This suggests that the problem of pain presents itself to us largely because of the limitations of our knowledge and imagination. If we could see as God sees, it would, for all we know, be transparently obvious that the sufferings of the present time are not worthy to be compared with the glory that shall be revealed in us, and indeed that the sufferings were instrumental to the glory.

This is perhaps as far as one can get towards a solution from philosophical considerations; they are almost entirely negative in their scope. But the Christian religion, with its teaching of union with Christ and of reparation for sin, provides a positive technique for dealing with evil, both moral and physical. "Consider

[1] *Mysticism and Logic*, ch. iii.

the fact of suffering," writes Mr. F. J. Sheed, "Christianity answers . . . that suffering would be altogether intolerable if there were no God, but can be turned to the highest uses of man if there be a God. Atheism answers that the fact of suffering proves that there is no God. But this does not reduce the world's sufferings by one hair-breadth, it only takes away hope."[1] "The Christian idea of God," writes the Abbé Nédoncelle, "has lighted up the ugliness of evil, and has shown itself to be the best and most practical weapon with which to fight suffering and sin. Christianity has done something better than expound the nature of evil: it has provided mankind with a ferment which dissolves it. It has produced the beatitude of the Saints and the radiance of their healing influence. Christ has shown us, once and for all, how suffering should be faced, and we have only to imitate him. He suffered in achieving the impossible: in turning suffering—something which is hateful and bad—into action, into the most fruitful of all actions, into one which clothes us in humility, and establishes us in a utter disinterestedness."[2]

ADDITIONAL NOTE D TO CHAPTER XII

NATURAL THEOLOGY AND THE DOCTRINE OF THE TRINITY

As we have seen, traditional theism asserts that the consideration of finite beings, while it can assure us of the existence of God, is powerless to give us any quidditative knowledge of his interior essence; it follows from this that the Doctrine of the Trinity falls outside the proper sphere of natural theology. This conclusion is in no way contradicted by the fact that St. Augustine has seen an analogue of the three divine Persons in the natural structure of the human soul,[3] or by the universal analogism of St. Bonaventure, in virtue of which the latter saint can write that "a creature of the world is, as it were, a book in which there shines forth, is depicted and can be read the Trinity that made it";[4] for, as the very reluctance of these two great Christian thinkers to separate natural

---

[1] *Communism and Man*, p. 187.
[2] *Baron Friedrich von Hügel*, p. 120.   [3] *De Trin.*, ix, x, xiv.
[4] "*Creatura mundi est quasi quidam liber in quo relucet, repræsentatur et legitur Trinitas fabricatrix.*" (*Breviloquium*, II, 12, 1; quoted Gilson, *Phil. of St. Bonaventure*, E.T., p. 214.)

from revealed theology would suggest, this discernment of a
trinitarian structure in creation is not the product of natural
theology at all, but arises from a deliberate reflection upon the
created world from the standpoint of the Christian revelation.
This *ex post facto* character is even more clear in such a case as that
of Hegel, with his extraordinary identification of the distinctions
of his secondary triad with the Persons of the Trinity.[1] And it
seems to be generally agreed that the parallels to the Christian
Trinity which can be found in certain non-Christian religions are
very remote indeed.[2] We need not, however, deny that, once the
doctrine has been accepted, we may then be able to see how the
three Persons each participate in their several modes in the work
of creation. Thus, St. Thomas himself, after vigorously asserting
that "all things caused are the common work of the whole Godhead" and hence that "to create is not proper to any one Person,
but is common to the whole Trinity," immediately adds that, just
as "the craftsman works through the word conceived in his mind,
and through the love of his will regarding some object," so also
"God the Father made the creature through his Word, which is
his Son, and through his Love, which is the Holy Ghost."[3] Indeed,
he goes on to affirm with St. Augustine[4] that in creatures there is
necessarily found a trace (*vestigium*) of the Trinity. "In rational
creatures," he tells us, "there is found the representation of the
Trinity by way of *image*," since the processions of the Son and the
Spirit are analogous to the rational operations of intellect and
will, but "in all creatures there is found the *trace* of the Trinity,"
since as substances they represent the cause and principle which
is the Father, as possessing form and species they represent the
Son, and as having relation of order they represent the Holy
Ghost.[5] And he refers back to an earlier article in which, after
denying (since the creative power of God belongs to the unity of
the essence and not to the distinction of the Persons) that God can
be known as Trinity from the consideration of created things, he
has nevertheless admitted that reason can confirm that God is
Trinity, when this has already been accepted on other grounds.[6]
And he admits that some of the Greek philosophers had an obscure
awareness of some kind of plurality in the Godhead, though he

[1] Cf. McTaggart, *Studies in Hegelian Cosmology*, ch. viii.
[2] See, e.g., Dr. Berriedale Keith in *E.R.E.*, XII, s.v. "Trimūrti."
[3] *S. Theol*, I, xlv, 6, *sed contra* et *resp*.   [4] *De Trin.*, vi, 10.
[5] *S. Theol.*, I, xlv, 7c. Cf. Hooker, *Eccl. Pol.*, V, lvi, 5.
[6] Ibid., I, xxxii, 2c et ad 2.

adds that it was partial and inaccurate. We may not unreasonably suspect that, had he known about it, he would have made a similar admission about the Hindu *Trimūrti*.

From a similar *ex post facto* standpoint it can be seen that the doctrine of the Trinity provides the great bulwark against the tendency, which we have seen to be so prominent in modern theistic philosophy, to view the world as necessary to God in order that God shall have an arena for his self-expression and an object for his love. In theory, of course, we can assert simply that in the contemplation of his own perfection and the love of his own goodness God has an entirely adequate sphere for the exercise of his supremely full and vital activity. But, in practice, unless we believe in the eternal generation of the divine Word and the eternal spiration of the Spirit of love, we shall probably find ourselves saying with Dr. Tennant that "God without a world, or a Real other, is not God, but an abstraction."[1] We shall then argue with him that, while "a self or subject does not depend, *quâ* an existent or as to its being, upon any object to which it stands in the relation of presentation and attention," yet "relation or *rapport* is essential for any existent's assuming the rôle of, and being, a subject,"[2] without realizing that this is exactly the kind of argument which, in conjunction with the notion of *internal* relations, a trinitarian will use in support of the doctrine of the Trinity.[3] We may add that Tennant's criticism of this cardinal doctrine of the Christian Faith does not seem very convincing. According to him, it claims for the three persons a status between the substantival and the adjectival which is inconceivable.[4] But here he has surely missed the point. The three Persons are distinct and substantival (not, be it observed, three *substances*, but three *substantives*, three *hypostases*), but this does not involve that they are three Gods, simply because the processions within the being of God are *necessary*. Of course, if the creation of the world was necessary too, this would place the Second and Third Persons on the same level as the world itself, and we should be involved in something rather akin to Arianism. But the traditional view of creation stands or falls with the contingency of the world. It is because the creation of the world is contingent, whereas the processions of the Persons are necessary, that we can at the same time assert that God without the world is still God, and that the three Persons are not three Gods.

[1] *Phil. Theol.*, II, p. 168.   [2] Ibid., II, p. 167.   [3] Cf. p. 177, n. 1 *supra*.
[4] *Phil. Theol.*, II, Appendix: Note D, p. 267 f. Cf. G. L. Prestige, *God in Patristic Thought*, p. xxviii.

In conclusion, some very tentative suggestions might be made here as to the way in which the "trace" of the Trinity is to be observed in the created world.

There are in the world two great contrasts which force themselves upon our attention. The first is the contrast between the actual and the possible; the second the contrast between permanence and change.

(a) The contrast between the actual and the possible has come in recent years very much to the front in modern philosophy, although the distinction between a realm of experience and a realm of ideas is at least as old as Plato. The materialistic-scientific philosophy of the last century tried to obliterate the distinction completely. It was claimed that a sufficient account could be given of the universe by supposing it to consist of an aggregate of material particles moving under the direction of a few simply defined mathematical laws. As a matter of fact, even if this claim were true, it would still be necessary to account for the initial configuration of the particles at some arbitrarily chosen zero of time, and to explain why the laws governing their motions should be those that were actually observed to hold rather than any of the multiplicity of other laws which could, without any violation of logic, be equally easily imagined. But Victorian science, under the baneful shadow of Herbert Spencer, was content to ignore these awkward questions and to take the world of experience as a self-obvious axiomatic fact. In recent years, however, the breakdown of the materialistic theory has forced scientific philosophers to recognize the essential contingency of the universe. Different scientists at the present day give us different models of the ultimate constitution of the physical world; but whether they correlate phenomena by the concepts of q-numbers, probability-waves, matrices or what not, it is clear that the universe which we experience possesses no logical necessity. (We have commented on the unconvincingness of Eddington's attempt to show that the actual world is inevitable.[1]) The fundamental thesis of Whitehead's cosmology is, as we have seen, the distinction between the realm of possibility and that of actuality, between "eternal objects" and the "actual occasions" into which these are ingredient; and the ultimate problem, which he tries to overcome by the two notions of actual entities as units of creativity and of God as the ideal locus of all eternal objects, is to explain why

[1] See p. 51 *supra*.

the eternal objects are ingredient into the actual occasions in the particular modes in which they *are* ingredient rather than in others which are equally possible.

(*b*) The second contrast is that between permanence and change, and it is well to note that these two notions of permanence and change, though they are often felt to be contradictory, are both necessarily involved if there is to be any experience of a world at all. I can only say "*A* is permanent" if there is something by whose change I measure the passage of time. I can only say "*B* has changed" if, *in some sense*, *B* has remained the same; otherwise instead of *B* having changed, we shall have two totally different entities, a B_1 which is annihilated and a B_2 which appears in its place. Like the first one, this contrast has come to be recognized as fundamental in modern philosophy. Leaving out of account the wilder forms of "philosophy of change," we need again only think of Whitehead's self-creative actual occasions. Incidentally, this same contrast lies behind the Aristotelian and Thomist doctrine of potentiality and act.

In consequence, therefore, of these two contrasts we are presented with three fundamental and irreducible, yet mutually implicated, facts of experience which can be summarized as follows:

(i) There is an infinite realm of abstract possibility.

(ii) There is, selected from this realm, a limited realm of actual concrete occurrence.

(iii) In contrast with the former realm, there is in this latter realm a process of change.

The suggestion which is here made is that these three facts are to be correlated (in Thomist language, "appropriated") to the three Persons of the Trinity, as, in virtue of their mutual coinherence, they all concur in the unity of the creative act.

God the Father, the great Catholic Creed asserts, is the Maker (*Factor*, Ποιητής) of all things visible and invisible, while through God the Son all things "came into being" (*facta sunt*, ἐγένετο). This is the obvious force of ἐγένετο, and it is perhaps not without point to remark that *facta sunt* is at least as much the active of *fio* as it is the passive of *facio*. Thus the Creed affirms that, while in the last resort everything derives from the Father, who is the ground of all possibility, the concrete existence of the actual world is the outcome of the peculiar mode of action of the

Son. (We are tempted to identify Whitehead's principle of "concretion" or "decision" with the Son, but in view of Whitehead's radically unorthodox doctrine of actual entities as self-creative, we could do so only with many reservations.) If we remember that the Son is also the Father's Word, the complete expression and inner reduplication of himself, the *God from God* who is the Father's Image, this will not seem fantastic. In the perfect intellectual act which is the eternal generation of the Word, the whole realm of possibility which is rooted in the divine fecundity will receive its ideal expression; as St. Thomas tells us, the ideas of all created things are, in a certain way, in God.[1] They are, we might say, uttered by the Father to himself in the generation of the Son as his Image. But the selection and expression of ideas in the created realm will then fall to the Son "by whom all things come into being." Thus, as St. Paul writes, "To us there is one God the Father, *of* whom are all things (ἐξ οὗ τὰ πάντα) . . . and one Lord, Jesus Christ, *by* whom are all things (δι' οὗ τά πάντα) . . ."[2] The subtle distinction between εκ and διά gives the exact shade of meaning required to bring out the difference between the rôles played by the Father and the Son in the creative act.[3]

Can we now associate the third fact, that of change, with the Holy Spirit? Can we "appropriate" to him the "becomingness" of the universe? The Nicene Creed tells us that the Spirit is "the Lord, the Giver of Life" (*Dominum et vivificantem*, τὸ Κύριον τὸ ζωοποιόν), and the essence of life in the material realm is movement, adaptability and change. It is surely not fanciful to see the peculiar action of the Holy Spirit, no less than that of the creative Word, in every event of the world's history. There is a variant reading of a text in the first chapter of St. John's Gospel, which tells us that that which was made was life in the divine Word, and if we can take this in conjunction with the truth that the Spirit is the Giver of Life, we can then recognize that at the heart of the world's process is the peculiar work of the Holy Ghost. St. Thomas tells us that "seeing that the Holy Ghost proceeds by way of love, and that love is an impelling and moving force, any movement

---

[1] *S. Theol.*, I, xv. *S.c.G.*, I, li; liii *ad fin.*   [2] 1 Cor. viii, 6.
[3] It may be remarked that Bulgakov sees the divine Essence rather than the Logos as the *locus* of the ideas to be realized in creation, apparently on the "Bonaventuran" ground that creation reflects not just the Father but the tripersonal Godhead. See *The Wisdom of God*, ch. ii. Cf. also p. 140, n. 1 *supra*. The two views do not appear irreconcilable.

that God causes in things is rightly appropriated to the Holy Ghost,"[1] and he interprets this, not only of the movement of living creatures, but also, on the strength of *Genesis* i, 2, of the initial origination of created being.

While emphasizing again the speculative nature of this exposition, we may sum it up as follows. Creation is not, as the deists conceived it, an isolated occurrence which happened once for all in the remote past; it is the act of love and power, continuous from our standpoint but timeless from God's, by which the triune Deity sustains the world in being. In this creative act, all the three Persons take part; and, just as they are not three Gods but three Persons united in one indivisible Godhead, so there are not three acts but three elements indivisibly combined in one act. At the root of all created being there is the infinite potentiality of all possible existence, grounded in God the Father and imaged in the eternal generation of the Word; superimposed upon this there is the contribution of the Divine Word, the principle of decision and concretion, resolving pure potentiality into the actuality of occurrence; while the full character of the being as embodied in the world-process is completed by the inbreathing of the Holy Spirit, who confers upon it the character of temporality and becomingness which makes it an actual member of the finite, temporal world.

Thus, it may be suggested, the doctrine of the Trinity may be seen to be directly relevant to cosmology, although it is not itself to be deduced from the consideration of the created realm.[2]

[1] *S.c.G.*, IV, xx.

[2] Chambat, in *Présence et Union*, argues very strongly that, in the Thomist doctrine, the principle that the acts of God *ad extra* are acts of the one nature and not of the three Persons applies only in the order of efficient causality, and that in the order of exemplary causality creation is an extension into the finite order of the processions of the divine Persons.

CHAPTER XIII

CONCLUSION

COMPARATIVELY little need be added in bringing this book to its end. It may, however, be well to summarize briefly the course that the argument has followed.

We began, in the Introduction, by distinguishing between the *ordo essendi*, the order in which things ultimately exist, and the *ordo cognoscendi*, the order in which we come to know them, and remarked that from the former, though not from the latter, standpoint the doctrine of God is the primary doctrine of the Christian Religion. Observing in passing the universal belief of mankind in a Being who, however dimly he may be apprehended, is the Being whom the theist identifies as God, we then saw how Christian theism, with its two main sources of Judæo-Christian and Græco-Roman origin, respectively, received a coherent, and for Western Christendom, a normative formulation in the transformation which Aristotelianism underwent in the hands of St. Thomas Aquinas.

In the Second Chapter, as a preliminary to investigating the question of the existence of God, we endeavoured to elucidate the precise meaning of he word "God" in Christian usage. Definition by genus and difference was seen to be impossible, for the reason that God does not belong to any genus. We then examined the Anselmian definition of God as *aliquid quo majus nihil cogitari potest*, with its implication of infinity as the formal constituent of the nature of God, and noted that, in contrast, the Thomist conception of God as *ipsum esse subsistens*, while practically equivalent to it, gives this place to the notion of being.

The Third Chapter began by asking the question: Why do we believe that God exists?, and it was seen that in all probability no two persons would answer this question in the same way. Rejecting the view that there is a natural human faculty by which we could apprehend God with the same directness as we apprehend material objects, we went on to divide the grounds on which belief in God has been alleged to be justified into three: religious experience, revelation, and reason. Our judgment on religious experience was that, while it might be overwhelmingly convincing

191

to the person who was its subject, it was far too inexpressible to provide by itself the basis of a formulated argument; we observed also that Catholic theology had been very reluctant to admit, even in genuine mystical experience, any direct apprehension or immediate knowledge of the essence of God. We then glanced at the contention of many neo-Protestants that the only knowledge of God that is not hopelessly perverted is that given in the revelation of Jesus Christ, and concluded with some discussion of the relation between natural and revealed theology.

The next three chapters were devoted to an examination of the traditional approach to the problem of God's existence. In Chapter Four the Ontological Argument of St. Anselm was seen to have three vulnerable points; in particular in its attempt to pass from the realm of logic to that of concrete existence. Attention was then turned to arguments from the existence of finite being, and especially to the one general argument of which, according to Fr. Garrigou-Lagrange, the five classical arguments of St. Thomas are refinements.

In the Fifth Chapter the Thomist "Five Ways" were considered in detail, while in the Sixth Chapter an attempt was made to estimate their significance and validity. The criticisms brought by Professor Broad against all arguments of the cosmological type were seen to be inconclusive, and indeed to rest upon the attribution to traditional theism of a view which it vigorously repudiates. It was seen that the arguments depend upon the recognition of finite beings as possessing both being and finitude. They are arguments from finite being as such, and not from any special kind of finite being; and, while they cannot give us a knowledge of what God is in his inner essence, they can tell us a great deal about him from the fact that he is the ultimate source of all being other than his own. The question as to whether the Five Ways all necessarily pointed to the same ultimate being as one another led us to consider how far the syllogistic form really represented the bearing of the arguments in their essential nature. We came to the conclusion that syllogistic statement was primarily a device for persuading our minds to apprehend finite beings in their radical finitude and thus, in so apprehending them, to apprehend the existence of the God who is their Creator. The implications of this conclusion were developed at some length, and an explanation was offered of the difficulty experienced by modern people in accepting the validity of the theistic arguments.

This led us, in Chapter Seven, to investigate the relation between intellect and intuition, since the position arrived at in the previous chapter obviously involved the attribution to the human mind of the capacity to achieve some kind of intuition of the essence of the beings which it experiences. Against all epistemological theories of sensationalist type it was asserted that the intellect is by its very nature equipped to abstract from finite beings their intelligible content and to grasp, however partially and obscurely, their inner essence. We saw that this doctrine was at the heart of Fr. D'Arcy's extremely impressive argument for the theistic interpretation of the world; and we also saw that it, or something very like it, was absolutely necessary if any answer was to be found to one of the most important problems of philosophy, which sensationalist systems were quite powerless to solve, namely, the problem of induction. A note was added on the inter-relations of Certainty and Certitude.

The Eighth Chapter took as its subject God and the World, and developed the doctrine of *analogia entis*. In it we maintained that the whole course of the preceding argument compelled us to believe, on the one hand, that the world is entirely dependent upon God, while, on the other, God is in no way dependent on the world, so that the relation between God and the world is an entirely one-sided one. On the part of God, therefore, creation is an extra-temporal act and is not really distinct from preservation. Two great questions were then dealt with. The first was how, if God is the fullness of being, anything can exist other than God; the second, why, granted that God can create a world, he should decide to do so.

The answer to the first question was seen to lie in the fact that, since God is strictly infinite, God and the world do not "add up." The second we admitted to enshrine an ultimate mystery; but we pointed out that the very impossibility of answering it is a direct consequence of the position that we have adopted. No answer, other than the freedom of the divine will, can be given either to the question why God should create a world at all, or to the question why, if he does create one, it should be this one rather than any other. Any world that God makes must be good, but no world can be the best of all possible worlds, for any world that God could make would fall infinitely short of his own perfection and therefore leave room for an infinite number of better ones. We concluded this chapter with some criticisms of Dr. W. R.

Matthews, and added a note on the teaching, in many respects
similar, of the late James Ward.

In Chapter Nine we discussed the Divine Attributes, so far as
they were relevant to our main line of argument. The consideration of freedom and omnipotence led on to some brief remarks on
miracles.

In the Tenth Chapter we considered at some length the
Transcendence and Immanence of God. The two elements were
seen to be mutually related, and it was asserted that to lay stress
on one to the exclusion of the other leads to religious interpretations which are not only erroneous but also unstable. As instances
of transcendentalist error we mentioned Deism and Mohammedanism. The former was seen to pass easily over into a
formalistic immanentism; while in the latter a compensating
factor for its extreme transcendence was found in the development
of Sufi mysticism. An obvious example of modern transcendentalism within the sphere of Christianity appeared in the guise
of the neo-Protestant revival, with its strongly marked anti-
mystical trend.

Typical instances of unbalanced immanentism were found in
the religions of Asia: Brahmanism, Buddhism and Taoism. As
formulated European systems of immanentist type we considered
the writings of two modern Eastern Orthodox thinkers, Professor
Nicolas Berdyaev and Fr. Alexis van der Mensbrugghe. We ended
this chapter by pointing out how, both in sociology and in mystical
theology, it is essential to keep the balance between immanence
and transcendence. The mystical doctrine of Gardeil was summarized, and it was seen, in consequence, that the Catholic
notion of the *analogia entis* between God and the world made it
possible to construct a mystical theology which was not vulnerable
to the attacks of the neo-Protestants.

In the following two chapters we discussed, in the light of the
conclusions already drawn, the approaches to theism of two of the
most typical and distinguished of modern natural theologians,
Professor A. N. Whitehead and Dr. F. R. Tennant. In both of
them we discovered certain defects. Whitehead's adoption of
"creativity" as the fundamental characteristic of finite beings was
seen to have diverted his attention away from the existence of
things to their behaviour, and so to have caused him to be satisfied
with the notion of a purely immanent deity, while his neglect of

the concept of *analogia entis* left him at last with only a finite God. Tennant's position was far more satisfactory. His arguments for the reality of the soul and of the extra-mental world were recognized as of the highest value. But a certain hesitation to follow these arguments to their natural conclusion and an unfortunate introduction of "faith," rather than of some kind of intuition, in order to solve the problem of induction led him to a final position which, while it is indeed far more acceptable than that of Whitehead, falls short of that of traditional theism. Two notes were added in which a brief discussion was made of two important questions falling outside the strict limits of this book: namely, the Moral Argument, with the closely related Problem of Evil, and the connections between Natural Theology and the revealed doctrine of the Holy Trinity.

Whether the attempt that has been made in this book to vindicate the traditional doctrine of God and of his relation to the world be judged as a success or as a failure, we cannot leave the subject without emphasizing its supreme importance. For, on the one hand, unless God is, in his essential nature, altogether exalted above his world and independent of it, we shall have no absolute standard by which human exploits are to be judged; the logical outcome of unbalanced immanentism is the moral relativism which, both in personal life and in world affairs, is so evident at the present day. On the other hand, unless, at the very heart of its being, the world is in constant and intimate contact with God, God will be so disconnected from the world as to be irrelevant to it; and the logical outcome of unbalanced transcendentalism is a doctrine of God as unknowable by man which can be counterbalanced only by an anti-rational revelationism. Dr. Demant has written, in words which we have quoted before, that if the faith has steadily lost its transforming power over the last three centuries, "the reason is to be found in the Christian mind having split, in its innermost outlook, into cosmic interpretations which bring God within the world process and purely redemptive theologies which take man as religious out of it, leaving his actual existence at the mercy of its floods."[1] If in this book we have been concerned more with rebutting the immanentist than the transcendentalist error, the reason is that it is the former towards which

[1] *The Religious Prospect*, p. 214. See p. 142 *supra*.

natural theology has tended in recent years; the transcendentalist extreme is almost entirely represented by a certain recent but very influential school of theologians to whom the very idea of natural theology is anathema.

In English-speaking countries it is still unfashionable, though less so than formerly, to avow oneself to be an atheist; there is thus a temptation to those who do not believe in the God of traditional Christian theology to apply the word "God" to whatever entity or influence or principle they may suppose to underlie the phenomenal world and then to ask what God is like. The result is that man's conception of God changes with every fashion of thought. In contrast, the traditional approach of Christian philosophy has been first to formulate the Christian conception of God, and then to inquire whether he exists or not. In other words, the traditional attitude has considered the primary problem for investigation to be that of the *existence* of God, while the "modern" attitude has considered the primary problem to be that of his *nature*. This is more than just a difference of method. It touches the very nerve of the Christian life, for while the traditional approach judges man by the measure of God, the "modern" approach at least tends to judge God by the measure of man. The famous Aberdonian epitaph—

> "Here lie I, Martin Elginbrodde;
> Ha'e mercy o' my soul, Lord God,
> As I would do, were I Lord God
> And ye were Martin Elginbrodde"—

puts in a nutshell the anthropocentrism of this type of thought. How different in effect is the ejaculation attributed to St. Augustine: "O my God, if I were God and thou Augustine, I would wish that thou wert God and I Augustine!"

For only a God who is, in St. Anselm's phrase, "something than which nothing greater can be thought," or, as St. Thomas puts it, "subsistent Being itself," can be the adequate object of Christian devotion, which has always believed itself to reach its climax in the sheer adoration in which the creature, knowing its own entire insufficiency and its relative nothingness, casts itself in complete abasement before the majesty and holiness of a God whom it recognizes as being altogether complete without it and yet as conferring upon it its very existence and tending it with the most gentle and intimate love. "Religion is adoration," wrote Baron von Hügel in a never-to-be-forgotten phrase,[1] and the name of its Object is *I am*. If there is nothing in reality corresponding to this concept, then the Christian life is based upon an utter and tragic error, and the whole structure of Christian devotion falls into ruins. The Catholic Christian, if he is convinced that no such being exists, will not say that, after all, God is not so great as he thought; he will say quite simply that, after all, there is no God. *Dicet in corde suo, Non est Deus.* God may or may not exist, but the Catholic will either believe in a God who is the self-existent Being than which nothing greater can be thought, or he will cease to claim that, in any sense in which he is interested in the word, there is a God at all. *Aut Deus aut nihil* will be his motto; and whether God exists or not, his glory he will not give to another. To adore any being less than one who comprises in himself all possible perfection would be to the Catholic a kind of conceptual idolatry. The point at issue is well brought out in the dialogue between St. Augustine and Evodius which Fr. M. C. D'Arcy quotes in his essay on "The Philosophy of St. Augustine." "If," the Saint says to Evodius, "we can find something indubitably superior to our reason, would you hesitate to call that, whatever it be, God?" And the answer of Evodius, with which Augustine agrees, is, "I would not straightway . . . call that God. For it is not one to whom my reason is inferior whom I would call God, but one who has no superior."[2] And from the religious point of view, the reason why Professor A. E. Taylor's conclusion is so profoundly satisfactory in comparison with that of Whitehead or Tennant is to be found in the place which it leaves for adoration.[3] It is true that he finds it not primarily in the metaphysical realm, but in that realm .of religious experience which we have considered as being, when taken in isolation, of doubtful evidential value. On the other hand, it must be recognized that he does not take it in isolation, but as the culmination of a threefold argument whose primary steps are provided by cosmological and moral considerations. And we have also agreed with Fr. D'Arcy, on the ground that the classical arguments lead us not merely to intellectual acquiescence in a proposition but to a genuine appre-

---

[1] Cf. *Essays and Addresses*, II, p. 224. "The most fundamental need, duty, honour and happiness of man, is not petition, nor even contrition, nor again even thanksgiving; these three kinds of prayer which, indeed, must never disappear out of our spiritual lives; but *adoration*." Cf. also I, p. 90; II, p. 233.

[2] *A Monument to St. Augustine*, p. 167.

[3] I do not, of course, suggest that this is an argument for its truth.

hension of God as present by immensity at the ontological root of finite beings, that, while the argument from religious experience must not be taken in isolation, there is a presentation of it in which it appears as an interior view of the argument from contingency,[1] and therefore has a real, though subsidiary, validity. In any case, our conclusion remains, that the God of traditional theism is identical with the God of Catholic devotion. Reason, as St. Thomas says, tells us that God exists, rather than what, in his inner nature, he is; but reason is supplemented by revelation and, although all knowledge of God in this life must be through his effects, when those effects are the unfolding of his secrets to the soul as it lives in the Revelation itself, as it advances in its sharing of the divine nature through the deepening of its sacramental union with the humanity of the Incarnate Word, we can achieve here upon earth a knowledge of God by grace as not merely the God of the philosophers and scholars, nor even as just the God of Abraham, Isaac and Jacob, but as the God and Father of our Lord Jesus Christ, who is the effulgence of the Father's glory and the very image of his substance: a knowledge in comparison with which all that the greatest philosophers can tell us fades into insignificance. Nevertheless, grace does not destroy nature, but perfects it; reason is not annihilated by revelation, but supplemented and transformed by it. And, while the Angelic Doctor himself left his great theological work unfinished on the ground that he had seen something in comparison with which all that he had written was as straw, he did not wish, like Faust, to burn his books. To be the handmaid to theology is, for philosophy, a great dignity, which confirms, instead of destroying, philosophy's autonomy in her own sphere. Philosophy comes to theology like the Queen of Sheba when she visited King Solomon, bearing with her treasures of inestimable price and yet awed into silence by the glory that confronted her. *Dominus meus et Deus meus!* cried the Apostle Thomas as he fell at the feet of the Risen Lord. *Deus meus et omnia!* repeated St. Francis of Assisi through his night of prayer. And Anselm and Aquinas are but echoing their worship when they write that God is *Aliquid quo majus nihil cogitari potest* and *Ipsum esse subsistens.*

[1] See p. 92 *supra*.

FAITH AND REASON: ANSELM AND AQUINAS

I

TO suggest that St. Anselm and St. Thomas Aquinas have something very important in common in their several approaches to the problem of the existence of God will no doubt appear highly paradoxical, for it is notorious that the famous ontological argument, which St. Anselm believed to be his supreme contribution to Christian thought, was emphatically and repeatedly rejected by St. Thomas as demonstrably invalid.[1] Nevertheless, I believe that they were in fundamental agreement upon the very basic question of the relation between rational argumentation for the existence of God and the great organic corpus of Christian revelation and tradition, and that this fact is not in any way weakened by their deep disagreement as to what type of rational argumentation for the existence of God is valid and what is not.

Students have often commented on the puzzling fact that both St. Anselm's ontological argument and St. Thomas Aquinas's *quinque viae* are embedded in a context in which the existence of God is already taken for granted. In the *Proslogion* the very title of the work shows that it is constructed as an address to a God who is already believed to exist, and the detailed working out of the contents confirms this indication; the chapter which immediately precedes that in which the ontological argument is expounded concludes with a prayer that God will grant the author to understand that which he already believes. In the *Summa Theologiae* of St. Thomas the point is made less flamboyantly but is equally unmistakable. The *Pars Prima* opens with the exposition of the nature of sacred doctrine as something beyond the reaches of the human reason and revealed by God through *sacra Scriptura*; and, although this is immediately succeeded by a solid slab of natural theology in which the five ways of "proving that there is

[1] *S. Th.* I. ii. 1 ad 2; *C. Gent.* I. x et xi; *In Boet. de Trin.* I. iii ad 6; *De Ver.* x. 12 ad 2; in these last two places Anselm is mentioned by name. It is clear from Anselm's remarks in the Prooemium to the *Proslogion* that it is the proof in the *Proslogion* and not that of the *Monologion* to which he attached supreme importance.

a God" hold the central place, St. Thomas has a disconcerting
way of inserting even into this latter a number of references to
Scripture and Christian doctrine without any apparent consciousness of breaking the rules. Attempts have indeed been made to
establish that St. Anselm was not in fact really writing rational
theology and that what appear, in both the *Monologion* and the
Proslogion, to be arguments for the existence of God are not
intended as arguments at all (it is rather more difficult to make the
corresponding assertion about St. Thomas!). Thus Dom Anselm
Stolz has asserted that "Anselm had not the slightest intention
of proving the existence of God" and that the *Proslogion* was "an
essay in mystical theology".[1] Dr. A. Koyré and Dr. A. Jacquin
are quoted to the same effect.[2] And Karl Barth has made a
heroic—and in my view a heroically perverse—attempt to show
that Anselm was really a Barthian before his time. For Anselm,
he writes, "it is a question of the proof of faith by faith which
was already established in itself without proof. And both—faith
that is proved and faith that proves—Anselm expressly understands
not as presuppositions that can be achieved by man but as
presuppositions that have been achieved by God."[3] How much
is true and how much is false in this interpretation I shall try to
show. But that, in contrast to Barth, Anselm is not an anti-
rationalist is, I think, clearly shown by two things. The former is
that in replying to the objections brought by Gaunilo against
the proof in the *Proslogion*, Anselm meets his opponent with purely
rational arguments. He never suggests that Gaunilo is a bad man
or a man who is lacking in the virtue of faith, but addresses him
as a *catholicus*. He is, in fact, too courteous to identify him with
the *insipiens*, though he does take him as the *insipiens*' mouthpiece,
catholicus pro insipiente.[4] And, addressing the *insipiens* in the person
of his advocate, Anselm does not accuse him either of the crime
of malice or of infidelity; he treats him as a man who has simply
gone wrong in an argument, a man who has not got his head
screwed on straight. Here Barth seems to me to score one of those
near-misses which are as good as a mile. "The *insipiens*", he writes,

[1] 'Zur Theologie Anselms im Proslogion', in *Catholica*, ii (1933), pp. 1–24. I take
this and the following reference from J. Pieper, *Scholasticism*, p. 70.
[2] A. Koyré, *L'Idée de Dieu dans la philosophie de St. Anselme*, p. 195; A. Jacquin,
Mélanges Mandonnet, ii (1929), pp. 67 f.
[3] *Fides Quaerens Intellectum*[2] (Zollikon, 1958), p. 163; E.T. (1960), p. 170.
[4] *Contra Gaun.*, prol. The *insipiens* is, of course, the "fool" in the Psalm who "says
in his heart, There is no God".

"can think of God as not existing. Anselm does not deny this fact. Neither does he ascribe it to lack of intellectual capacity or to malevolent inconsistency on the part of the *insipiens*. But only to the simple fact that he is an *insipiens* and as such thinks on a level where one can only think falsely—though without violating the inner consistency of that level . . . If there is anything at all that can serve to make him cease from being a fool it will be just this insistence—the presupposition on which the thought of God's non-existence is impossible: knowing God himself."[1] It is the last part of this passage with which I disagree, for it seems to me to be inconsistent with the whole tenor of Anselm's reply. I do not suppose this "knowing God himself" which Barth considers the fool to lack is, in Barth's view, some sort of mystical experience, for Barth and all those who think with him flee in horror from all forms of mysticism; I take it to be the experience of faith, conceived in the Barthian manner as excluding and repudiating the use of the reason altogether. But clearly, whether it is a matter of mystical experience or of faith, this is not what Anselm conceives the fool to lack. The *Liber apologeticus contra Gaunilonem* is not an appeal either to faith or to mystical experience, but to logic. It may be bad logic, as many including St. Thomas have thought, but it is undeniably logic. And the second reason why I take St. Anselm not to be an anti-rationalist is that he says so himself. In the Prooemium to the *Proslogion* he tells us that the name which he originally intended to give to the work was *Fides quaerens intellectum*, "Faith seeking to understand", and at the end of the first chapter he describes his aim in the following words: "I do not seek to understand in order that I may believe, but I believe in order that I may understand. For I believe this also, that I shall not understand unless I have believed."

Anselm is in fact a whole-hearted intellectualist, far more so in aim indeed than St. Thomas. Furthermore, he has a far greater confidence than St. Thomas in the power of human reason to demonstrate the truths of the Christian Faith. In the Preface to the *Monologion* he announces his intention to base his exposition upon reason and not upon the Scriptures, and he includes in his scope the doctrine of the Trinity, which St. Thomas will declare to be one of those truths which reason is powerless to discover.[2] Similarly, in the Preface to the *Cur Deus Homo* he tells us that, "leaving Christ out of the question as if nothing ever had been

<hr>

[1] Op. cit., pp. 158–9 = E.T., pp. 165–6.   [2] *S. Th.* I. xxxii. 1.

known of him", he is going to prove "by necessary arguments" (*rationibus necessariis*) that the whole man, body and soul, is made for a blessed immortality and that this end can only be brought about through this God-man Christ. Anselm is, of course, convinced that this understanding can only be brought about by means of "faith"; if it is understanding that is being sought, it is faith that seeks it. But this does not mean that the understanding which is being sought is itself a kind of faith; and how faith seeks it we shall inquire later on. My present point is that, unlike Barth, Anselm does not think that the desire to understand is either irreligious or futile. He is enough of a realist (in the modern sense) to know that the human reason is fallible and in need of divine illumination; he is also enough of an Augustinian to believe that this illumination is forthcoming. But he is not in the least ashamed of wanting to understand, though we have only to read the *Monologion* to see that this desire is both stimulated by and issues in a deep and burning love. And when he is arguing, whether he is expounding the ontological argument or answering Gaunilo's objections to it or proving that man can be saved only by a divine incarnation, he is arguing and doing nothing else, not preaching or appealing to revelation or testifying to a mystical experience.

Where, then, does faith come into the ontological argument? Primarily, I think, in providing Anselm with the definition of God from which he starts. It is true that the phrase *aliquid quo nihil majus cogitari potest*, "that than which nothing greater can be thought", does not occur in Scripture or, apparently, in any earlier Christian writer; it is Anselm's own invention. In this it differs from St. Thomas's more biblical assertion that "He who is" (*Qui est*) is the more proper name of God.[1] But Anselm is quite clear that in his definition he is only rendering explicit the essential character of the God of Christian faith. "We *believe*", he writes, "*credimus*, that thou art that than which nothing greater can be thought."[2] No such definition could apply to the first mover of Aristotle or the *demiourgos* of Plato's *Timaeus*, with their need of prime matter, pre-existent as themselves, as the necessary condition of their cosmological functions. And, although Anselm's definition might seem not unfittingly to apply to the One of Plotinus, it would be to the One of Plotinus as understood by Augustine rather than as understood (if indeed the word "under-

[1] Ibid., xiii. 11.   [2] *Pros.* ii.

stood" is applicable here) by Plotinus.[1] The matter has been stated
with his usual clarity by Étienne Gilson:

> That no trace of [Anselm's argument] exists in Greek thought is
> quite undisputed, but it does not seem to have occurred to anyone
> to ask either why the Greeks never dreamt of it, or why, on the
> contrary, it was perfectly natural that Christians should be the
> first to conceive it.
> Once the question is asked the answer is obvious. Thinkers like
> Plato and Aristotle, who do not identify God and being, could
> never dream of deducing God's existence from his idea; but when a
> Christian thinker like St. Anselm asks himself whether God exists
> he asks, in fact, whether Being exists, and to deny God is to affirm
> that Being does not exist. That is why the mind of St. Anselm was
> so long filled with the desire of finding a direct proof of the existence
> of God which should depend on nothing but the principle of con-
> tradiction. . . . The inconceivability of the non-existence of God
> could have no meaning at all save in a Christian outlook where
> God is identified with being, and where, consequently, it becomes
> contradictory to suppose that we think of him and think of him as
> non-existent.[2]

Leaving on one side, then, the question whether St. Anselm's
argument is valid or not—and I would agree with Gilson that
"to show that the affirmation of necessary existence is analytically
implied in the idea of God would be, as Gaunilo remarked, to
show that God is necessary if he exists, but would not prove
that he does exist"[3]—it must, I think, be recognized that the first
point in which the influence of the Christian revelation is to be
seen in Anselm's proof is in the very definition which he gives of
the word "God". I do not think it could occur to anyone who
was not in the tradition of Judeo-Christian monotheism to define
God as *aliquid quo nihil majus cogitari potest*. It must be admitted
that no Christian before the eleventh century seemed to have
thought of defining him in precisely those terms either.[4] Ideas,
however, have their own inertia, and their implications may need
long years to make themselves evident; and as we look back it is

---

[1] On the transformation of the Plotinian triad by Augustine, cf. E. Gilson, *The
Christian Philosophy of St. Augustine*, pp. 199 f.
[2] *The Spirit of Mediaeval Philosophy*, p. 59.   [3] Ibid., p. 62.
[4] St. Augustine does, however, use the phrase *quo esse aut cogitari melius nihil possit*
(*De Moribus*, ii. 11. 24), and St. Anselm, who is a professed Augustinian, may have
picked it up. I am indebted to Dr. H. Chadwick for this reference. Barth (*Fides
Quaerens Intellectum*, p. 85) quotes a similar phrase from *De doct. chr.* i. 7.

not difficult for us to see that St. Anselm's definition is the unforced development, by a logician of the first order, of the content of the Christian understanding of God as the supremely transcendent Being. A pagan might indeed have conceived of God as *that than which nothing greater exists*, he might even have postulated God or the One as lying beyond the utmost bounds of both being and intelligibility, but only in the tradition of Judeo-Christian monotheism can we expect to find a thinker who will define God as *that than which nothing greater can be thought* and at the same time claim that God's existence can be the conclusion of a rational demonstration.[1]

Having now, as I hope, established that St. Anselm's argument in chapter ii of the *Proslogion* is an exercise in pure ratiocination, although the definition of God on which it is based is derived from the Christian revelation, we must now attend to the remarkable fact from which this discussion began, namely that this purely rational argument for the existence of God is embedded in an exuberant and devout address to the God of Christian belief and is alleged to be the process (or at any rate one of the processes) by which a Christian can learn to understand his faith. Admitted that Anselm believed in God before he had thought of the ontological argument and that he wished this belief to issue in understanding, and admitted that he thought later on of the ontological argument and that it seemed to him to be valid, we might still wonder why the attempt to understand his belief should take the form of a recital of the ontological argument rather than of a pious and prayerful contemplation of the mystery of faith itself. Why, in short, should he have thought, as he obviously did, that the ontological argument was not merely intellectually enjoyable but of direct *religious* value? I think the answer is twofold. First, Anselm quite unashamedly believed that the human intellect was something which God had made and which he could assist to function aright; to despise the human reason with Luther or to despair of it with the modern sceptics or to dismiss an argument about religion on the ground that it was "purely intellectual" would have seemed to Anselm both absurd and irreverent. To call an argument "purely intellectual" would be to pay it the highest possible compliment. And secondly, it seems

[1] Thus I think that Barth is right when he says: "This Existence of God which is accepted in faith is now to be recognised and proved on the supposition of the Name of God likewise accepted in faith and is to be understood as necessary for thought" (*Fides Quaerens Intellectum*, p. 73 = E.T. p. 78).

to me that Anselm was so passionately convinced, *on grounds of faith*, of the absolute self-sufficiency and self-consistency of God, of the fact that nothing concerning God is contributed to him from outside but everything concerning him is included in his essential being, that it seemed obvious that if only we could discover how to express that essential being in words we should not only *believe* but *see* that his existence derives from himself and not from any outside agency. This is surely the explanation of the wrestlings which Anselm so movingly describes in the Prooemium to the *Proslogion*, "to find some one argument which should need no other argument beside itself to prove it and which would suffice to prove that God truly exists." In other words, if God is what faith assures us that he is, he is of such a nature that reason should be able to prove his existence; for faith tells us that he exists necessarily, and necessary existence is something that reason ought to be able to prove. It is therefore fully consistent with the fundamentally religious character of the *Proslogion* that it should contain a purely rational proof of the existence of God. If God's existence could not be proved by reason, he would not be the kind of God that faith assures Anselm that he is. No doubt Anselm's attitude will seem perverse to those for whom it is axiomatic that faith and reason are prima facie in tension, if not indeed in conflict, and to those for whom faith would lose its merit if reason came to its aid. For Anselm, religion means *credo ut intelligam*, not *credo quia absurdum*. Among all the great theologians of Christendom he stands out for the confidence which he had in the capacity of the human reason, when enlightened by God, to penetrate the mysteries of the Faith and for the intrepidity with which he attempted to show the rational necessity of revealed truths.[1] Where he attempted to prove the necessity of God's activities *ad extra* in creation and revelation he was, I think, mistaken, for in all these matters God is bound by no necessity; nevertheless, even here his discussions are of value for the congruity which they show to characterize God's dealings with his creation. Where he attempted to probe by argument the inner secrets of God's triune being, I think he forced human reason beyond its proper sphere, though even here congruity can be discerned. But where he attempted, on grounds of faith,

[1] Cf. E. Gilson: 'By means of Logic alone, Anselm has achieved a rational understanding of Christian faith—the same faith as that of Augustine, but a different understanding' (*Reason and Revelation in the Middle Ages*, p. 26).

to prove the existence of God on grounds of reason, I think he was right in his intention but wrong in his actual reasoning. For I think there are rational arguments for the existence of God, though Anselm's ontological argument is not one of them. And St. Thomas Aquinas thought this too.

2

From the time of St. Anselm onwards there have never been lacking critics who, while admiring the ingenuity of the ontological argument and recognizing the significance of its emergence in Western Christendom of the eleventh century, have held it to be rationally fallacious. It has also had its defenders and its repairers, and of these Descartes in the seventeeth century is probably the most significant.[1] The fundamental weakness of the argument lies in the fact which some modern philosophers, with their bias towards logic, have expressed in the aphorism "Existence is not a predicate" and which Gilson has more metaphysically stated in the assertion that "existence" (*esse*) is affirmed in a judgment and is not included, as a constituent of essence, in a concept. Thus, for example, whereas the essence of a horse will be different according as it is white or brown, it will not be different according as it exists or does not exist. This does not mean that existence is unimportant or trivial, quite the reverse; it simply means that existence is not a constituent of essence. Hence the attempt to prove the existence of any being, whether God or the perfect island of Guanilo or anything else, from its essence is doomed to failure. Existence is not included in essence and therefore cannot be extracted from it; if one attempts to include it all one suceeds as including is a purely conceptual substitute, what some of the later scholastics have, perhaps not too happily,[2] called *existentia ut significata* in contrast to the *existentia ut exercita* by which things exist in full-blooded reality in the actual universe. Thus, in the conceptual order in which Anselm's argument moves, it is just not possible to compare existence-in-reality-

---

[1] Cf. ch. iv, *supra*.

[2] "Not too happily", because *existentia* is an abstract noun (as, unfortunately, is our word 'existence') and therefore can only too easily suggest something of the same order as *essentia*. St. Thomas avoids the word *existentia*, and prefers *esse*, the infinitive of the verb "to be" employed as a noun. (The word *existentia*, which occurs in the Commentary on the Divine Names of Dionysius, is not an abstract noun but the plural of the participle *existens* of the verb *existere*, and this verb is only used because it occurs in the Latin version of Dionysius. St. Thomas's own word for "exist" is not *existere* but *esse*.)

and-in-the-intellect with existence-in-the-intellect-only by adding existence-in-reality to the latter; all that you can add is a purely conceptual substitute for existence-in-reality, and so the most that you can succeed in achieving is a demonstration that to *think of* something as existing in reality as well as in the intellect is more than to *think of* it as existing in the intellect alone.

For Gilson, the first Christian philosopher who fully apprehended the radical difference between *esse* and *essentia* was St. Thomas Aquinas. In his fascinating book *Being and some Philosophers* he traces the history of this obstinate transcendental "Being" from Plato down to Kierkegaard.[1] The Platonists, he argues, and especially the neo-Platonists, evaded the problem of existence by placing the ultimate reality, the One, above being altogether. (Incidentally, this involves the view that Erigena is not a pantheist, for, although he says that God is the *being* of all things, he does not think of God in terms of being at all; God is *above* or *beyond* being.) Nor is Aristotle in much better case; for, although he recognizes the importance of existence, when he asks what it is to exist his reply is that it is to be a particular kind of thing, to be an *essence*. In consequence—and this is one of Gilson's most provocative points—whatever St. Thomas is he is not an Aristotelian, though he makes as much use of Aristotle, "the philosopher", as he wishes. The Muslim Avicenna, who, as much as any Christian, believed in *creation* (though, unlike any Christian, in creation of a very deterministic kind), tried to escape from essentialism by making existence an *accident* of being; this was a step in the right direction, but it was far too crude, and the reaction came with Averroës, who removed individual existents from the concern of philosophy altogether. What St. Thomas did, however, was to take the whole Aristotelian doctrine of substances, forms, and essences and to supplement it with an entirely distinct metaphysical doctrine of existence, of *esse*, which transforms it from top to bottom. The key to Thomist philosophy is chapter 54 of *Contra Gentiles*, book ii, in which it is argued that to be composed of *substantia* (in this context, the same as *essentia*) and *esse* is not the same as to be composed of matter and form. We are not concerned here with the rest of Gilson's story, which continues, via Scotus and Suarez, to Descartes, Leibnitz, Spinoza, Wolff, Kant, Hegel, and Kierkegaard. We might, however, note in passing two striking

[1] *Being and some Philosophers* was published at Toronto in 1949. The French version, *L'Être et l'Essence*, published in Paris in 1948, has a not entirely identical text.

judgments which Gilson delivers. If Kant, he tells us, had really understood what was involved in his recognition that existence is not a predicate, modern philosophy might have been very different from what it is. And Kierkegaard's work was a tragic reaction, "the exasperated protest of a religious conscience against the centuries-old suppression of existence by abstract philosophical thinking. But it was the protest of existence against philosophy, not an effort to reopen philosophy to existence."[1]

To return to St. Thomas, it was in Gilson's view the supreme achievement of the Angelic Doctor to grasp with full understanding the "sublime truth" that in God, and only in God, *esse* and *essentia* are identical:

> The essence of God is his *esse*. Moses was taught this sublime truth by the Lord, when Moses asked the Lord [Exod. iii. 13 f.], "If the children of Israel ask me, What is his name?, what shall I say to them?" And the Lord replied: "I am Who am. Thus thou shalt say to the children of Israel: He Who Is has sent me to you", showing that his proper name is *Who Is*. But every name is intended to signify the nature or essence of a thing. Hence it remains that the divine *esse* is God's essence or nature.[2]

On a casual reading this might seem to give away the whole case to St. Anselm, for, we might reason, if the essence of God is *esse*, that is to say existence, we have only to know his essence to know that he exists. But this would be to misunderstand St. Thomas's meaning. In passages such as that just quoted he is contrasting the being of God, in whom essence and *esse* are identical, with that of all other beings in whom they are really distinct. In all other beings that exist their existence derives from God, that is from a source outside themselves; in him alone it is underived. In all beings existence and essence are correlative; that is to say, the act by which a being exists must be appropriate to the kind of being it is. A being whose essence is that of a horse cannot exist by the same kind of existential act as a being whose essence is that of a toadstool. Now since God's very essence is to be self-existent (for his proper name is "He Who Is"), in his case essence and existence are identical, for it is clearly contradictory to say that, although self-existent Being exists, circumstances might occur in which it would not. But we can only say this when we know that he already exists. In fact it is precisely the identity of essence and existence in God that makes the ontological argument invalid,

[1] Op. cit., p. 153.   [2] *C. Gent.* i. xxii; *S. Th.* i. iii. 4 to the same effect.

for, since his essence is *to exist*, it is only if he does exist that he has any essence at all. Unless God exists the ontological argument has no starting-point, but if he does exist we do not need it. St. Thomas's identification of essence with existence in God is somewhat cryptic, but I do not think there is any doubt about his meaning. In his whole metaphysic it is existence not essence that is primary. There are not a lot of essences, some of which happen to exist; there are existing beings exercising acts of existing, and the character of any being's act of existing is its essence. The kind of being it is arises out of the way in which it exists. In every case but one this act is non-self-sustaining and has to be maintained by creative activity from without. In one case alone, that of God himself, is it self-sustaining. If we ask what *his* essence is, what kind of being *he* is, the answer can only be that he is the kind of being that needs nothing outside itself in order to exist. And in this sense, therefore, we must say that his essence is existence. But all this talk would be simply vacuous unless in fact God existed; as Gilson says, "it is the *esse* which absorbs the essence and not *vice versa*".[1]

In the light of what has now been said, St. Thomas's direct reply to St. Anselm becomes fully intelligible. If, he says in effect, we define God as Anselm defines him (and he does not suggest that this is wrong), then the idea of God which we have in our mind will be that of a being that really exists; but whether in fact it really exists is quite another matter.[2] However, in the body of the article in which the reply is given St. Thomas seems to be saying that there is a purely logical and *a priori* argument for the existence of God, though, at any rate in this life, we cannot see it; and this requires a little attention.

The question at issue, is whether "the fact that God exists" (*Deum esse*) is *per se notum*, and Anselm's argument is taken as claiming that it is. Something, we are told, can be *per se notum*[3] in either of two ways, either in itself and not to us (*secundum se et non quoad nos*) or in itself and to us as well (*secundum se et quoad nos*). In either case a proposition is *per se notum* because the predicate is logically implied (*includitur*) in the meaning (*ratio*) of the subject; the example given is "Man is an animal", in which animality is included in the meaning of "man". If, therefore,

---

[1] *The Christian Philosophy of St. Thomas Aquinas*, p. 456, n. 27.
[2] *S. Th.* I. ii. I ad 2; cp. *C. Gent.* I. xi.
[3] The earlier English Dominican translation of the *Summa* translates this by "self-evident", but I think this may be misleading.

everybody knows what the predicate and subject severally mean
(*quid sit*), the preposition will be *per se nota* to all; otherwise it
will not.

Now, the Angelic Doctor somewhat puzzlingly proceeds, the
proposition "God exists" (*Deus est*) is *per se nota*, because, as we
shall show later on, God is his own *esse* and so the subject and
predicate are identical. But, because we do not know what
God's nature is (*de Deo quid est*), the proposition is not *per se nota*
to us; and so we have to arrive at God's existence in another way,
namely from his effects, which are better known to us. The problem this raises is that the argument seems now to have been
shifted to a purely logical plane; if our definition of God does not
include his existence, then his existence will not be *per se nota* to
us, but if we adopt a definition that does then it will be. In fact,
the parallel with the proposition "Man is an animal" suggests
that the Angelic Doctor has abandoned the radical existentialism
of which Gilson has acclaimed him as the great champion and
inaugurator in Christian philosophy and has slipped back into the
most abject essentialism. Are we forced to this depressing verdict?

I do not think we are, but I do not think, with all respect, that
we can altogether exonerate St. Thomas from a certain lack of
caution in expressing himself. I suspect that the illustration from
man and his animality is one of those familiar illustrations which
he sometimes introduces into the *Summa Theologiae* in order to
make things easier for the *incipientes* (not *insipientes*!)[1] for whom
he wrote it but which sometimes make his meaning less clear to
the professional philosopher or theologian. My reason for thinking this is that when he criticizes Anselm in his less elementary
works he seems to be quite explicit that the reason why God's
existence is not *per se nota* to us is that we have not in this life a
direct and intuitive acquaintance with the divine Being. Thus in
his Commentary on Boethius *De Trinitate*, the reason given is
that *ejus essentiam non videmus*.[2] In the *Contra Gentiles* he writes:
"As it is *per se notum* to us that the whole is greater than the part,
so as to those who see the divine essence itself the fact that God
exists is *per se notissimum*, because his essence is his *esse*. But because
we cannot see his essence we have to approach the knowledge
that he is, not through him but through his effects."[3] In the *De*

---

[1] *Propositum nostrae intentionis in hoc opere est, ea quae ad Christianam religionem pertinent,
eo modo tradere, secundum quod congruit ad eruditionem incipientium* (*S. Th.* I, prol.).
[2] Prooem. i. 3 ad 6.   [3] *C. Gent.* I. xi.

Veritate he is even more explicit: "Because the quiddity of God is not known to us the fact that God exists is not *per se notum* to us, but needs demonstration. However, in the fatherland, where we shall see his essence, the fact that God exists will be more fully *per se notum* to us than it is now *per se notum* that affirmation and negation are not simultaneously true."[1] And now, to return to the *Summa*, we may observe that even there St. Thomas goes on to say that the proposition "God exists" is not *per se nota* to us because "we do not know concerning God *quid est*" and we must recall that the phrase *scire de Deo quid sit*, as contrasted with *scire quia est*, is regularly used to denote that knowledge of God's being which is not open to us here below, where we know him only by his effects. In spite of first appearances, I do not think St. Thomas held that anyone who had been told that "God" means self-existent being would be able on the strength of this definition to construct a valid ontological argument for God's existence. What he undoubtedly did hold was that, when we see God face to face in the infinite plenitude of his uncreated glory, it will then be manifest to us, beyond all possibility of doubt and all need of argument, that he exists in his own right and by his own power in a way that transcends and subsumes, and is at the same time the archetype of, all finite necessity, metaphysical, physical or logical.

It seems thus to be clear that, when we ask about either St. Anselm or St. Thomas why the saint inserts into a treatise that presupposes divine revelation an argument of a purely rational type for God's existence, the answer is in either case the same, namely that the notion of God which he has received from divine revelation is that of a God whose existence should be rationally demonstrable. St. Anselm is in the essentialist tradition which goes back at least to St. Augustine, for whom God was the unchanging ground of a changing universe: it is natural that he should define God's transcendence in a logical way and try to show that his existence can be proved by logic. St. Thomas, on the other hand, is, if not the founder, at least the great exponent of the existentialist tradition, for which God is the self-existent ground of a universe that is contingent and yet exists; it is therefore natural for him to define God's transcendence in a meta-

---

[1] *De Ver.* x. 12 resp. St. Thomas's own thought may, of course, have undergone development, as has been argued by Père G. Lafont in his *Structures et Méthode dans la Somme Théologique de Saint Thomas d'Aquin.* I must not, however, claim Père Lafont's authority for my own interpretation.

physical way and to argue to his existence from the existence of the universe. *Quo majus nihil cogitari potest* is the Essence that is above all change; *Qui est* or *ipsum esse* is the Self-existent on which all other existents depend. The one is idea, the other is act; but in their several orders each is altogether transcendent.

It is not difficult to see why Barth feels so much sympathy for St. Anselm, in spite of the fact that Anselm has had the presumption to do what Barth would never dare to attempt, namely to prove the existence of God. It is because Anselm's definition refers to God without apparently saying anything about him. It does not even say that we can think about God, though presumably when we have the definition in our minds we are thinking about him in *some* sort of way; all it says is that we cannot think about anything greater. That, for St. Thomas, is of course the definition's weakness, for the fact that we cannot think about anything greater might simply arise from the definition having no intelligible content at all; it might not refer to anything that *could* exist in reality. This is, however, for Barth its great glory. "It contains nothing in the way of statements about the existence or about the nature of the object described. Thus nothing of that sort is to be derived from it on subsequent analysis. . . . It is a genuine description (*significatio*), one name of God, selected from among the various revealed names of God for this occasion and for this particular purpose, in such a way that to reach a knowledge of God the revelation of this same God from some other source is clearly assumed."[1] This is, I think, in fact true, but St. Anselm did not think it was, or he never would have put forward his ontological argument, which professes *not* to need a revelation of God from some other source. And when Barth writes that "clearly it [sc. the definition] is *deliberately chosen* in such a way that the object which it describes emerges as something completely independent of whether men in actual fact conceive it or can conceive it",[2] he may be saying what he would have intended to do if he had been Anselm but he is not saying what Anselm intended to do. Anselm would no doubt have admitted that he was describing God *quasi ignotum*, but he goes on to deduce from the definition a surprising number of things about him; there is no appeal to revelation in chapters v to xii, in which God is shown to be sensible, almighty, compassionate, impassible, just, merciful,

---

[1] *Fides Quaerens Intellectum*, p. 71 = E.T., p. 75.
[2] Ibid., p. 70 = E.T., p. 74 (italics mine).

and living. (St. Thomas, we may recall, also says that *de Deo scire non possumus quid sit, sed quid non sit.*)[1] Anselm's definition may indeed have been empty of content, but that was not what he intended. What for Barth was a triumph was for Anselm a calamity, and this is a measure of the distance that separates Anselm from Barth. So perhaps Barth is wise in admitting that he cannot identify himself completely with Anselm's views.[2]

3

I should like at this point to draw attention to one of the most illuminating discussions I have yet seen of the precise status and purport of the Five Ways in the theological system of St. Thomas, that which is contained in Fr. Edward Sillem's book *Ways of Thinking about God.* After a very penetrating and original critique of the arguments which have been adduced by various present-day philosophers against the very possibility of a rationally respectable philosophical theism, he provocatively remarks that for theists of Thomist proclivities the most perplexing and absorbing problem is neither the diversity of interpretations put upon the "traditional" arguments by those who have never studied them in their historical context nor the objections brought against them by contemporary philosophers, but the diversity of interpretations put upon the Five Ways by those who have studied them most meticulously and sympathetically.[3] To clear up this puzzle he insists that we must for a while stop worrying about their bearing upon issues and attitudes that had never existed when St. Thomas was writing, but must ask what it precisely was that the Angelic Doctor himself was concerned to do. And the answer given is that, in the earlier questions of the *Pars Prima*, and especially in the famous second question upon the existence of God, he was not arguing as a philosopher to convert atheists but, in accordance with the title of the whole great work, as a theologian against certain other theologians. "He is writing in the interests of sound theology about and against a theological opinion current during the thirteenth century. He is rejecting the view that we have some kind of intuitive knowledge of God's existence, and trying to show that naturally human reason has no intuitive certainty

---

[1] *S. Th.* I. iii. prol.   [2] Op. cit., p. 9.   [3] Sillem, op. cit., p. 14.

of the truth that God exists. We have to establish this truth by reasoning."[1] To quote Fr. Sillem again:

> [St. Thomas] is expounding in a methodical manner the truths of faith he believes and which he has been commissioned to teach, giving reasons to justify them to the mind, and showing how reason stands in their regard. In article 2 writing as a theologian, he is pointing out that since the things we know in experience are the effects of God's creative activity, we must be able in principle to argue from them to the existence of God. In the actual arguments (as given in article 3), however, St. Thomas reasons, not from his knowledge that things are the effects of God, but from the way things reveal themselves to us in experience; he argues that, being imperfect in various ways as they are, they must be the effects of some cause. He avoids *petitio principii* because he gives us, not his own arguments, but those of pagan philosophers who knew nothing of the Christian doctrine of creation.[2]

Again:

> The first Quaestiones of the *Summa Theologica* were written neither for nor against philosophers, but for, and to a certain extent against, theologians. St. Thomas wrote articles 1 and 2 [of question ii] to refute the widely accepted view of theologians of his day that we need not prove the being of God, the ESSE DEI, but only the divine attributes, and thence to show how we can think of each of them.[3]

This, we are told, explains two otherwise puzzling facts: first, that the proofs, both as they are found in the *Summa Theologiae* (1. ii. 3) and as in the *Contra Gentiles* (1. xiii), are not all the proofs that had been used by earlier Christian thinkers but come straight from Aristotle and his commentators, and secondly that, in spite of the fact that Aristotle did not believe in anything like the God of Christianity and even in some cases did not identify the terminus of his arguments as "God" in any sense at all, St. Thomas rounds each of them off with a casual remark such as "Everyone understands this as God". To put this in my own words, Fr. Sillem's point is that St. Thomas is in effect saying to the fellow-Christians whom he is assuming as his readers: "If you understand God as Christians understand him, that is as the self-existent Being, the *Qui est*, upon whose creative act the existence of the world depends, you will see that the unmoved first mover, the absolutely necessary being and all the others to which Aristotle's arguments lead are

[1] Op. cit., p. 53.   [2] Op. cit., p. 54.   [3] Op. cit., p. 57.

in fact identical with one another and with the Christian God."
Or, to view the matter the other way round, the notion of God
which St. Thomas has received from divine revelation, from
Sacra doctrina, is that of a God whose existence should be rationally
demonstrable from his effects, though not, as St. Anselm thought,
demonstrable from his very definition. And this leads on to a
further point made by Fr. Sillem. Although, when we have proved
that there is a first mover, we can say that we all agree in calling
this "God", we have not at this stage *proved* that it is what Christians assert God, in his fundamental character, to be. So, Fr.
Sillem argues very persuasively, St. Thomas's argument for the
existence of God is not complete until, having, in the subsequent
quaestiones, successively established that "God", the terminus
of the various Aristotelian arguments, is entirely simple, absolutely
perfect, good, infinite, ubiquitous, immutable, and eternal, he is
able to show that they coalesce in unity and can then say without
qualification, in article 3 of question xi, not just that we all agree
in calling this "God", but quite simply *Et hoc est Deus*. So St.
Thomas's argument for the existence of God is not the perfunctory
thing that it may well appear to be if we confine ourselves to
article 3 of question ii; it extends all the way thence to question
xi and is only complete when God has been shown to be "one".

There is, however, one point on which I must dissent from Fr.
Silem. He appears to hold that from question iii onwards St.
Thomas progressively imports into his exposition more and more
material derived from revelation, though he still considers the
argument to be a "reasoned" one. Thus he writes:

> All St. Thomas is trying to show in the Five Ways is that reason
> is capable of attaining some minimum knowledge of God, that this
> knowledge is adequate enough as a foundation on which faith can
> build its fully developed teaching, and that faith must inevitably
> presuppose such a minimum knowledge of God as attained by
> reason, even as grace presupposes the existence of nature which it
> too perfects . . . From Quaestio iii onwards St. Thomas ceases to
> be interested in the philosophers, even though some of the ideas
> of God he deals with in this Quaestio may have been known to
> them. . . . The fourth Quaestio, on the perfection of God, definitely
> takes us beyond anything that reason had been able to attain
> by its own unaided powers. From now onwards St. Thomas takes
> us deeper and deeper into the theology of the unity of God's Being.
> No pagan philosopher had ever conceived of the goodness, the in-
> finity, the transcendence and immanence of God to creation,

nor of the immutability and eternity of God as these are presented
to us by reasoned argument in Quaestiones v to x. . . . In Quaestio
iv and onwards he leaves ground which is reachable by philosophers
on their own to explore what reason can come to know under the
positive guidance of faith.[1]

I may perhaps have failed to grasp Fr. Sillem's precise meaning
and we may be nearer to each other here than we seem to be;
I am not quite sure of the force to be attributed to the words
"reasoned" and "reason" in this passage. But Fr. Sillem certainly
seems to be saying that from question iv onwards St. Thomas is
less and less concerned to argue philosophically and more and
more concerned to expound revealed truths, and this does not
seem to me to be true when I examine the actual text. Admittedly
in the *Sed-contras* of these questions St. Thomas almost invariably
quotes a text from Scripture or one of the fathers, but this is
common form and means very little. The significant fact is
that the body of each article is purely philosophical throughout
and makes no direct appeal to revelation. I agree with Fr. Sillem's
most illuminating assertion that the argument for the existence
of God is not limited to question ii but is spread out all the way
to question xi, but I cannot agree that it is not a purely rational
argument. What I think revelation provides is the concept of
God in terms of which the question of God's existence is proposed
for rational investigation and with which the argument operates.
As I see it, what St. Thomas is saying is this: "For Christians 'God'
means, not some first principle within the order of finite causality,
but Self-existent Being. Never mind for the moment whether we
know from revelation that a Being answering to this notion
exists. Can we prove the existence of such a Being by purely
rational argument? St. Anselm thought we could by pure logic,
but for reasons which I have stated I think his argument was
fallacious; furthermore it is not immediately evident that his
definition *Aliquid quo majus nihil cogitari potest* is logically equivalent
to our definition *Qui est* or (though this is another question) that
is equally scriptural. From what then can we argue in order to
prove the existence of self-existent Being? Being which is not
self-existent would seem to be an obvious starting-point, for if such
being does exist this can only be because self-existent Being is
its cause. And when we look at the world around us (of which,

[1] Op. cit., pp. 107–8.

of course, we ourselves are really part) we see it to be composed of beings whose mutability, contingency, imperfection and the like show it to be just of this type. Aristotle never quite saw this; he never properly grasped that which this mutability and the rest involve. He saw that mobility implies an immobile mover, that contingency implies a necessary ground, that imperfection implies a perfect archetype. We shall all agree that these are what we know as 'God', but Aristotle did not know this, for it never occurred to him that mutability and the rest are the marks of *non-self-existent being*. But once this has been recognized all the rest follows, and in my well-known Five Ways I showed that starting from mutability or any of the other four characteristics which I selected we can then see not merely that there is an unmoved first mover, an absolutely necessary ground and so on, which might conceivably be identical with the world or with some part or aspect of it, but that there is a Self-existent Being, the *Qui est* of Christian faith. Once this stage has been reached, we can go on, still remaining within the bounds of rational argumentation, to show that this Self-existent Being is entirely simple, absolutely perfect, good, infinite, ubiquitous, immutable and eternal and that he is one, not merely numerically but ontologically. This is what I did in questions iii to xi. I still had not said anything about the great revealed truths about God which the human reason is altogether incapable of discovering, for example that God is the Blessed Trinity; but I had at least shown enough about him to justify me in summing up my discussion in the words *Et hoc est Deus*."

The question on which, unless I misunderstand him, I differ from Fr. Sillem is simply whether the movement from question iii to question xi involves an appeal to Christian revelation or is purely rational in structure. In the final chapter of his book, in which Fr. Sillem most entertainingly imagines the Angelic Doctor explaining his position to a gathering of modern philosophers, St. Thomas is represented as saying:

The second stage of the argument, as I conceived it, consists before all else in a carefully planned course of reasoning about the biblical teaching concerning God as from certain first principles. In the second stage of my proof, then, the theologian steps on to the scene to show that divine revelation provides us with the best possible, and indeed the only conceivable way of understanding what you were left asking at the end of the first stage of the

argument, namely what are we to understand by necessary, uncaused, unlimited being.[1]

Then, when he goes on to state what the theologian does in the
second stage (that is, from questions iii to xi), St. Thomas, as
interpreted by Fr. Sillem, says that it is to introduce a new metaphysic, which conceives being as not merely an essence but as
"positivity of existing", so that there is a real distinction between
essence and existence in finite beings, while God is pure existence.
My reply to this would be that this metaphysic has in fact been
operative in the argument from the start, but that even so it
does not make the argument any less purely rational. The choice
of a metaphysic may be due to revelation, in the sense that it
is revelation which has redirected the metaphysician's vision when
it has strayed from its proper focus, but this does not make the
argument any the less metaphysical or any more theological, in
the strict sense of that term. Fr. Sillem has usefully pointed out
that St. Thomas includes under the consideration of God's
"essence" the whole range of questions from ii to xxvi and that
the proofs of God's existence fall within this range,[2] but I do not
think that this removes them from the realm of philosophy into
that of theology. I think, as I have said earlier, that what revelation provides for St. Thomas is a conception of God's "essence"
in virtue of which God's existence would seem to be rationally
demonstrable, and that this is why, without any sense of incon-
gruity, the Angelic Doctor places within a treatise on dogmatic
theology a purely rational proof of God's existence. Having
criticized Fr. Sillem on this one point I would repeat my very
warm admiration and appreciation of his book and especially
of his brilliant realization that questions ii to xi of the *Pars Prima*
must be taken as a whole.

4

We can now say something about a question of quite fundamental importance; namely, whether the definitions of God

---

[1] Op. cit., pp. 139-40. Cf. the previous statement: "The argument is metaphysical
in character throughout, but in the first stage it consists in reason arguing from the
universe, and in the second stage in reason arguing from what God has revealed"
(p. 139). However, on p. 148 Fr. Sillem appears to hold that St. Thomas *might* have
written a purely philosophical second stage of his argument, although in fact he did
not do so.

[2] *S. Theol.* i. ii prol. Cf. Sillem, p. 43.

adopted by St. Anselm and St. Thomas have any intelligible content whatever. There is, of course, a widely held belief among modern philosophers that not only these but no other definition of God that could satisfy the demands of religion is in the last resort anything else than a meaningless combination of words; this is true not only of the position of Professor A. J. Ayer in his logical-positivist days[1] but also of that of Professor A. G. N. Flew, for whom all assertions about God evaporate into thin air when subjected to "the death by a thousand qualifications".[2] I am concerned here, however, with the specific cases of two particular definitions, Anselm's *aliquid quo nihil majus cogitari potest*, and Thomas's *Qui est* or *Ipsum esse*.

Barth rightly points out that Anselm does not define God as the highest that man has in fact conceived or as the highest that man ever will conceive and says that the definition "denies neither the former reality nor the latter possibility, but leaves open the question of the givenness of them both".[3] His previous translation of the definition by *Un être tel qu'on n'en peut concevoir de plus grand* or *Quelque chose dont on ne peut rien concevoir de plus grand* and by *Etwas über dem ein Grösseres nicht gedacht werden kann* seems to me to be unfortunate, for *un être, quelque chose*, and *Etwas* suggests an existence in reality that Anselm is deliberately leaving open at this stage. Indeed, even the word "conceive" seems a little question-begging, for, although it is clear that in some sense the object of the definition can "be thought" (*cogitari*)—even the famous "round square" can *in some sense* be "thought"— Anselm, whether deliberately or not, avoids the word "be conceived" (*concipi*) altogether. Barth's main point, however, stands, and we must notice that, although, as I have said, there is *some* sense in which the object of the definition can be "thought", the definition does not define it as something that can be thought but only as that than which nothing greater can be thought; in what sense, therefore, God, as thus defined, can be thought is not specified and it is certainly not assumed that he can be "thought" in the sense in which the definition assumes that other beings can be "thought". This is, of course, precisely one of the grounds on which the ontological argument has been alleged to be fallacious. It is thus noteworthy that Duns Scotus was led to

---

[1] Cf. *Language, Truth and Logic, passim.*
[2] Cf., e.g., his essay in *New Essays in Philosophical Theology* (1955), pp. 96 f.
[3] *Fides Quaerens Intellectum*, p. 70 = E.T., p. 74.

redefine "God" as *quo cogitato sine contradictione majus cogitari non potest sine contradictione*, "that which can be thought without contradiction, but than which nothing greater can be thought without contradiction" and then to assert that only when God so defined has been shown to be "thinkable" is the ontological argument valid.[1] We are not, however, concerned at the moment with the truth or falsehood of the ontological argument as such, and what I have to say about that I have said elsewhere;[2] what we are concerned with is the intelligibility of the definition in any other than a purely verbal sense. Can we be sure, not yet that there *is in fact* a being corresponding to the definition, but even that the definition *could as a matter of logic* have anything corresponding to it? May it not be as self-contradictory as the definition of "an integer than which no greater integer can be thought" or "a line than which no more crooked line can be thought"?

It is precisely on such grounds as this that the definition has been condemned as inadequate for human purposes; St. Thomas says in effect that, although God and the blessed in heaven can no doubt see that it is a satisfactory definition of God, since they see him "as he is", we cannot know this until we already know that God exists.[3] For Barth, however, the completely vacuous character of the definition appears to be its chief title to glory: "It contains nothing in the way of statements about the existence or about the nature of the object described. Thus nothing of that sort is to be derived from it on subsequent analysis."[4] This I think is true, but it is not what Anselm himself thought. However, for Barth it is Anselm's great achievement to have produced, under the impression that he had found the most compelling of all arguments for the existence of God, an argument that was radically fallacious.

Nevertheless, even if the existence of God cannot be proved from Anselm's definition, we need not therefore reject it as a definition. We may well hold, as we should if we were considering any other being than God, that it is not the purpose of a definition to supply an argument for existence. We may think, with St. Thomas, that God's existence is to be proved in some other way or,

---

[1] *Op. Ox.* i, d. 2, q. 2, n. 32 (Ed. Vives, viii, p. 479).
[2] Cf. ch. iv *supra*; *Existence and Analogy*, ch. ii.
[3] *C. Gent.* i. xi; *S. Theol.* i. ii. 1 ad 1 et 2; and the very acute remark in *De Ver.* x. 12 ad 2, "Hoc quod Deus potest cogitari non esse, non impedit quin etiam sit quo majus cogitari non possit."
[4] Op. cit., p. 75.

with Barth, that it is not to be proved at all, and still leave the
question open whether the definition is satisfactory as a definition.
Now, I do not think that any Christian theist will deny that the
definition is accurate as a description of God, once he has been
convinced that it is not self-contradictory. Once he has become
convinced, whether by reason or by blind faith, that God does
exist, he is not likely to deny that God *is* "that than which nothing
greater can be thought" and therefore he must presumably
hold that the definition is self-consistent. What I think he will find
very difficult, unless he goes outside the framework of the definition, will be to extract any definite content from it, without
appealing to our experience of the finite world. We can agree
that there can be nothing greater than God and, if we believe
that God exists, we shall also hold that God is greater than everything else; the difficulty comes when we try to give a content to
"greater", and it is significant that Anselm himself, as soon as
he has proved God's existence and disposed of the "fool", goes on,
in chapter v, to argue that God has made everything else out of
nothing and only on this basis proceeds further to show that
God is immaterial, omnipotent, merciful, impassible, and the
rest.

When we come to St. Thomas we have a very different situation.
No doubt it would be possible, with a little ingenuity, to argue that
Anselm's *quo nihil majus cogitari potest* is equivalent to St. Thomas's
Qui est, but we could do this only if we interpreted *Qui est* in an
essentialist and not an existential way. That is to say, we might
argue that the notion of a being than which nothing greater
could be thought, if it was a self-consistent notion at all, was the
idea of a being which derived nothing from any outside source.
This, however, does not seem to be what St. Thomas understood
by *Qui est* or *Ipsum esse*. For starting from the fact of the world's
contingent existence he had argued to the existence of a Being
who is actually and not merely conceptually self-existent as its
creator, for a Being that was merely conceptually self-existent
could not create anything. It is only when he has convinced
himself that God is this self-existent act of Being that he goes on
to discuss what God is like, and, as we shall see, he does this
in a very odd but very significant way. This, I think, explains
the puzzling fact that, having said, in the Prologue to question
ii of Book I, that he is going to consider "the things that belong
to the essence of God", as soon as he has proved God's existence

he hastens to tell us that this essence is nothing less than God himself and that it is in fact identical with God's *esse* or act of existence.[1] Thus, in any ordinary sense of the words, God does not *have* any essence at all; for in so far as we can talk of his essence it is identical with his *esse*, and his *esse* is not what he has but what he *is*. Clearly the whole distinction between what a thing is and how it exists breaks down when we try to apply it to God; and this is fully in line with the Thomist principle that there is a real distinction between essence and *esse* in every being other than God.

We know then that the God whose proper name is *Qui est* or *Ipsum esse* does in fact exist, and we know this from our consideration of finite beings.[2] But how much does this tell us about him? What content of *Ipsum esse* does it disclose to us? St. Thomas tells us, rather disconcertingly, that we do not know what God is but only *that* he is and *how* he is, or rather how he is *not*;[3] later he tells us that "we know his relation to creatures, namely that he is their cause, and their difference from him, namely that he is not any of the things which are caused by him, and that they are not distant from him because of any defect in him but because he is far above them".[4] As to the source of this knowledge "that God Is", St. Thomas is quite clear: "Although we cannot know concerning God *what he is*, nevertheless we make use in this teaching of his effects, whether of nature or of grace, instead of a definition, in order to consider in this teaching things concerning God; as in some philosophical sciences something is demonstrated about a cause from its effect, by taking the effect in place of the definition of its cause."[5] But concerning the extent which St. Thomas thought this knowledge *de Deo quid non sit* covers, his interpreters differ very greatly. Fr. Victor White considers it is very small indeed and even quotes Barth as unwittingly agreeing with St. Thomas;[6] he stresses the force of the words "whether of nature *or of grace*" in the passage just quoted, and we should perhaps remember that for St. Thomas it is only in the beatific vision that God can be even partially "comprehended", since there and only there his own essence takes the place of that "intelligible species" which, on Thomist theory, is the necessary

---

[1] *S. Th.* I. iii. 3 et 4.
[2] For a discussion of the way in which the Thomist "Five Ways" operate, cf. my *Existence and Analogy*, ch. iv, or E. Sillem's *Ways of Thinking about God*, ch. v.
[3] *S. Th.* I. ii Prol.: cp. iii Prol.   [4] Ibid. I. xii. 12c.
[5] *S. Th.* I. i. 7 ad 1.   [6] *God The Unknown*, chs. i–iii and p. 32.

condition of human knowledge.[1] On the other hand Jacques Maritain writes:

> All knowledge which does not attain the essence *in itself* belongs to *scire quia est* . . . The inviolable secret of the deity does not, then, prevent the Divine Essence being known by us, not in itself, but because it communicates a created participation of itself to what is not itself—that word "participation" expresses in the ontological order the same thing expressed by the word "analogy" in the noetic order. . . . The Divine Nature remains veiled, not revealed, to our metaphysical gaze. It is not objectivised according to what it is in itself. And yet, thanks to ananoetic intellection, it is constituted the object of an absolutely stable knowledge, of a science which contemplates, and delineates in it, determinations which imply negation only in our mode of conceiving.[2]

Maritain seems to me to be nearer the truth in this matter than Fr. White, for, when we recall that the doctrine of creation as Christianity understands it means that God is the direct cause of everything that a creature has and is, to know God "in his effects" is to know him in a very close and intimate way. And certainly St. Thomas goes on to deduce a very large number of facts about God once he has proved that God exists. Furthermore we must remember that it is extremely difficult to draw a sharp line between what we know by reason and what we know through grace, since the two are in practice normally concurrent and co-operative. (As Fr. Rahner observes, we can experience grace without recognizing that it is grace that we are experiencing.[3]) And grace is experienced primarily by that "knowledge by connaturality" or *per modum inclinationis*[4] which is "felt" rather than reasoned about. Therefore, although St. Thomas says, as we have seen, that, whether by nature or by grace, we can know God only through his effects, this knowledge need by no means be trivial or sketchy; in fact it takes St. Thomas all the way from question iii to question xi of the *Pars Prima*, even when we eliminate any contribution that grace may be making.

It seems to me, therefore, that, while St. Anselm's definition of God fails to give any intelligible content to the notion simply because it attempts to approach God in total independence of any of his works, St. Thomas's doctrine, because it is rooted in

[1] *S. Th.* I. xii. 2 ad 3.
[2] *The Degrees of Knowledge* (trans. of 1959), pp. 230–1.
[3] Cf. *Theological Investigations*, i, p. 300.
[4] Maritain, op. cit., p. 260. Cf. *S. Th.* I. i. 6 ad 3.

the act of being which is analogically common to God and his creatures, gives us a process by which we can transform the *via negativa* into the *via eminentiae* and, without trying to escape from our creaturely status, can achieve a real knowledge of God in this life. As Maritain pointed out in the passage just quoted, there is a direct connexion between the ontological dependence of creatures upon God in the real metaphysical order and the fact that we are able to talk about God in language derived from our experience of finite beings. For if we experience finite beings as they really are we experience them as God's creatures and so we mediately experience him, not, of course, *sub ratione deitatis* but *sub ratione creatoris*, as the loving Creator of both them and us.

After this somewhat rambling discussion it will be well to return to the question from which I began, namely why it is that both St. Anselm and St. Thomas embed what professes to be a purely rational proof of the existence of God in the early part of a writing which quite clearly assumes from the start that God exists and is what the Christian revelation asserts him to be. My answer is that each of these great Christian thinkers begins with a definition of God which has come to him, as he believes, from the Christian revelation, but that the definition is of such a character that the existence of the being to which it corresponds would seem to be capable of a purely rational proof; the definition comes from revelation, the argument does not. The two definitions are very different, and even more different are the two metaphysical contexts in which they are placed. One is that of Being identified with essence, the other that of Being identified with *esse* or existence. Where they are both profoundly Christian is in identifying God with Being. From the Thomist's point of view St. Anselm's argument was a brilliant and praiseworthy, but unsuccessful, first attempt at a task which St. Thomas discovered how to perform successfully. But both the *Doctor Magnificus* and the *Doctor Angelicus* were, as I see it, concerned with the same Christian work, *fides quaerens intellectum, philosophari in fide*.

BIBLIOGRAPHY

[In each case the edition mentioned is the one that has been made use of in this book; other editions are referred to in parentheses where such mention seemed relevant. The dates given are normally those on the title-pages.]

ALEXANDER, S. *Space, Time and Deity.* London: Macmillan. 1927. (1st. ed., 1920.)

ANDREWES, Lancelot. *A Pattern of Catechistical Doctrine and other Minor Works.* Oxford: Parker. 1846.

Anglicanism. The Thought and Practice of the Church of England, illustrated from the Religious Literature of the Seventeenth Century. Compiled and edited by P. E. More and F. L. Cross. London: S.P.C.K. 1935.

ANSELM, St. *The Devotions of St. Anselm.* Ed. by C. C. J. Webb. London: Methuen. 1903.

AUGUSTINE, St. *Confessions.* E.T. by E. B. Pusey. Oxford: Parker. 1843.

AYER, A. J. *The Foundations of Empirical Knowledge.* London: Macmillan. 1940. *Language, Truth and Logic.* 2nd. ed. London: Gollancz. 1946.

BAILLIE, John. *Our Knowledge of God.* Oxford Univ. Press. 1939.   ⟵

BALMFORTH, H. *Is Christian Experience an Illusion?* London: S.C.M. Press. 1923.

BARNES, E. W. *Scientific Theory and Religion. The World described by Science and its Spiritual Interpretation.* Cambridge Univ. Press. 1933.

BARTH, Karl. *Credo. A Presentation of the Chief Problems of Dogmatics with Reference to the Apostles' Creed.* E.T. by J. S. McNab. London: Hodder & Stoughton. 1936.
The Knowledge of God and the Service of God according to the Teaching of the Reformation. E.T. by J. L. M. Haire and I. Henderson. London: Hodder & Stoughton. 1938.

→ BERDYAEV, Nicolas. *Freedom and the Spirit.* E.T. by O. F. Clarke. London: Geoffrey Bless. 1935. *Ch. 2. esp. (attacks doctrine of analogy)*
Solitude and Society. E.T. by G. Reavey. London: Geoffrey Bles. 1938.

BEVAN, Edwyn. *Symbolism and Belief.* London: Allen & Unwin. 1938.

BEVAN JONES, L. *The People of the Mosque. An Introduction to the Study of Islam with special reference to India.* London: S.C.M. Press. 1932.

BEVERIDGE, William. *Theological Works.* Oxford: Parker. Vols. VII–IX. 1845–7.

Bible of the World, The. Ed. by R. O. Ballou. London: Kegan Paul. 1940.

BLACK, M. *The Nature of Mathematics. A Critical Survey.* London: Kegan Paul. 1933.

BLOSIUS, L. *A Book of Spiritual Instruction (Institutio Spiritualis).* E.T. by B. A. Wilberforce. (Vol. I of the 7-vol. ed. of *The Works of Louis de Blois.*) London: Burns, Oates. 1925.

BOX, H. S. *The World and God. The Scholastic Approach to Theism.* London: S.P.C.K. 1934.

BRABANT, F. H. *Time and Eternity in Christian Thought.* London: Longmans. 1937.

→ BRADLEY, F. H. *Appearance and Reality. A Metaphysical Essay.* London: Allen & Unwin. 2nd ed., 1897. (1st ed., 1893.)

BREMOND, Henri. *A Literary History of Religious Thought in France from the Wars of Religion down to our Own Times.* 3 vols. so far published. London: S.P.C.K. 1928–36. (French original: *Histoire littéraire du sentiment religieux en France depuis la fin des guerres de religion jusqu'à nos jours.* Paris: Bloud et Gay. 1916–1932.)

BROAD, C. D. *Examination of McTaggart's Philosophy.* Cambridge Univ. Press. 2 vols. in 3 parts. 1933, 1938.

BRUNNER, Emil. *The Mediator. A Study of the Central Doctrine of the Christian Faith.* E.T. by Olive Wyon. London: Lutterworth Press. 1924. (German original: *Der Mittler.* Tübingen: Mohr. 1927.)

BULGAKOV, Sergius. *The Wisdom of God. A Brief Summary of Sophiology.* E.T. by P. Thompson, O. F. Clarke and X. Braikevitch. London: Williams & Norgate. 1937.

BURNABY, John. *Amor Dei. A Study of the Religion of St. Augustine.* London: Hodder & Stoughton. 1938.

BUTLER, Cuthbert. *Western Mysticism. The Teaching of SS. Augustine, Gregory and Bernard on Contemplation and the Contemplative Life. Neglected Chapters in the History of Religion.* London: Constable. 2nd ed., 1927. (1st ed., 1922.)

BUTLER, Joseph. *Works.* Ed. by W. E. Gladstone. 2 vols. Vol. I: *The Analogy,* etc. Oxford: Clarendon Press. 1897.

CARNAP, Rudolf. *Philosophy and Logical Syntax.* London: Kegan Paul. 1935. *The Unity of Science.* E.T. by M. Black. London: Kegan Paul. 1934.

CHAMBAT, Lucien. *Présence et Union: Les Missions des Personnes de la Saint-Trinité.* Ed. de Fontenelle. 1944.

CHAPMAN, H. John. *The Spiritual Letters of Dom John Chapman.* Ed. by R. Hudleston. London: Sheed & Ward. 2nd ed., 1935. (1st ed., 1935.)

CHARLES, P. *Prayer for All Times.* E.T. by Maud Monahan. London: Sands. 3 vols. 1929, 1930. (French original: *La Prière de toutes les heures.* Paris: Desclée de Brouwer. 1936.)

CHESTERTON, G. K. *The Everlasting Man.* London: Hodder & Stoughton. People's Library ed. 1927. (1st ed., 1925.)

COHEN, M. R. *A Preface to Logic.* London: Routledge. 1946.

CONFUCIUS. *The Analects, or the Conversations of Confucius with his Disciples and certain others.* E.T. by W. E. Soothill. Ed. by Lady Hosie. Oxford Univ. Press. 1937.

COOMARASWAMY, Ananda. *Buddha and the Gospel of Buddhism.* London: Harrap. 1916.

D'ARCY, M.C. *The Nature of Belief.* London: Sheed & Ward. 1931. *Thomas Aquinas.* London: Benn. Oxford Univ. Press. 1930.

DAWSON, Christopher. *Enquiries into Religion and Culture.* London: Sheed & Ward. 1933.

DEMANT, V. A. *The Religious Prospect.* London: Muller. 1939.

DENZINGER, H. *Enchiridion Symbolorum Definitionum et Declarationum de rebus fidei et morum.* 11th edition, ed. by C. Bannwart. Friburgi Brisgoviae: Herder. 1911.
DEWAR, Lindsay. *Man and God. An Essay in the Psychology and Philosophy of Religious Experience.* London: S.P.C.K. 1935.
Dogma in History and Thought. Studies by various writers. London: Nisbet. 1929.

EDDINGTON, A. S. *The Nature of the Physical World.* Cambridge Univ. Press. 1928.
New Pathways in Science. Cambridge Univ. Press. 1935.
The Philosophy of Physical Science. Cambridge Univ. Press. 1939.
ELWIN, Verrier. *Christian Dhyāna or Prayer of Loving Regard. A Study of " The Cloud of Unknowing."* London: S.P.C.K. 1930.
EMMET, D. M. *Whitehead's Philosophy of Organism.* London: Macmillan. 1932.
Encyclopædia Britannica. London: Encyc. Brit. Co. 14th ed. 1929.
Encyclopædia of Religion and Ethics. Ed. by J. Hastings. Edinburgh: T. & T. Clark. 13 vols. 1908–26. (Vol. XII, 1921.)
Essays Catholic and Critical. By Members of the Anglican Communion. Ed. by E. G. Selwyn. London: S.P.C.K. 3rd ed., 1929. (1st ed., 1926.)

FRANÇOIS DE SALES, St. *Introduction à la Vie dévote.* Paris: Nelson. n.d.

GABRIEL OF ST. MARY MAGDALENE, Fr. *St. John of the Cross, Doctor of Divine Love.* E.T. by a Benedictine of Stanbrook. London: Thomas Baker. 1940.
GARDEIL, A. *La Crédibilité et l'Apologétique.* Paris: Gabalda. 2nd ed., 1912.
La Structure de l'Âme et l'Expérience mystique. Paris: Gabalda. 2 vols. 3rd ed., 1927. (1st ed., 1926.)
GARRIGOU-LAGRANGE, R. *Dieu, son Existence et sa Nature.* Paris: Beauchesne. 1st ed., 1915. (E.T. by Bede Rose, *God, his Existence and Nature.* St. Louis, Mo.: Herder. 2 vols. 1934.)
Perfection chrétienne et Contemplation, selon S. Thomas d'Aquin et S. Jean de la Croix. Paris: Desclée. 2 vols. 7th ed., 1923.
Le Sens du Mystère et le clair-obscur intellectuel. Paris: Desclée de Brouwer. 1934.
GILSON, Étienne. *God and Philosophy.* New Haven: Yale Univ. Press; and London: Milford. 1941.
The Mystical Theology of St. Bernard. E.T. by A. H. C. Downes. London: Sheed & Ward. 1940. (French original: *La Théologie mystique de saint Bernard.* Paris: Vrin. 1934.)
The Philosophy of St. Bonaventure. E.T. by I. Trethowan and F. J. Sheed. London: Sheed & Ward. 1938. (French original: *La Philosophie de saint Bonaventure.* Paris: Vrin. 1925.)
The Christian Philosophy of St. Thomas Aquinas. E.T. by L. K. Shook. London: Gollancz. 1957. (French original: *Le Thomisme. Introduction au Systeme de saint Thomas d'Aquin.* Paris: Vrin. 5th ed., 1945.)

Reason and Revelation in the Middle Ages. New York and London. Scribner. 1939.

The Spirit of Medieval Philosophy. E.T. by A. H. C. Downes. London: Sheed & Ward. 1936. (French original: *L'Esprit de la Philosophie médiévale.* Paris: Vrin. 2 vols. 1932.)

The Unity of Philosophical Experience. London: Sheed & Ward. 1938.

Christianisme et Philosophie. Paris: Vrin. 1936.

History of Christian Philosophy in the Middle Ages. London: Sheed & Ward. 1955. Adapted from *La Philosophie au Moyen Age.* Paris: Payot. 1944.

God. Edited by C. Lattey. London: Sheed & Ward. 1931.

GONSETH, F. *Les Fondements des mathématiques. De la Géometrie d'Euclide à la Relativité générale et à l'Intuitionisme.* Paris: Blanchard. 1926.

HARRIS, C. R. S. *Duns Scotus.* Oxford: Clarendon Press. 2 vols. 1927.

HEIN, Karl. *God Transcendent: Foundation for a Christian Metaphysic.* E.T. London: Nisbet. 1935.

HERBERT, A. P. *Misleading Cases in the Common Law.* London: Methuen. 1927.

HORTON, W. M. *Contemporary Continental Theology. An Interpretation for Anglo-Saxons.* London: S.C.M. Press. 1938.

HULME, T. E. *Speculations. Essays on Humanism and the Philosophy of Art.* Ed. by Herbert Read. London: Kegan Paul. 1924.

HUXLEY, Aldous. *Ends and Means.* London: Chatto & Windus. 1937. *Grey Eminence. A Study in Religion and Politics.* London: Chatto & Windus. 1941.

INGE, W. R. *Christian Mysticism.* London: Methuen. 1899.

JACKSON, Thomas. *Works.* Vol. V. Oxford Univ. Press. 1844.

JAMES, William. *The Varieties of Religious Experience. A Study in Human Nature.* London: Longmans. 2nd ed., 1902.

JOHN OF THE CROSS, St. *Works.* E.T. by E. Allison Peers. London: Burns, Oates. 3 vols. 1934. (Spanish original is the critical edition of P. Silverio de Santa Teresa. Burgos. 1929–31.)

JOSEPH, H. W. B. *An Introduction to Logic.* Oxford: Clarendon Press. 2nd ed., 1916.

JULIAN OF NORWICH. *Revelations of Divine Love.* Ed. by G. Warrack. London: Methuen. 1901.

KARRER, O. *Religions of Mankind.* E.T. by E. I. Watkin. London: Sheed & Ward. 1936.

KEYNES, Lord. *A Treatise on Probability.* London: Macmillan. 1921.

KIMBLE, G. W. T. *Geography in the Middle Ages.* London: Methuen. 1938.

LAIRD, J. *Theism and Cosmology.* London: Allen & Unwin. 1940. *Mind and Deity.* London: Allen & Unwin. 1941.

LEIBNITZ, G. W. *Philosophical Writings.* London: Dent. Everyman's ed. 1934.

LEWIS, C. S. *The Problem of Pain.* London: Centenary Press. 1940.

MACKINNON, D. M. *God, the Living and the True.* London: Dacre Press. 1940.

MACMURRAY, John. *Creative Society.* London: S.C.M. Press. 1935.
The Structure of Religious Experience. London: Faber. 1936.
McTAGGART, J. McT. E. *Studies in Hegelian Cosmology.* Cambridge Univ. Press. 2nd ed., 1918. (1st ed., 1901.)
Malvern, 1941. The Life of the Church and the Order of Society. Being the Proceedings of the Archbishop of York's Conference. London: Longmans. 1941.
MAQUART, F. X. *Elementa Philosophiæ.* Paris: Blot. 3 vols. 1937–8.
MARÉCHAL, Joseph. *Studies in the Psychology of the Mystics.* E.T. by Algar Thorold. London: Burns, Oates. 1927. (Selected from French original: *Études sur la Psychologie des mystiques.* Paris: Desclée de Brouwer. 2 vols. 1924, 1937.)
MARITAIN, Jacques. *The Degrees of Knowledge.* E.T. under the supervision of G. B. Phelan. London: Geoffrey Bles. 1959. (French original: *Distinguer pour unir.* Paris: Desclée de Brouwer. 4th ed., 1946.)
Freedom in the Modern World. E.T. by R. O'Sullivan. London: Sheed & Ward. 1935. (French original: *Du Régime temporel et de la Liberté.* Paris: Desclée de Brouwer.)
→ *An Introduction to Logic.* London: Sheed & Ward. 1937.
An Introduction to Philosophy. E.T. by E. I. Watkin. London: Sheed & Ward. 1930. (French original: *Introduction générale à la Philosophie.* Paris: Téqui.)
Redeeming the Time. London: Geoffrey Bles. 1943.
Religion and Culture. E.T. by J. F. Scanlan. London: Sheed & Ward. 1931. (French original: *Religion et culture.* Paris: Desclée de Brouwer. n.d.)
St. Thomas Aquinas. E.T. by J. F. Scanlan. London: Sheed & Ward. 1938. (First English impression, 1931.) (French original: *Le Docteur Angélique.* Paris: Desclée de Brouwer. 1929.)
Scholasticism and Politics. London: Bles. 1940.
True Humanism. E.T. by M. R. Adamson. London: Geoffrey Bles. 1938. (French original: *Humanisme intégral.* Paris: Aubier. 1936.)
De la Philosophie chrétienne. Paris: Desclée de Brouwer. 1933.
Réflexions sur l'Intelligence et sur sa vie propre. Paris: Desclée de Brouwer. 2nd ed., 1926. (1st ed., 1924.)
MASCALL, E. L. *Christ, the Christian and the Church. A Study of the Incarnation and its Consequences.* London: Longmans. 1946.
MATTHEWS, W. R. *God in Christian Thought and Experience.* London: Nisbet. 1930.
The Purpose of God. London: Nisbet. 1935.
Monument to St. Augustine, A. Essays on some aspects of his Thought written in commemoration of his 15th Centenary. London: Sheed & Ward. 1930.
MURRAY, G. G. A. *Five Stages of Greek Religion.* London: Watts. 1935.

NÉDONCELLE, M. *Baron Friedrich von Hügel. A Study of his Life and Thought* E.T. by Marjorie Vernon. London: Longmans. 1937.
NEWMAN, J. H. *An Essay in aid of a Grammar of Assent.* London: Burns, Oat 4th ed., 1874. (1st ed., 1870.)
NIEBUHR, Reinhold. *The Nature and Destiny of Man. A Christian Interpretc* Vol. I, *Human Nature.* London: Nisbet. 1941.

NYGREN, A. *Agape and Eros. A Study of the Christian Idea of Love.* Part I. E.T. by A. G. Hebert. London: S.P.C.K. 1932. Part II in 2 vols. E.T. by P.S. Watson. London: S.P.C.K. 1938, 1939. (Swedish original: *Den kristna kärlekstanken.* Stockholm: Svenska Kyrkans Diakonistyrelses Bokförlag. 1930, 1932.)

OTTO, R. *The Idea of the Holy. An Inquiry into the Non-rational Factor in the Idea of the Divine and its Relation to the Rational.* E.T. by J. W. Harvey. Oxford Univ. Press. 3rd imp., with additions, 1925. (1st ed. 1923.) (German original: *Das Heilige.* 1st ed., 1917.)

PASCAL, B. *Thoughts.* E.T. by W. F. Trotter. London: Dent. 1904. (From French ed. of L. Brunschvicg. Paris: Hachette.)
PATTERSON, R. L. *The Conception of God in the Philosophy of Aquinas.* London: Allen & Unwin. 1933.
PECK, W. G. *The Salvation of Modern Man.* London: Centenary Press. 1938.
PEERS, E. Allison. *Spanish Mysticism. A Preliminary Survey.* London: Methuen. 1924.
PENIDO, M. T-L. *Le Rôle de l'Analogie dans la Théologie dogmatique.* Paris: Vrin. 1931.
PFLEGER, Karl. *Wrestlers with Christ.* E.T. by E. I. Watkin. London: Sheed & Ward. 1936. (German original: *Geister die um Christus ringen.* Pustet.)
PHILLIPS, R. P. *Modern Thomistic Philosophy.* London: Burns, Oates. 2 vols. 1934, 1935.
Pilgrim continues his Way, The. Trans. from the Russian by R. M. French. London: S.P.C.K. 1942.
POULAIN, A. *The Graces of Interior Prayer. A Treatise on Mystical Theology.* E.T. by L. L. Yorke Smith. London: Kegan Paul. 1910. (French original: *Des Grâces d'Oraison.* 6th ed., 1907.)
PRESTIGE, G. L. *God in Patristic Thought.* London: Heinemann. 1936.
PRINGLE-PATTISON, A. S. *The Idea of God in the Light of Recent Philosophy.* Oxford Univ. Press. 2nd ed., 1920. (1st ed., 1917.)
PRZYWARA, E. *Polarity. A German Catholic's Interpretation of Religion.* E.T. by A. C. Bouquet. Oxford Univ. Press. 1935. (The German original is an essay in Vol. II of *Handbuch der Philosophie*, ed. Baümber and Schröter. Munich. 1927–30.)

QUICK, O. C. *The Christian Sacraments.* London: Nisbet. 1928.

READE, W. H. V. *The Problem of Inference.* Oxford: Clarendon Press. 1938.
Revelation. Ed. by J. Baillie and H. Martin. London: Faber. 1937.
RHYS DAVIDS, Mrs. *Buddhism. A Study of the Buddhist Norm.* London: Williams & Norgate. 1912.
RICKABY, J. *Studies on God and his Creatures.* London: Longmans. 1924.
ROUSSELOT, P. *The Intellectualism of St. Thomas.* E.T. by J. E. O'Mahoney. London: Sheed & Ward. 1935. (French original: *L'Intellectualisme de saint Thomas.* 2nd ed.)

RUSSELL, Bertrand. *The Analysis of Mind*. London: Allen & Unwin. 1921.
An Inquiry into Meaning and Truth. London: Allen & Unwin. 1940.
An Introduction to Mathematical Philosophy. London: Allen & Unwin. 2nd ed., 1920. (1st ed., 1919.)
Mysticism and Logic, and other Essays. London: Allen & Unwin. 1917.
An Outline of Philosophy. London: Allen & Unwin. 1927.
(See also under "Whitehead and Russell.")

SCHMIDT, W. *The Origin and Growth of Religion*. E.T. by H. J. Rose. London: Methuen. 2nd ed., 1935. (1st ed., 1931.)
SERTILLANGES, A. D. *Le Christianisme et les Philosophies*. Vol. I. Paris: Aubier. n.d., but (?) 1939.
Foundations of Thomistic Philosophy. E.T. by G. Anstruther. London: Sands. 1931. (French original: *Les Grandes Thèses de la Philosophie thomiste*. Paris: Bloud et Gay. 1928.)
Saint Thomas d'Aquin. Paris: Alcan. 2 vols. 1925.
SHEED, F. J. *Communism and Man*. London: Sheed & Ward. 1938.
SMITH, Margaret. *An Early Mystic of Baghdad. A Study of the Life and Teaching of Hārith B. Asad al-Muhāsibī*. London: Sheldon Press. 1935.
Studies in Early Mysticism in the Near and Middle East. London: Sheldon Press. 1931.
SOLOVYEV. *God, Man and the Church. The Spiritual Foundation of Life*. E.T. by Donald Attwater from the French version of G. Tsebrikov and A. Martin. London: James Clarke. n.d. (Russian original: *Religiosnya Osnovy Zhizni*, written in 1882–4.)
SORLEY, W. R. *Moral Values and the Idea of God*. Cambridge Univ. Press. 2nd ed., 1921. (1st ed., 1918, but lectures delivered 1914–15.)
SPENS, W. *Belief and Practice*. London: Longmans. 2nd ed., 1917.
STEBBING, L. S. *Philosophy and the Physicists*. London: Methuen. 1937.
Studies in Comparative Religion. General editor: E. C. Messenger. London: Catholic Truth Society. 5 vols. n.d.

TAWNEY, R. H. *The Acquisitive Society*. London: G. Bell. 1924.
TAYLOR, A. E. *The Faith of a Moralist*. London: Macmillan. 2 vols. 1930.
TEMPLE, W. *Nature, Man and God*. London: Macmillan. 1934.
TENNANT F. R. *Miracle and its Philosophical Presuppositions*. Cambridge Univ. Press. 1925.
Philosophical Theology. Cambridge Univ. Press. 2 vols. 1928, 1930.
Philosophy of the Sciences, or The Relations between the Departments of Knowledge. Cambridge Univ. Press. 1932.
The Nature of Belief. London: Bles. 1943.
THOMAS AQUINAS, St. *De Potentia Dei*. E.T. by the English Dominican Fathers. London: Burns, Oates. 1932–4.
Summa contra Gentiles. E.T. by the English Dominican Fathers. London: Burns, Oates. 1924–9.
Summa Theologica. E.T. by the English Dominican Fathers. London: Burns, Oates. 1920–5.
Latin text with a French Translation by A. D. Sertillanges. Paris: Edition de la Revue des Jeunes, Société de S. Jean l'Evangéliste. Vol. I. 1925.
TURNER, W. *History of Philosophy*. New York: Ginn. 1903.

USHENKO, P. P. *The Problems of Logic.* London: Allen & Unwin. 1941.

VAN DER MENSBRUGGHE, Alexis. *From Dyad to Triad. A Plea for Duality against Dualism and an Essay towards the Synthesis of Orthodoxy.* London: Faith Press. 1935.

VERRIÈLE, A. *Le Surnaturel en nous et le Péché originel.* Paris: Bloud et Gay. New ed., 1934.

VON HÜGEL, F. *Essays and Addresses on the Philosophy of Religion.* London: Dent. 2 vols. 1921, 1926.
The Mystical Element of Religion as studied in Saint Catherine of Genoa and her Friends. London: Dent. 2 vols. 2nd ed., 1923. (1st ed., 1908.)

WARD, James. *Essays in Philosophy.* Cambridge Univ. Press. 1927.
Naturalism and Agnosticism. London: Black. 4th ed., 1915. (1st ed., 1899.)
The Realm of Ends, or Pluralism and Theism. Cambridge Univ. Press. 2nd ed., 1912. (1st ed., 1911.)

WATKIN, E. I. *The Philosophy of Mysticism.* London: Grant Richards. 1920.
Theism, Agnosticism and Atheism. London: Heritage. 1936.

WEINBERG, J. R. *An Examination of Logical Positivism.* London: Kegan Paul. 1936.

WHITEHEAD, A. N. *Adventures of Ideas.* Cambridge Univ. Press. 1933.
The Concept of Nature. Cambridge Univ. Press. 1920.
An Enquiry concerning the Principles of Natural Knowledge. Cambridge Univ. Press. 2nd ed., 1925. (1st ed., 1919.)
Modes of Thought. Cambridge Univ. Press. 1938.
⟶ *Process and Reality. An Essay in Cosmology.* Cambridge Univ. Press. 1929.
Religion in the Making. Cambridge Univ. Press. 1926. (There is an edition of 1927 with different pagination.)
Science and the Modern World. Cambridge Univ. Press. 1926. 8½ in. by 5¼ in. (There is another edition of the same date and from the same press on smaller pages with different pagination.) Also in Pelican Books, 1938. (References to this edition are given in parentheses.)
Symbolism, its Meaning and Effect. Cambridge Univ. Press. 1928.

WHITEHEAD, A. N. and RUSSELL, B. *Principia Mathematica.* Cambridge Univ. Press. 1st ed., 1910–13. (2nd ed., 1925.)

WHITTAKER, E. T. *The Beginning and End of the World.* Oxford Univ. Press. 1942.

WICKSTEED, P. H. *The Reactions between Dogma and Philosophy illustrated from the Works of S. Thomas Aquinas.* London: Williams & Norgate. 1920.

WILLIAMS, Charles. *He came down from Heaven.* London: Heinemann. 1938.

INDEX

[Where a number of references occur under one name the most important are indicated by heavy type.]